K14407

MORE PRAYERS FOR SUNDAYS

MORE
PRAYERS
·FOR·
SUNDAYS

For Use With the Revised Common
Lectionary or Any Other

Edited by

MICHAEL COUNSELL

HarperCollinsPublishers

HarperCollins*Liturgical*
Part of HarperCollins*Publishers*
77–85 Fulham Palace Road, London W6 8JB

First published in Great Britain
in 1997 by HarperCollins*Liturgical*

1 3 5 7 9 10 8 6 4 2

Copyright in this compilation © Michael Counsell

A catalogue record for this book is
available from the British Library

0 00 599373 3

Printed and bound in Great Britain by
Caledonian International Book Manufacturing Ltd, Glasgow

CONTENTS

FOREWORD

I have known Michael Counsell in his parish ministry both at St Peter's, Harborne, in Birmingham in the 1980s, and now at St Augustine's, Honor Oak Park in the Woolwich area of the Diocese of Southwark. He provided some years ago a fine collection called *Prayers for Sundays*, a compilation related to the Sunday themes of the ASB. This will for many more years be useful for those who want a collection of shorter prayers arranged by subject. The Church of England, however, has adopted a new lectionary which follows the gospels consecutively and is not thematic. So Michael has had another go – for use with the Revised Common Lectionary or any other. He has both a questing instinct and, as both volumes demonstrate, a gazetteering mind – but both are harnessed to a pastoral heart. Add a touch of linguistic discernment and scriptural orthodoxy and you are near to a good compiler of prayers of the present sort.

Knowing these characteristics, I came to this collection with both spiritual expectations and frankly earthly curiosity, and I have found both satisfied. Michael Counsell has ransacked critically a hundred other sources of prayers and prayer materials, has arranged the results by themes, and has duly acknowledged his sources (which, on my reading, I found to be weighted towards the Bible, Janet Morley and Michael Perry – a rich cocktail in themselves!). He is very ready to import his own craftsmanship, but it is not obtrusive; and he leads his users into not only material for leaders, but also prayers for congregational recitation, litany-type responsive material, and open-woven frameworks for extemporary insertions.

Prayer resources serve a variety of purposes and, clearly, thematic ones have a strong liturgical orientation. Among such collections I suppose all worship leaders develop their own favourites. Only time and personal predilection will determine how each of us views the range available; but I have a shrewd suspicion I shall be reaching for my new Counsell fairly frequently.

Rt Rev. Colin Buchanan, Bishop of Woolwich
Easter 1997

PREFACE

This book is for leaders of worship, in any context, who believe that worship can be moving and inspiring when it draws on beautiful and thought-provoking words from many sources and uses them within a fairly formal structure.

The welcome given to my first collection of *Prayers for Sundays* showed the need for a collection of the best ancient prayers and some new ones, but all in contemporary inclusive language, and arranged by themes. Worship is easier to participate in, and remains in the minds of the worshippers, if the different parts of the service are linked together by a common thread. The themes in *Prayers for Sundays* were those set for each week in the *ASB 1980* of the Church of England. This has not prevented worship leaders from other churches and fellowships using it, but the Church of England itself is talking of moving away from that lectionary soon. I hope that the themes in this book can be linked to the subject chosen by the preacher for the day.

Where extempore prayer is used, written prayers may serve to start it or draw it to a close. Where only limited variation is allowed in the liturgy, prayers from this or the earlier book may still be inserted at certain places. Those who are regulated about what they can do at the main Sunday worship of their congregation may find they have much greater freedom on weekdays, or out of the church buildings, or in schools, at conferences, in house groups, on camp, pilgrimage or retreat. Of course, worship leaders must always be sensitive to the balance between the need to be stimulated to fresh insights by new material, and the desire to feel secure with familiar phrases.

More Prayers for Sundays makes less use of the short prayer or collect than its predecessor, in favour of congregational participation by means of responsive prayers or litanies. For those who have the whole service printed out on a service sheet or an overhead projector this will present no problem, but in other circumstances it may be necessary to begin by saying something like, 'Every time I say … will you all please make the response …' Or initially the response (and its 'cue' or 'trigger') could be changed to something the congregation is familiar with. A chanted response such as those from Taizé or Iona could sometimes be used.

This book can be used as a quarry from which to extract nuggets of liturgy in one of three ways:

1) A theme may be already defined by the Church authorities or the Christian year. Worship leaders would look up that theme in the index of this book, and select a few items from the pages concerned.
2) A preacher might look up in this book's Scripture Index the readings which are appointed, then select a theme and ask the worship leaders to emphasize that in their planning of the service. The readings are almost all from the Revised Common Lectionary, and nearly all the passages in that lectionary occur at least once in these pages.
3) A community might decide on a certain Sunday or series of Sundays to develop a particular theme or themes in their worship, and in planning it they might choose from the suggested readings as well as from the prayers printed under those themes. The Liturgical Commission of the Church of England has designated the Sundays after Candlemas and those following Trinity Sunday as 'open seasons' when this could be done.

A service could be entirely planned around the prayers in this book, or a few sections could be inserted in an existing liturgy, or the ideas in these prayers might encourage worship leaders to write their own prayers.

I am grateful to all those who have given me permission to reprint copyright material. All the copyright holders* have said that permission is freely given to copy this material onto a service sheet which will be thrown away after its use on one occasion; but for more permanent copies, application should be made to the individual copyright holders in the Index of Sources and Acknowledgements.

Michael Counsell
Honor Oak, London, 1996

Notes
1) **Bold type** is used for all the words to be said by the whole congregation.
2) Kyries: these are printed for the congregation to say or sing '**Lord, have mercy**' after the leader, but they may alternatively be used with the congregational response once, twice or thrice without the

---

*Except those of *A Prayer Book for Australia*; and see *Liturgical Texts for Local Use* for the Central Board of Finance of the Church of England.

'cue' or 'trigger', or **'Lord, have mercy upon us'** or **'Kyrie eleison'** instead, or a suitable musical setting or Taizé chant could be sung softly throughout. It is inadvisable to use both a confession and a Kyrie.

3) Absolutions: 'you' and 'your' may optionally be changed to 'us' and 'our', or vice versa.

4) Collects: many of the prayers under this heading do not have the strict collect form, but are short prayers which can be used to introduce the readings. A wider selection will be found in *Prayers for Sundays*.

5) Prefaces: these are for inserting into any recognized Eucharistic Prayer or Great Thanksgiving; 'Longer Prefaces' replace everything between 'Lift up your hearts' and 'Holy, holy, holy'; and, to clarify the cue to the Sanctus for musicians, they have been altered so that all end with the same words.

6) Blessings: 'you' and 'your' may optionally be changed to 'us' and 'our', or vice versa. Where the ending is not printed in full, some variation on 'and may the blessing of God almighty, the Father, the Son and the Holy Spirit, be upon you and remain with you always' may be used.

7) An asterisk (*) in the text indicates that a prayer has been altered with the permission of the copyright holder.

1. ADVENT, THE COMING OF CHRIST, HOPE

See also JUDGEMENT, READINESS

1a **GREETING**
Our Lord says, 'Surely, I come quickly.'
Even so, come, Lord Jesus.

Revelation 22.20

1b **INVITATION TO CONFESS**
When the Lord comes he will bring to light things now hidden
in darkness, and will disclose the purposes of the heart. In that
light, we confess our sins.

In Penitence and Faith, No. 1,* Patterns for Worship, 1B1

1c **PENITENTIAL KYRIE**
Lord Jesus, you came to gather the nations into the peace of
your kingdom. Lord have mercy;
Lord have mercy.
You come in word and sacrament to strengthen us in holiness.
Christ have mercy;
Christ have mercy.
You will come in glory with salvation for your people. Lord
have mercy;
Lord have mercy.

Roman Missal

1d **ABSOLUTION**
God our heavenly judge declares you innocent, not by your
own righteousness, but by that of Jesus Christ, who came to
earth to save you from your sin. **Amen.**

Michael Counsell

COLLECTS
1e

God our deliverer, whose approaching birth still shakes the
foundations of our world, may we so wait for your coming
with eagerness and hope that we embrace without terror the
labour pangs of the new age, through Jesus Christ. **Amen.**

All Desires Known

1f

O God, whose love endures beyond the end of the age, give us
grace to bear the nights of darkness, that we may come at last to
see the morning star, and that you may be born again in us, so
that in the fulfilment of time, on the last great day, you may

come to life in us as the noonday sun, in the glory of the Christ who lived and loved, died and rose again for us, and reigns for ever in your presence. **Amen.**

Prayer in the Morning

1g SUITABLE SCRIPTURE PASSAGES
2 Samuel 7.1–11, 16; Isaiah 2.1–5; 7.10–16; 11.1–10; 12.2–6; 40.1–11; 61.1–4, 8–11; 64.1–9; Jeremiah 33.14–16; Ezekiel 37.1–14; Micah 5.2–5a; Zephaniah 3.14–20; Malachi 3.1–4; Baruch 5.1–9; Psalms 25.1–10; 42; 43; 80.1–7, 17–19; 85.1–2, 8–13; 89.1–4, 19–26; 122; 123; 126; 130.
Matthew 1.18–25; 3.1–12; 11.2–11; 24.1–14, 36–44; Mark 1.1–8; 13.24–37; Luke 1.26–38, 39–56, 67–79; 3.1–18; 21.25–36; John 1.6–8, 19–28; Romans 1.1–7; 8.12–25; 15.1–6; 13.11–14; 15.4–13; 16.25–27; 1 Corinthians 1.3–9; Ephesians 1.15–23; Philippians 1.3–11; Colossians 1.1–14; 1 Thessalonians 3.9–13; 5.1–11, 16–24; Hebrews 10.5–10; James 5.7–10; 1 Peter 1.3–9; 2 Peter 3.8–15a; 1 John 3.1–7; Revelation 22.12–14, 16–17, 20–21.

1h AFFIRMATION OF FAITH
We believe in the Gospel,
promised by God long ago through the prophets,
written in the Holy Scriptures.
We believe in God's Son,
our Lord Jesus Christ:
as to his humanity,
born a descendant of David;
as to his divinity,
shown with great power to be the Son of God
by his rising from death. Amen.

Romans 1.2–4, Bible Praying, 206

1i INTERCESSION
God of never–failing compassion, we pray for those who cannot forget the past; who are burdened by dark things they have done; who wish they could live their lives over again. Lord, come among them,
Be their Light and hope.

We pray for those who need you today: the poor and the rich … the old and the young … the sick and the healthy … the living and the dying … Lord, come among them,
Be their Light and hope.

We pray for those who fear the future, those who have no faith in you, those who are without any hope. Lord, come among them,
Be their Light and hope. Amen.

Companion to the Lectionary 6, p. 2

1j AT THE PEACE
The God of peace make us holy in all things that we may be ready at the coming of our Lord Jesus Christ.

1 Thessalonians 5.23, *Patterns for Worship*, 1R2, freely available

1k LONGER PREFACE
Blessed are you, gracious God, creator of heaven and earth; we give you thanks and praise through Jesus Christ our Lord, who in the fullness of time came among us in our flesh, and opened to us the way of salvation. Now we watch for the day when he will come again in power and great triumph to judge this world, that we, without shame or fear, may rejoice to behold his appearing. Therefore we praise you, joining our voices with angels and archangels, and with all the company of heaven, for ever praising you and saying/singing: ...

Canadian Book of Alternative Services, p. 219*

1l THANKSGIVING
Let us pray.
You keep us waiting.
You, the God of all time,
want us to wait
for the right time in which to discover
who we are, where we must go,
who will be with us, and what we must do.
So, thank you ... for the waiting time.

You keep us looking.
You, the God of all space,
want us to look in the right and wrong places
for signs of hope,
for people who are hopeless,
for visions of a better world which will appear
among the disappointments of the world we know.
So, thank you ... for the looking time.

You keep us loving.
You, the God whose name is love,
want us to be like you –

to love the loveless and the unlovely and the unlovable;
to love without jealousy or design or threat;
and, most difficult of all,
to love ourselves.
So, thank you ... for the loving time.

And in all this,
you keep us.
Through hard questions with no easy answers;
through failing where we hoped to succeed
and making an impact when we felt we were useless;
through the patience and the dreams and the love of others;
and through Jesus Christ and his Spirit,
you keep us.
So, thank you ... for the keeping time,
and for now,
and for ever.
Amen.

A Wee Worship Book, p. 32

1m SOLEMN BLESSING
May God the Father, who loved the world so much that he sent
his only Son, give you grace to prepare for eternal life. **Amen.**
May God the Son, who comes to us as Redeemer and Judge,
reveal to you the path from darkness to light. **Amen.**
May God the Holy Spirit, by whose working the Virgin Mary
conceived the Christ, help you bear the fruits of holiness.
Amen.
And the blessing ...

Michael Perham, *The Promise of His Glory*, p. 101

---

2. THE AGED, THE ELDERLY

See also LIGHT

2a OPENING RESPONSE
Lord, who may dwell in your tabernacle?
Who may abide upon your holy hill?
Those who lead a blameless life and do what is right,
who speak the truth from their heart.

Psalm 15.1–2, freely available

2b INVITATION TO CONFESS
Those may approach God who do not deceive, or do evil to
their friends, or pour contempt on their neighbours. Let us confess our sins as we come close to God.

Psalm 15.3, Michael Counsell

2c CONFESSION
Grant, Lord, to your faithful people pardon and peace,
that we may be cleansed from all our sins,
and serve you with a quiet mind,
through Jesus Christ our Lord. Amen.

BCP 1549,* Gelasian Sacramentary

2d ABSOLUTION
Whoever confesses their sins shall never be overthrown, and
may dwell with God in the eternal habitations. **Amen.**

Psalm 15.5, 1, Michael Counsell

2e COLLECT
O God, in your love you have kept us vigorously and joyfully
at work in days gone by, and now you send us joyful and con-
tented into silence and inactivity; grant us to find happiness in
you in all our solitary and quiet hours. In your strength, O God,
we bid farewell to all. The past you know: we leave it at your
feet. Grant us grace to respond to your divine call; to leave all
that is dear on earth, and go alone to you. Behold, I come quickly, says the Lord. Come, Lord Jesus. **Amen.**

Prayer of an elderly Indian priest,* Living Prayers for Today, p. 93

2f SUITABLE SCRIPTURE PASSAGES
Leviticus 19.1–3, 32; Deuteronomy 34.1–8; Proverbs 22.6–9;
23.22; Ecclesiastes 12.1–7; Isaiah 65.16–22; Zechariah 2.1–5;
8.4–5; Psalms 37.22–26; 71.5–22; 90.1–12.
Luke 2.22–38; John 21.15–24; 1 Timothy 4.11 – 5.10; Titus 2.1–5.

2g AFFIRMATIONS OF FAITH
(a) Holy God, Father, Son and Holy Spirit, I trust you, I believe
    in you, I love you.
(b) Jesus, remember me when you come into your kingdom.
(c) Lord, I believe: help my unbelief.
(d) Lord Jesus Christ, Son of God, have mercy on me, a sinner.
(e) Father, into your hands I commend my spirit.

Ministry at the Time of Death, p. 5

INTERCESSIONS

2h

O Lord God, look with mercy on all for whom increasing years bring isolation and distress. Give them understanding helpers and the willingness to accept help; and as their strength diminishes, increase their faith and their assurance of your love. We pray in the name of Jesus Christ our Lord. **Amen.**

A Prayerbook for Australia, p. 691

2i

Compassionate and holy God, we ask your blessing on all who care for elderly or infirm people. Give them skill in their ministrations; patience to face difficulties; strength when they are tired. Cheer them in times of depression and encourage them with the knowledge that they are sharing in your work of compassion and love. We thank you for their dedication and pray that we may be sensitive to their needs and ready to give support. This we pray through Jesus Christ our Lord. **Amen.**

Pamela Searle, All Year Round 1990, p. 9

2j AT THE PEACE

Sovereign Lord, your word has been fulfilled; my eyes have seen your salvation: now you let your servant go in peace.

Luke 2.29, Patterns for Worship, 0R29, freely available

2k PREFACE

And now we give you thanks because you are the Ancient of Days, the same yesterday, today and for ever, yet you make all things new, and have promised the kingdom of God to those who become as little children.

Michael Counsell

2l THANKSGIVING

Blest be the infant in me;
You know how she smiles
Looking, seeing, discovering
Your creation.

Blest be the child in me;
You know how she grows
Searching, learning, exploring
Your creation.

Blest be the mother in me;
You know how she loves
Sharing, giving, teaching
Your creation.

Blest be the old woman in me;
You know how she waits
Expecting, hoping, expressing
Your creation.

Thank you God for
The blessings through my life
From beginning to end.

Rosemary Cryle

2m BLESSING
Throughout the day, the good God encompass you.
Throughout the night, the saving God enfold you. Throughout
your life, the loving God behold you; and the blessing ...

The Open Gate, p. 111

---

3. THE ARTS, ARCHITECTURE, DANCE, MUSIC, WRITERS

See also THE SABBATH

3a CALL TO WORSHIP
All your works praise you, O God,
and your people give you thanks.
Let your people be joyful with glory,
let them rejoice and praise your name.
Sing for joy to the Lord, all the earth,
praise him with songs and shouts of joy.
Not to us, O God, not to us,
but to your name give the praise.

Michael Counsell, from Psalms 145.10; 149.5; 68.32; 115.1

3b INVITATION TO CONFESS
How shall we sing that majesty
which angels do admire?
Let dust in dust and silence lie;
sing, sing, O heavenly choir.
We shall, we fear, be dark and cold,
with all our fire and light;

yet when you, Lord, accept their gold,
still treasure up our mite.

John Mason*

3c **PENITENTIAL KYRIE**
Creator God, we fail to recognize your part in what we create.
Lord, have mercy;
Lord, have mercy.
Word of God, we fail to recognize our part in your work of
communication. Christ, have mercy;
Christ, have mercy.
Spirit of God, we fail to draw on the richness of your inspiration. Lord, have mercy;
Lord, have mercy.

Michael Counsell

3d **ABSOLUTION**
What God finds acceptable, let us not call unclean: where God
has inspired, we will fan the smouldering wick into a flame of
love. To those who repent, God will give beauty for ashes, the
oil of joy instead of mourning, the garment of praise for the
spirit of heaviness. **Amen.**

Michael Counsell, from Acts 11.9; Isaiah 42.3; 61.3

3e **COLLECT**
O God our dance, in whom we live and move and have our
being; so direct our strength and inspire our weakness that we
may enter with power into the movement of your whole creation, through our partner Jesus Christ. **Amen.**

All Desires Known

3f **SUITABLE SCRIPTURE PASSAGES**
1 Samuel 16.14–23; 2 Samuel 6.1–5, 12b–19; 2 Chronicles 2.1–14;
5.11–62; Zephaniah 3.14–20; Psalms 45; 92.1–4, 12–15; 98; 150.
Matthew 6.24–34; 26.26–30; Ephesians 5.15–20; Philippians
4.8–9; Colossians 3.12–17; Revelation 5.1–10, 11–14; 14.1–3.

3g **THE FAITH OF WILLIAM BLAKE**
To Mercy Pity Peace and Love
All pray in their distress:
And to these virtues of delight
Return their thankfulness.

For Mercy Pity Peace and Love,
Is God our Father dear:
And Mercy Pity Peace and Love,
Is Man his child and care.

For Mercy has a human heart
Pity, a human face:
And Love, the human form divine,
And Peace, the human dress.

Then every man of every clime,
That prays in his distress,
Prays to the human form divine
Love Mercy Pity Peace,

And all must love the human form.
In heathen, Turk or Jew,
Where Mercy, Love and Pity dwell,
There God is dwelling too.

'The Divine Image', William Blake

3h A BLESSING OF THE WHOLE PERSON
God our creator, you have made each one of us in every part.
Bless *us* through and through, that we may delight to serve you
to the full. Bless *our* eyes, that we may discern the beauty you
give. Bless *our* ears, that we may hear you in the music of
sounds. Bless *our* sense of smell, that your fragrance may fill
our being. Bless *our* lips, that we may speak your truth, and sing
your joy. Bless *our* hands, that they may play, write and touch
as you guide them. Bless *our* feet, that they may be messengers
of your peace. Bless *our* imaginations, that we may be fired
with wonder in your truth. Bless *our* hearts, that they may be
filled with your love. Bless *us* through and through, that we
may delight to serve you to the full, through Jesus Christ, who
took our nature to make us whole. **Amen.**

A Prayer Book for Australia, p. 221

3i AT THE PEACE
Worship the Lord in the beauty of holiness, for mercy and truth
have met together; righteousness and peace have kissed each
other.

Psalms 96.9; 85.10

3j PREFACE

Blessed are you, Lord God, our light and our salvation; to you
be glory and praise for ever! From the beginning you have created all things and all your works echo the silent music of your
praise. You make us in your image to reflect your glory. You
give us breath and speech, that with all the powers of heaven
we may find a voice to sing your praise: ...

Additional Eucharistic Prayers

3k THANKSGIVING

O Lord our God, we thank you for the privilege of living in a
world filled with variety and beauty, and for the challenge of its
mysteries.
For the gift of loving and being loved, for friendship and mutual understanding: O God, we give you thanks,
and lift up our hearts in praise.
For the richness of our world; for forests and fields; for mountains and oceans: O God, we give you thanks,
and lift up our hearts in praise.

For the delights of music and poetry, for other people's
thoughts and conversations, and for all good books and reading: O God, we give you thanks,
and lift up our hearts in praise.

For the refreshing power of the falling rain, for the strength and
vitality of the shining sun, and for every life-giving source: O
God, we give you thanks,
and lift up our hearts in praise.
Above all,
we thank you for the grace of your Spirit
flowing into our lives and recreating them
in the image of Jesus our redeemer. Amen.

Editors, Prayers for the People, 11.30

3l BLESSING

Be filled with the Spirit; speak to one another with psalms,
hymns and spiritual songs – sing and make music in your
hearts to the Lord; and the blessing ...

Ephesians 5.18–19, Bible Praying, 475

4. THE ASCENSION

See also AUTHORITY, KING

4a **OPENING RESPONSE**
You Christ are the King of glory;
the eternal Son of the Father.
You are seated at God's right hand in glory:
we believe that you will come and be our judge.

Te Deum, ICET

4b **INVITATION TO CONFESS**
Jesus is our high priest, tempted like us, yet without sin. He lives for ever in heaven to intercede for us. Through him we approach the throne of grace with confidence, and confess our sins.

Hebrews 4.15–16, *Patterns for Worship*, 7B8

4c **PENITENTIAL KYRIES**
God our creator, you have welcomed humanity into eternal glory. Lord, have mercy;
Lord, have mercy.
Jesus, you plead for us at the Father's side. Christ, have mercy;
Christ, have mercy.
Spirit, you have been promised to fill us with love. Lord, have mercy;
Lord have mercy.

Michael Counsell

4d **ABSOLUTION**
Who will condemn us? Not Jesus, who has been raised to God's side, where he pleads our case. No, God himself declares us not guilty. **Amen.**

Romans 8.33–34, Michael Counsell

4e **COLLECT**
O God, you withdraw from our sight that you may be known by our love; help us to enter the cloud where you are hidden, and surrender all our certainty to the darkness of faith in Jesus Christ. **Amen.**

All Desires Known

4f **SUITABLE SCRIPTURE PASSAGES**
2 Kings 2.1–12; Daniel 7.9–14; Psalms 47; 68.1–10, 32–35; 93; 97; 139.1–12.
Matthew 28.16–20; Mark 16.19–20; Luke 24.44–53; John 17.1–11;

Acts 1.1–14; Ephesians 1.15–23; Philippians 2.1–13; 1 Peter 4.12–14; 5.6–11.

4g AFFIRMATION OF FAITH
Let us proclaim the mystery of our faith:
We believe in one Lord Jesus Christ;
revealed in the flesh,
attested by the Spirit,
seen by the apostles,
proclaimed to the nations,
believed in throughout the world,
and taken up to glory. Amen.

1 Timothy 3.16, *Bible Praying*, 222

4h INTERCESSION
Let us seek the Father's blessing and the gifts of the Spirit, praying through Christ our Lord:
Lord Jesus Christ, pray to the Father.
Lord, send us your Spirit.

Jesus Christ, great high priest, ever living to intercede for us, pray for the Church, your broken body in the world … Lord Jesus Christ, pray to the Father.
Lord, send us your Spirit.

Jesus Christ, king of righteousness, enthroned at the right hand of the Majesty on high, pray for the world, and subject it to your gentle rule … Lord Jesus Christ, pray to the Father.
Lord, send us your Spirit.

Jesus Christ, son of man, drawing humanity into the life of God, pray for your brothers and sisters in need, distress or sorrow … Lord Jesus Christ, pray to the Father.
Lord, send us your Spirit.

Jesus Christ, pioneer of our salvation, bringing us to glory through your death and resurrection, surround with your saints and angels those who have died trusting your promises … Lord Jesus Christ, pray to the Father.
Lord, send us your Spirit.

Jesus Christ, Lord over all things, ascending far above the heavens and filling the universe, pray for us who receive the gifts you give for work in your service … Lord Jesus Christ, pray to the Father.
Lord, send us your Spirit.

Jesus Christ, keep the Church in the unity of the Spirit and in the bond of your peace, and bring the whole created order to worship at your feet; for you are alive and reign with the Father and the Holy Spirit, one God, now and for ever. **Amen.**

Michael Perham, *Enriching the Christian Year*, 5C1, adapted in *Patterns for Worship*, 7H10

4i AT THE PEACE

Jesus says: Peace is my parting gift to you, my own peace, such as the world cannot give. Trust in God always; trust also in me.

John 14.1, 27, Michael Perham, *Enriching the Christian Year*, 5G1

4j PREFACE

He has passed beyond our sight, not to abandon us but to be our hope, that where he is we might also be and reign with him in glory.

An Australian Prayer Book 1978

4k THANKSGIVING

Creator God, we give you thanks and praise that in awesome power you made us, and in tender love you care for us, so that we do not need to be dismayed by change or chance or evil. For you are the true and living God:
You are our everlasting King.

Saviour Jesus, we give you thanks and praise that in steadfast grace you came into our world, and with fervent love you died and rose in our midst, so that we can trust in your authority to save us from all that is wrong in ourselves, and in others. For you are the true and living God:
You are our everlasting King.

Holy Spirit, we give you thanks and praise that in constant kindness you bear us up, and with radiant goodness you shine through us, so that we can worship God in Spirit and in truth and spread the Good News of peace and joy. For you are the true and living God:
You are our everlasting King.

Gracious God, Creator, Saviour, Spirit, we give you thanks and praise that from your truth we receive wisdom in loving, and from your justice, the ability to tell right from wrong. Help us to continue in your way and to grow in your compassion. For you are the true and living God:
You are our everlasting King.

Companion to the Lectionary 6, p. 70

13

4l BLESSING

Christ our exalted King pour upon you his abundant gifts and bring you to reign with him in glory; and the blessing ...

A Prayer Book for Australia, p. 156

4m SOLEMN BLESSING

God the Father, who has given to his Son the name above every name, strengthen you to proclaim Christ Jesus as Lord. **Amen.**
God the Son, who is our great high priest passed into the heavens, plead for you at the right hand of the Father. **Amen.**
God the Holy Spirit, who pours out abundant gifts upon the Church, make you faithful servants of Christ our king. **Amen.**
And the blessing ...

Michael Perham, *Enriching the Christian Year*, 5F1*

5. ASSURANCE, CONFIDENCE

See also FAITH, HOPE, PROVIDENCE

5a OPENING RESPONSE

This is what the Holy God says: Turn back and rest in me, and you shall be saved;
in quietness and confidence we shall find strength.

Isaiah 30.15

5b INVITATION TO CONFESS

Seek the Lord, for he may be found, pray to him, for he is near. Let the wicked leave their way of life and change their way of thinking. Let them return to the Lord, and he will have mercy; to our God, and he will freely pardon. 'For my thoughts,' says the Lord, 'are not like yours, and my ways are different from yours. As high as the heavens are above the earth, so high are my ways and thoughts above yours.' Let us then confess our sins to God, confident in his desire to forgive.

Isaiah 55.6–9, Michael Counsell

5c KYRIE

Forgive us, God, loving Father of your prodigal children; for we have doubted that your love reaches out to welcome us home. Lord, have mercy;
Lord, have mercy.

Forgive us, Jesus our brother; we have not trusted that upon the cross you have done all things needful for our salvation. Christ, have mercy.
Christ, have mercy.
Forgive us, Spirit of God within us; we have not used the powers with which you have filled us. Lord, have mercy.
Lord, have mercy.

Michael Counsell

5d ABSOLUTION
'Be still and know that I am God,' says the Lord. The mighty Lord is with you, the God who saves you is your refuge. **Amen.**

Psalm 46.10–11, Michael Counsell

5e COLLECT
O God, at whose table we are no longer strangers; may we not refuse your call through pride or fear, but approach with confidence to find our home in you through Jesus Christ. **Amen.**

All Desires Known

5f SUITABLE SCRIPTURE PASSAGES
1 Kings 18.20–21, 30–39; Jeremiah 20.7–13; Lamentations 3.1–9, 19–24; Zephaniah 3.14–20; Psalms 22.1–15; 31.1–5, 19–24; 31.9–16; 46; 121; 130.
Matthew 6.24–34; 10.24–29; 2 Corinthians 3.1–6; Hebrews 10.11–14, 19–25.

5g AFFIRMATION OF FAITH
This is a true saying:
If we have died with Christ Jesus
we shall also live with him.
If we continue to endure,
we shall also reign with him.
If we deny him,
he also will deny us.
If we are unfaithful,
he remains faithful,
because he cannot be false to himself.

2 Timothy 2.11–13

5h PRAYER
O Lord God, in whom we live and move and have our being, open our eyes that we may behold your loving presence always around us. The Lord is our helper,
we will not be afraid.

Draw our hearts to you with the power of love. The Lord is our helper,
We will not be afraid.
Teach us in nothing to be anxious. The Lord is our helper,
We will not be afraid.
When we have done what you have given us to do, help us to leave the outcome to your wisdom. The Lord is our helper,
We will not be afraid.
Take from us all doubt and distrust. The Lord is our helper,
We will not be afraid.
Lift our thoughts up to you, and make us know that all things are possible to us, in and through your Son our Redeemer, Jesus Christ our Lord. **Amen.**

Adapted from Brooke Fosse Westcott

5i   AT THE PEACE
Peace to you, says the Lord; do not fear, you shall not die.

Judges 6.23

5j   LONGER PREFACE
Heavenly Father, we give you thanks and praise through Jesus Christ your Son, our Lord. For he is your living Word; through him you have created all things from the beginning, and have formed us in your own image.
You are worthy, O Lord our God,
to receive glory and honour and power.
For you created all things,
and by your will they have their being.

We praise you through Jesus Christ your Son, because you have given him to be born of Mary and to die upon the cross for us. We praise you for raising him from the dead and exalting him to your right hand on high. So we join the eternal praise of heaven, for ever praising you and saying/singing: ...

Additional Eucharistic Prayers*

5k   THANKSGIVING
Father, you gave up your Son for us all: you give us all things with him; you call us, justify us, glorify us. Father in heaven:
we give you thanks and praise.

Jesus Christ died, was raised to life, and pleads for us at your side. Who can separate us from your love? Father in heaven:
we give you thanks and praise.

For your sake we face death all day long. In your world we face trouble and hardship, persecution, famine, nakedness, danger and death. Father in heaven:
we give you thanks and praise.

But nothing separates us from your love: neither death nor life, neither angels nor demons, neither the present nor the future, nor any heavenly powers, neither the world above nor the world below: nothing in all creation can separate us from your love in Jesus Christ. Father in heaven:
we give you thanks and praise.

In all these things we are more than conquerors through him who loves us, and has freed us from our sins and made us a kingdom and priests to serve you for ever, even Jesus Christ our Lord. **Amen.**

Romans 8.23–39, *Patterns for Worship*, 13P17*

51 BLESSING
Now unto him that is able to do exceedingly abundantly, above all that we ask or think, according to the power that is at work in us, to him be glory in the Church by Christ Jesus, throughout all ages; and may the blessing ...

Ephesians 3.20

6. AUTHORITY, GOVERNMENT, LEADERS

See also THE ASCENSION, KING

6a INVITATION TO WORSHIP, IN AN OLD CHURCH
We welcome you to this parish church of ... here in ... built on a site hallowed by the people of this place for the worship of God during ... years. Here, through the centuries, preceding generations have come to celebrate occasions of joy and to seek strength in times of fear and sorrow. Here they have known the unity of a common citizenship and the meaning of a common purpose in the service of God and each other. Let us now follow where they have gone before, and fill this place with our praise and prayer to him who makes us one, and calls us to live together in peace and mutual service.

*Services for Special Occasions**

6b PENITENCE

Teach us, O Lord, to have done with anger, suspicion and envy, which are the seeds of discord, and in all our dealings to look for the best in one another, and not for the worst. O Lord, hear us:
O Lord, help us.

Teach us, O Lord, to carry in our care the lonely, the deprived, and those whose way of life is different from our own. O Lord, hear us:
O Lord, help us.

Teach us, O Lord, to use people's labour justly, and to practise so wise a husbandry of the earth and the seas as may banish want and hunger from the world. O Lord, hear us:
O Lord, help us.

Teach us, O Lord, to honour the vows of marriage; to cherish our homes and family life, and to serve each other courteously. O Lord, hear us:
O Lord, help us.

Teach us, O Lord, to believe that we may be mistaken; teach us how to repent; teach us how to forgive and be forgiven, teach us obedience to the life-fulfilling will of God. O Lord, hear us:
O Lord, help us.
O Lord God, whose will is our peace,
forgive what we have been,
sanctify what we are,
direct what we shall be,
for Jesus Christ's sake. Amen.

*Services for Special Occasions**

6c ABSOLUTION

May the almighty and merciful Lord grant us pardon and peace through Jesus Christ our Lord. **Amen.**

The Promise of His Glory, p. 249

COLLECTS

6d

Christ our Lord, you refused the way of domination and died the death of a slave. May we also refuse to lord it over those who are subject to us, but share the weight of authority so that all may be empowered in your name. **Amen.**

All Desires Known

6e

Eternal God, Fount of wisdom; we ask you to bless the representatives we have elected; grant that through their discussions and decisions we may solve our problems effectively, enhance the well-being of our nation, and achieve together a fairer and more united society. **Amen.**

A New Zealand Prayer Book, p. 139

6f   SUITABLE SCRIPTURE PASSAGES
Genesis 37.1–4, 12–28; Numbers 11.4–6, 10–16, 24–30; 1 Kings 2.10–12; 3.3–14; 1 Kings 19.15–16, 19–21; Isaiah 45.1–7; Micah 5.2–5a; Psalm 105.1–6, 16–22, 45b.
Matthew 21.23–32; 22.15–22; Mark 6.14–29; 10.32–45; Luke 7.1–10; Acts 1.15–17, 21–26; Galatians 1.11–24; 1 Timothy 2.1–7.

6g   AFFIRMATION OF FAITH
We believe in Christ,
the image of God the invisible,
first-born of creation;
in whom were created
all things in heaven and earth,
seen and unseen:
states, powers, rulers and authorities;
all things were created through him and for him.
Christ is before all things,
in him all things hold together;
Christ is the head of the body, the church;
he is the beginning
and the first-born from the dead.
Christ over all things is supreme;
it is God's pleasure
for all his fullness to live in him,
and by him to reconcile all things to himself,
making peace through the blood of the cross. Amen.

Colossians 1.15–20, *Bible Praying*, 219

6h   INTERCESSION
Let us pray.
Lord God,
Through ocean's surge and spider's web,
By crushing armies and cradling children,
Your power is known in strength and gentleness.
We ask for your power in the world today,
To pull down the mighty who abuse their privilege,
And to help the frail and powerless to lose their fear.

(*A silence in which names or situations may be mentioned.*)
Lord, in your mercy,
hear our prayer. (*Or a response may be sung.*)

Lord God,
You planned the secrets of the earth,
And know the bounds of human knowledge.
We ask for your wisdom in the world today,
To enable the knowledge and technology of the few
to be put at the disposal of all your children;
To ensure that earth's rulers and planners
perceive the gifts and plight of the poor.

(*A silence in which names or situations may be mentioned.*)
Lord, in your mercy,
hear our prayer.

Lord God,
In the dawn of creation,
And in the presence of your Son,
Your light shattered the force and lure of darkness.
We ask for your help today
For those who, in public and personal life,
Are in the grip of that which is wicked:
For those who deal in rumours and perpetrate cheap gossip,
For those who are slaves to a vice they fear to name,
For those who have traded openness for secrecy,
    morality for money,
    love for lust.
We ask for a light not to blind them,
But to show them a way out of their darkness.

(*A silence in which names or situations may be mentioned.*)
Lord, in your mercy,
hear our prayer.

Lord God,
Teach us today to rely on your strength,
learn from your wisdom,
walk in your light,
And enjoy the company of your Spirit.
Thus, though citizens of earth,
May we live as the commonwealth of heaven,
For your love's sake.
Amen.

A Wee Worship Book, p. 6

6i   AT THE PEACE
Violence shall no more be heard in your land, nor destruction
within your border; the Lord will make righteousness your
taskmaster, and your rulers shall be peace.

Isaiah 60.18, 27

6j   PREFACE
And now we give you thanks because Christ gave authority to
his disciples, saying, As the Father has sent me, so I send you;
that they might confess his name before the rulers of this world.

US BCP 1979, p. 381*

6k   THANKSGIVING
Praised be God in power and glory; the Creator of all, from
everlasting to everlasting; our Saviour and Redeemer; the Holy
Spirit, our helper and comforter. We praise God, who judges
the world in righteousness; we praise God, who waits upon us
in eternity; we praise God, who will bring to an end all that is
temporal; we praise God, who, having begun the work, will
now make it perfect. **Amen.**

Faith and Order Conference, 1937

6l   BLESSING
May God grant you a vision of our land
as God's love would make it:
a land where the weak are protected,
and none go hungry or poor;
a land where the benefits of civilised life are shared,
and everyone can enjoy them;
a land where different races and cultures
live in tolerance and mutual respect;
a land where peace is built with justice,
and justice is guided by love;
and may he grant you the inspiration and courage to build it;

and the blessing of God, the source of all authority,
King of kings and Lord of lords ...

Adapted from *Services for Special Occasions*

---

7. BAPTISM, WATER

7a   OPENING RESPONSE
There is one body and one Spirit:
one Lord, one faith, one baptism.

Ephesians 4.5, *Patterns for Worship*, p. 319

7b   INVITATION TO CONFESS
Because God was merciful, he saved us through the water of
rebirth, and the renewing power of the Holy Spirit. But through
sin we have fallen away from our baptism. Let us return to the
Lord and renew our faith in his promises by confessing our sins
in penitence.

Titus 3.5, Michael Perham, *Enriching the Christian Year*, 17A1

7c   CONFESSION
God of truth, you are faithful to the covenant you have made
with us; look in mercy on your people. Cleanse us, Lord, from
all our sins:
Wash us, and we shall be pure.

We have broken the pledges of our baptism, and failed to be
your disciples. Cleanse us, Lord, from all our sins:
Wash us, and we shall be pure.

Though we are saved by Christ and dead to sin through the
deep waters of death, we have not witnessed to his grace by
our manner of life. Cleanse us, Lord, from all our sins:
Wash us, and we shall be pure.

We have shown indifference to those in need and have been
afraid to stand up for justice and truth. Cleanse us, Lord, from
all our sins:
Wash us, and we shall be pure.

We have been slow to forgive, and have failed to remember your repeated forgiveness of our sins. Cleanse us, Lord, from all our sins:
Wash us, and we shall be pure.

Today we rejoice and give thanks because your Son humbled himself to be baptised in the Jordan. Through the waters you have given us the mystery of baptism for the remission of sins. Cleanse us, Lord, from all our sins:
Wash us, and we shall be pure.

Through water and Spirit you give us new life as the people of God, and pour out upon us the gifts of your new covenant. Cleanse us, Lord, from all our sins:
Wash us, and we shall be pure.

The Promise of His Glory, p. 229*

7d   ABSOLUTION
Now you are washed, you are sanctified, you are justified; in the name of the Lord Jesus and by the Spirit of our God. **Amen.**

1 Corinthians 6.11, *Bible Praying*, 156

7e   COLLECT
Almighty God, who at the baptism of your blessed Son Jesus Christ in the river Jordan revealed the glory of his divine nature: let the light of his presence shine in our hearts, and his glory be shown forth in our lives; through the same Jesus Christ our Lord. **Amen.**

Scottish Prayer Book 1929

7f   SUITABLE SCRIPTURE PASSAGES
Genesis 1.1–5; 7.1–5, 11–18; 8.6–18; 9.8–13; Exodus 14.19–31; 17.1–7; 2 Kings 5.1–15a; Isaiah 12.2–6; 35.4–7a; 42.1–9; 43.1–7; 55.1–11; Jeremiah 2.4–13; 31.31–34; Ezekiel 36.25a, 26–28; Psalms 29; 46; 78.1–4, 12–16; 114.
Matthew 3.13–17; 28.16–20; Mark 1.4–11, 9–15; Luke 3.15–17, 21–22; John 1.6–8, 19–28; 2.1–11; 3.1–8; 4.5–15, 19–26, 39–42; 5.1–9; Acts 1.1–11; 2.14a, 36–41; 8.14–17, 26–40; Acts 10.34–43, 44–48; 11.1–18; 16.9–15, 16–34; 19.1–7; Romans 6.3–11; 1 Corinthians 1.10–18; 12.12–13; Galatians 3.23–29; 1 Peter 3.13–22; Revelation 21.10, 22 – 22.5.

7g   AFFIRMATION OF FAITH
We believe in God
who, in the beginning, in love created all things
and, at the end, in love will gather all things to himself.

**We believe in Jesus Christ
who came to earth,
one of us and one with us,
with whom, in baptism,
we die and are buried
that we may rise in his resurrection life.**

**We believe in the Holy Spirit,
who led us to Christ,
who is given to us again in baptism
that we may love and serve the Lord
with all our being.**

**We believe in the Church,
of which, through faith and baptism,
we are made members,
one with Christ in his body.**

**We believe in the Christian calling to live in the world;
to live under the obedience of Christ
in his love, his joy and his peace.**

Michael Walker, *Baptist Praise and Worship*, 420

7h   INTERCESSION
God and Father of us all, in Christ you give us one Lord, one
faith, one baptism: look in your love upon the Church, the fel-
lowship of the baptized, and renew her life in unity and peace
... In faith we pray.
We pray to you our God.

Your Christ has commanded us to go and teach all nations,
baptizing them in the name of the Father, the Son and the Holy
Spirit: look in your love upon the world, redeemed by his
blood, and work out your purpose for the whole creation ... In
faith we pray.
We pray to you our God.

As a mother brings her child to birth in pain and yet in joy, you
bring us to new birth in the waters of baptism and make us
your own by adoption and grace: look in your love upon each
one of your children, and bless with your presence every home
and every family ... In faith we pray.
We pray to you our God.

We have accepted the baptism with which Christ was baptized, your children suffer various trials, testing their faith, as they await the salvation of their souls: look in your love upon those who walk in deep darkness and those who suffer beyond endurance ... In faith we pray.
We pray to you our God.

Christ is risen, the first-fruits of the harvest of the dead. In baptism we die with him in order that we may be alive with him: look in your love on all who are passing through the deep waters of death ... May they walk in newness of life. In faith we pray.
We pray to you our God.

Michael Perham, Enriching the Christian Year, 17C2

7i   AT THE PEACE
We are baptised into Christ: live in the Spirit of Christ.

Patterns for Worship, 8R8, freely available

7j   PREFACE OF THE BAPTISM OF OUR LORD
At his baptism your Holy Spirit was seen as a dove. He heard your voice from heaven, showing him to be your Son made flesh, and anointing him with joy as the Christ, sent to bring salvation to all people.

Melanesian Prayer Book Draft 1984*

7k   THANKSGIVING FOR WATER
Father, for your gift of water in creation:
we give you thanks and praise.
For your Spirit, sweeping over the waters, bringing light and life:
we give you thanks and praise.
For your Son, Jesus Christ our Lord, baptized in the river Jordan:
we give you thanks and praise.
For your new creation, brought to birth by water and the Spirit:
we give you thanks and praise.
For your grace bestowed upon us your children, washing away our sins:
we give you thanks and praise.

*So, Father, accept our sacrifice of praise; by the power of your life-giving Spirit bless these waters of your new creation:
we give you thanks and praise.

*May your servants who are washed in them be made one with your Son, who took the form of a servant:
we give you thanks and praise.
*May your Holy Spirit, who has brought us to new birth in the family of your Church, raise us in Christ, our anointed Lord, to full and eternal life:
we give you thanks and praise.

For all might, majesty and dominion are yours, now and for ever.
Alleluia! Amen.

*Paragraphs marked * should be omitted when this section is not being used in connection with sacramental water.*

Patterns for Worship, 8P13

71 BLESSING
May the living waters of Christ cleanse us, may the Spirit descend upon us, and the blessing of God be with us, this day/night and always. **Amen**.

Celebrating Common Prayer, p. 132

---

8. THE BIBLE, BIBLE SUNDAY,
THE GOSPEL, SCRIPTURE, THE WORD

8a OPENING RESPONSE
Grace and peace to you from God.
God fill you with truth and joy.

A New Zealand Prayer Book, p. 404

8b INVITATION TO CONFESS
The Word of God is living and active. It judges the thoughts and the intentions of the heart. All is open and laid bare before the eyes of God to whom we give account. We confess our sins in penitence and faith.

Hebrews 4.12, Patterns for Worship, 11B13,* freely available

8c CONFESSION
**Lord, we have not obeyed your word,
nor heeded what is written in the Scriptures:
we repent with all our heart,
and humble ourselves before you.
In your mercy forgive us;**

grant us your peace
and the strength to keep your laws;
through Jesus Christ our Lord. Amen.

2 Kings 22.13–20, *Bible Praying*, 70

8d   KYRIE
May your loving mercy come to us, O Lord, and your salvation
according to your word: Lord, have mercy;
Lord have mercy.
Your word is a lantern to our feet and a light to our path. Christ
have mercy;
Christ have mercy.
O Lord let your mercy come to us that we may live, for your
law is our delight: Lord, have mercy;
Lord, have mercy.

Portsmouth Cathedral*

8e   ABSOLUTION
It is on your mercy and grace that we daily depend. Open our
hearts and minds to receive your forgiveness and to hear your
word afresh. **Amen.**

Written to Teach

COLLECTS
8f

O God our disturber, whose speech is pregnant with power and
whose word will be fulfilled; may we know ourselves unsatis-
fied with all that distorts your truth, and make our hearts atten-
tive to your liberating voice, in Jesus Christ. **Amen.**

All Desires Known

8g

Heavenly Father, give us wisdom and understanding. As we
listen to your Word, may we know you better, love you more,
and learn to please you in all we do; through Jesus Christ our
Lord. **Amen.**

A Prayer Book for Australia, p. 23

8h   SUITABLE SCRIPTURE PASSAGES
Deuteronomy 18.15–20; 30.9–14; Nehemiah 8.1–4a, 8–12; Isaiah
45.22–25; 55.1–11, 10–13; Jeremiah 1.4–10; 15.15–21; 23.23–29;
28.5–9; 31.7–14; Ezekiel 2.1–5; Psalms 19.7–14; 33.1–12; 50.1–6;
99; 119.1–8, or 9–16, or 33–40, or 105–112, or 129–136; 147.12–20.
Matthew 7.21–29; 13.1–9, 18–23; 24.30–35; Mark 1.9–15; Luke
4.14–24; 24.13–35, 36b–48; John 1.1–14; 5.36b–47; 17.6–19; Acts
8.26–40; Romans 1.1–7; 10.5–15; 15.1–13; 1 Corinthians 9.16–23;

Galatians 1.1–12; Colossians 3.12–17; 2 Timothy 2.8–15; 3.14 –
4.5; Hebrews 4.12–16; James 1.17–24; 1 Peter 4.1–8; 1 John 1.1 –
2.2.

8i   AFFIRMATION OF FAITH
In the beginning was the Word,
the Word that shares the heavenly throne.
That Word was God; till he was heard
the Word and God were quite alone.

God spoke the Word, through whom all things
began to be; no thing was formed
apart from him; in him light springs
to life, and by it we are warmed.
That light was life for all mankind;
the beacon-Word shines in the night;
it strives with darkness in the mind,
and darkness cannot swallow light.

He formed the world with his own hand:
it would not recognise his name;
his chosen people, in his land,
would not accept him when he came.
To those who welcomed true light's dawn,
who marked his footsteps where he trod,
he gave the power to be born
as sons and daughters of our God.

The Word became a mortal man;
among us dwelt the one above,
God's only Son, such was his plan;
we saw his glory, truth and love.
In this full love he let us share;
he poured upon the human race,
on those who love him, everywhere,
love upon love, and grace on grace.

John 1.1–16, *The Secret Name*

8j   INTERCESSION
We pray for all Christian people, knit together by your word of
life; for leaders of the Church; and all who teach the faith;
May your word dwell in their hearts.

We pray for those who study and translate the Scriptures; for those who wrestle to search out and interpret their meaning for our time;
May your word dwell in their hearts.

We pray for the work of the Bible Society; for those employed at its headquarters; for those who represent the society at local level; and for all who serve under its direction;
May your word dwell in their hearts.

We pray for those who long to know you, and your living word; for those who are mocked and persecuted for their faith; for those who are tempted to forsake your way;
May your word dwell in their hearts.

We pray for those whose hearts are hardened and unfeeling; for those who threaten war and violence; and especially, we remember ...
May your word dwell in their hearts.

We pray for those who feel themselves in some way fettered; for all who are bowed down with grief, fear or sickness; especially, we remember ...
May your word dwell in their hearts.

Giving thanks for those who have died in the faith of Christ, we rejoice with all your saints, trusting in the promise of your word fulfilled. Lord of the Church,
Hear our prayer and make us one in heart and mind, to serve you in Christ our Lord. Amen.

Written to Teach

8k   AT THE PEACE
God will speak peace to his people, to those who turn to him in their hearts.

Psalm 85.8; 1 Samuel 12.20, *Patterns for Worship*, 0R24, freely available

8l   PREFACE
And now we give you thanks because the wisdom of your word sustains all things, and reveals you to us in your fullness.

Patterns for Worship, 11N22

8m   PRAYER AFTER COMMUNION
Lord God, you feed us with the living bread from heaven; you renew our faith, increase our hope, and strengthen our love. Teach us to hunger for Christ who is the true and living bread,

and to live by every word that comes from your mouth,
through Jesus Christ our Lord. **Amen.**

Westcott House, *Patterns for Worship*, 11J29

8n   THANKSGIVING
Thank you, Lord, for the Bible: for its ability to give us each day
new vision and new power; for its capacity to reach the roots of
inner life and to refresh them; for its power to enter mind and
spirit and fashion them anew, to beget new life and to sustain it;
we give you thanks and praise, through Jesus Christ our Lord.
Amen.

More Prayers for Today's Church, No. 35

8o   BLESSING
Hear the teaching of Jesus: 'Blessed are those who hear the word
of God and obey it.' Go now to do God's will. And the blessing ...

Patterns for Worship, 11T30

---

9. CHILDREN, EDUCATION, THE YOUNG

See also THE NEEDY, THE WORLD

9a   CALL TO WORSHIP
Young men and girls, old and young together,
Praise the name of the Lord.

Psalm 148.12–13, Michael Counsell

9b   INVITATION TO CONFESS
God loves us and wants to be friends. But we have all done
things which make us ashamed to face God. So let us own up,
certain that God will forgive us.

Michael Counsell

9c   CONFESSION
O God, our gracious Father,
we confess that we have sinned against you
and done many things to grieve you:
we have often been selfish,
we have sometimes forgotten to pray to you,
and we have not loved you as we should.
For these and all other sins
forgive us, we pray,
through him who died for us,
Jesus Christ our Lord. Amen.

C. S. Woodward, adapted by the editors of *Prayers for the People*, 14.15

9d ABSOLUTION
Hear the word of the Lord: My child, your sins are forgiven for
the sake of Christ. **Amen.**

1 John 2.12, *Bible Praying*, 161

9e COLLECT
Heavenly Father, whose children suffered at the hands of
Herod though they had done no wrong: help us to defend all
your children from cruelty and oppression; in the name of Jesus
Christ who suffered for us, but is alive and reigns with you and
the Holy Spirit, one God, now and for ever. **Amen.**

Church of Ireland *Alternative Prayer Book* 1984

9f SUITABLE SCRIPTURE PASSAGES
Exodus 1.15 – 2.10; Deuteronomy 6.1–9; 1 Samuel 1.20–28;
2.18–20; 3.1–10; 1 Kings 17.17–24; Proverbs 1.1–9; Ecclesiastes
11.9 – 12.1; Isaiah 9.2–7; 40.28–31; Psalms 25.1–7; 34.11–20;
71.1–17; 103.1–5; 119.9–16; 127.1–4; 139.1–18, 23–34; 148.
Matthew 2.13–23; Mark 5.21–43; 9.30–37; 10.2–16; Luke 2.41–52;
7.11–17; 1 Timothy 4.12 – 5.2; 2 Timothy 3.10–17.

9g AFFIRMATION OF FAITH
I believe in God who made
the earth and stars above.
I believe in Jesus Christ
who tells me God is love.

I believe the Holy Spirit
helps me every hour.
I believe that prayer unites
me with eternal power.

I believe the Church is where
all Christians learn to live.
I believe that here I learn
to love and to forgive.

I believe that God wants me,
at home and everywhere,
to be a friend, to tell the truth,
to trust, obey and care.

Queen's Park URC, *All Year Round 1990*, p. 152

31

9h INTERCESSION
We pray for strength to follow Jesus, saying: Saviour, we hear your call:
help us to follow.

Jesus said: 'If one of you wants to be great, you must be everyone's servant.' Saviour, we hear your call:
help us to follow.

Jesus said: 'Unless you change and become humble like little children, you can never enter the kingdom of heaven.' Saviour, we hear your call:
help us to follow.

Jesus said: 'Happy are the humble; they will receive what God has promised.' Saviour, we hear your call:
help us to follow.

Jesus said: 'Be merciful as your Father is merciful; love your enemies and do good to them.' Saviour, we hear your call:
help us to follow.

Jesus said: 'Love one another, as I love you; there is no greater love than this, to lay down your life for your friends.' Saviour, we hear your call:
help us to follow.

Jesus said: 'Go to people everywhere and make them my disciples, and I will be with you always, to the end of time.' Saviour, we hear your call:
help us to follow.

God of mercy:
**you know us and love us
and hear our prayer:
keep us in the eternal fellowship
of Jesus Christ our Saviour. Amen.**

Author unknown, adapted from *Church Family Worship*

9i AT THE PEACE
Jesus took the children in his arms and blessed them. Let us share with one another the love we have received from him.

Michael Counsell

9j THE GREAT THANKSGIVING

The following Great Thanksgiving may be used either as a framework within which insertions may be made or as a continuous whole.

The Lord is here.
God's Spirit is with us.
Lift up your hearts.
We lift them to the Lord.
Let us give thanks to the Lord our God.
It is right to offer thanks and praise.

The presiding priest gives thanks to God for the work of creation and God's self-revelation. The particular occasion being celebrated may also be recalled. The following or any other suitable words are used:

It is indeed right, always and everywhere, to give thanks to you, the true and living God, through Jesus Christ. You are the source of life for all creation and you made us in your own image.

The presiding priest now gives thanks for the salvation of the world through Christ. The following or any other suitable words are used:

In your love for us you sent your Son to be our Saviour. In the fullness of time he became incarnate, and suffered death on the cross. You raised him in triumph and exalted him in glory. Through him you send your Holy Spirit upon your church and make us your people.

If the Sanctus is to be included, it is introduced with these or similar words:

And so, we proclaim your glory, as we say:
Holy, holy, holy Lord, God of power and might:
heaven and earth are full of your glory.
Hosanna in the highest.

Then follows:

To you indeed be glory, almighty God, because on the night before he died, your Son, Jesus Christ, took bread; when he had given you thanks, he broke it, gave it to his disciples, and said: 'Take, eat; this is my body, which is given for you; do this to remember me.' After supper he took the cup; when he had

Children

given you thanks, he gave it to them, and said: 'This cup is the new covenant in my blood, poured out for you; do this as often as you drink it, to remember me.'

The people may say this or some other acclamation:
Christ has died,
Christ is risen,
Christ will come in glory.

Then follows:

Therefore, loving God, recalling now Christ's death and resurrection, we ask you to accept this our sacrifice of praise. Send your Holy Spirit upon us and our celebration that we may be fed with the body and blood of your Son and be filled with your life and goodness. Strengthen us to do your work and to be your body in the world. Unite us in Christ and give us your peace.

The presiding priest may add further prayer that all may receive the benefits of Christ's work and renewal in the Spirit.

The prayer ends with these or similar words:

All this we ask through your Son Jesus Christ our Lord, to whom with you and the Holy Spirit be all honour and glory now and for ever. **Amen.**

A New Zealand Prayer Book, p. 512

9k   **THANKS FOR FAMILIES**
God, when we know that you love us,
more than any parent could,
your love flows through us in love for each other.
We thank you for forming us into families,
(*and for giving us this child to love.*
Through the love of God we welcome him/her;)
with the love of God we will care for each other;
by the love of God we will direct our lives;
and in the love of God may we all abide for ever. Amen.

Adapted by Michael Counsell

91 BLESSING

The love of the Lord Jesus draw you to himself, the power of
the Lord Jesus strengthen you in his service, the joy of the Lord
Jesus fill your hearts; and the blessing ...

William Temple

---

10. CHRISTMAS, THE INCARNATION

10a GREETING

Behold, I bring you tidings of great joy which shall be to all
people: for unto you is born *(this day)* in the city of David a
Saviour who is Christ the Lord.
Thanks be to God.

Luke 2.10–11, *Church of Ireland Alternative Prayer Book 1984*

10b INVITATION TO CONFESS

Christ the light of the world has come to dispel the darkness of
our hearts. In his light let us examine ourselves and confess our
sins.

The Promise of His Glory, p. 165

10c KYRIE

Forgive us, Lord. You send your eternal light into the world,
but so often we choose to remain in darkness. Lord, have
mercy.
Lord, have mercy.
Forgive us, Lord. You show your love for us by sending your
Son into the world; but so often we do not love one another.
Christ, have mercy.
Christ, have mercy.
Forgive us, Lord. You offer us the privilege of becoming your
children; but so often we do not recognize or receive Jesus your
Son. Lord, have mercy.
Lord, have mercy.

Companion to the Lectionary 6, p. 21

10d ABSOLUTION

May almighty God, who sent his Son into the world to save sinners, bring you his pardon and peace, now and for ever. **Amen.**

The Promise of his Glory, p. 185

10e COLLECT

Lord Jesus, before whom the wise men laid their gifts, and
whom humble shepherds worshipped, accept our praises as we
celebrate your birth at Bethlehem, and be born in our hearts

today; for you are alive and reign, with the Father and the Holy Spirit one God, for ever and ever. **Amen.**

Prayers for Sundays

10f SUITABLE SCRIPTURE PASSAGES
Isaiah 7.10–16; 9.2–7; 52.7–10; 62.6–12; Micah 5.2–5a; Ecclesiasticus 24.1–12; Psalms 96; 97; 98.
Matthew 1.18–25; 2.13–23; Luke 1.26–38, 46–55 (Magnificat); 2.1–20, 41–52; John 1.1–18; Galatians 4.4–7; Philippians 2.1–13; Titus 2.11–14; 3.4–7; Hebrews 1.1–4; 4.12–16; 5.1–10; 10.5–10; 1 John 1.1 – 2.2.

10g AFFIRMATION OF FAITH
Christmas invites us to celebrate again an incredible hope. Let us stand and affirm our faith.
**In the shepherds,
the angels and all who were wise
we affirm the possibility
of recognising our God.
Faced with power and violence,
destruction and alienation,
in the child of Bethlehem
we celebrate all that saves us.
In the whole of history
beginning with the Word
we proclaim with joy
the presence of the Christ.
To be human is to be linked with God;
to be powerless is not the last word;
the ordinary may be the shelter
for the highest hopes of the world.
This we affirm in faith
because love has indeed come to us.**

*Pitt Street Uniting Church**

10h INTERCESSION
(*During the day substitute 'on this holy day' for 'in this holy night'.*)

Father, in this holy night your Son our Saviour was born as a human child. Renew your Church as the Body of Christ. Lord, in your mercy:
hear our prayer.

In this holy night Christians the world over are celebrating his birth. Open our hearts that he may be born in us today. Lord, in your mercy:
hear our prayer.

In this holy night there was no room for your Son in the inn. Protect with your love those who have no home and all who live in poverty. Lord, in your mercy:
hear our prayer.

In this holy night Mary in the pain of labour brought your Son to birth. Hold in your hand (... *and)* all who are in any kind of pain or distress today. Lord, in your mercy:
hear our prayer.

In this holy night your Christ came as a light shining in the darkness. Bring comfort to (... *and)* all who suffer in the sadness of our world. Lord, in your mercy:
hear our prayer.

In this holy night shepherds in the fields heard good tidings of joy. Give us grace to preach the gospel of Christ's redemption. Lord, in your mercy:
hear our prayer.

In this holy night the angels sang 'Peace to God's people on earth'. Strengthen those who work for your peace and justice in (... *and in)* all the world. Lord, in your mercy:
hear our prayer.

In this holy night strangers found the holy family, and saw the baby lying in the manger. Bless our homes and all whom we love, and help us to live as the holy family. Lord, in your mercy:
hear our prayer.

In this holy night heaven is come down to earth and earth is raised to heaven. Keep in safety (... *and)* all those who have gone through death in the hope of heaven. Lord, in your mercy:
hear our prayer.

In this holy night angels and shepherds worshipped at the manger throne. Receive the worship we offer in fellowship with Blessed Mary and all the saints. Merciful Father,
accept these prayers

**for the sake of your Son,
our Saviour Jesus Christ. Amen.**

Michael Perham, *The Promise of His Glory*, p. 178

10i AT THE PEACE

Glory to God in the highest, and peace on earth to all on whom
his favour rests.

Luke 2.14, *Patterns for Worship*, 2R3

10j PREFACE

By the power of the Holy Spirit he was born of the Virgin Mary
his mother, and we have seen his glory, glory as of the only Son
from the Father.

An Australian Prayer Book 1978

10k THANKSGIVING AFTER COMMUNION

At night:

God our Father, tonight you have made known to us again the
power and coming of our Lord Jesus Christ; may our Christmas
celebration confirm our faith and fix our eyes on him until the
day dawns and Christ the morning star rises in our hearts.
To him be glory both now and for ever. Amen.

Daytime:

Gracious Father, our eyes have seen the King in his beauty; by
this living bread and saving cup let his likeness be formed in us
and grow until the end of time; through Christ our Lord.
Amen.

The Promise of His Glory, pp. 182–3

10l SOLEMN BLESSING

May the Father, who has loved the eternal Son from before the
foundation of the world, shed that love upon you his children.
Amen.
May Christ, who by his incarnation gathered into one things
earthly and heavenly, fill you with joy and peace. **Amen.**
May the Holy Spirit, by whose overshadowing Mary became
the Godbearer, give you grace to carry the good news of Christ.
Amen.
And the blessing ...

The Promise of His Glory, p. 183

11. THE CHURCH, THE BODY OF CHRIST

See also THE EUCHARIST, THE TEMPLE, THE UNITY OF
THE CHURCH

11a GREETING
Peace and mercy to the people of God. **Amen.**

Galatians 6.16, *Bible Praying*, 11

11b INVITATION, CONFESSION AND ABSOLUTION
Let us pray.
Lord, Jesus Christ,
We are your body,
Not because we have chosen that name,
But because you have given it to us.
While we marvel at this great privilege,
We also regret our failures.

(Spoken or preferably sung)
Lord, have mercy on us, *or* **Kyrie eleison**
Christ, have mercy on us.

If through false pride or selfish independence,
We have said 'I am not part of the body ...'
Lord, have mercy on us,
Christ, have mercy on us.

If through superiority or lack of love,
We have said 'I don't need you ...'
Lord, have mercy on us,
Christ, have mercy on us.

If we have known that other parts of your body suffer,
And have refused to share their pain ...
Lord, have mercy on us,
Christ, have mercy on us.

If we have seen other parts of your body rejoice,
And have suspected or scorned their happiness ...
Lord, have mercy on us,
Christ, have mercy on us.

If, in place of you, the head of the body,
We have served our own theology, tradition or prejudice,

And loved only those who loved or looked like us ...
Lord, have mercy on us,
Christ, have mercy on us.

(Silence.)

Let the Body of Christ join hands
and become one.
(All join hands.)
Lord Jesus, here is your body:
It is frustrated and fallible;
It is flawed and gullible;
It is tired,
But through you it can be made new.
As your body, we wait on your word.
(Silence.)

Jesus says: 'Come to me,
you who are weary and heavily burdened
And I will give you rest.'
Jesus says: 'In the world you will have trouble.
But don't be afraid. I have overcome the world.'
Jesus says: 'I love you,
I want you,
And I am with you ... always.'
(Silence.)

In the name of Christ our Lord.
Amen.

A Wee Worship Book, pp. 20–21

11c KYRIE
God of all grace, you love the church and call us to care for one
another, but we have been careless about each other's feelings.
Lord, have mercy,
Lord, have mercy.
God of all grace, you love the church and call us to be one
together, but we have shown our divisions to the world. Christ,
have mercy,
Christ, have mercy.

God of all grace, you love the church and call us to rely on each other, but we have been jealous and independent. Lord, have mercy,
Lord, have mercy.

Companion to the Lectionary 6, p. 214*

11d COLLECT

Lord God, whose Son was content to die to bring new life, have mercy on your church, which will do anything you ask, anything at all, except die and be reborn.

Lord Christ, forbid us unity which leaves us where we are: welded into one company, but extracted from the battle: engaged to be yours but not found at your side.

Holy Spirit of God, reach deeper than our inertia and our fears: release us into the freedom of the children of God. **Amen.**

Wind and Fire

11e SUITABLE SCRIPTURE PASSAGES

Isaiah 5.1–7; Wisdom 10.15–21; Baruch 5.1–9.
Matthew 16.13–20; John 15.1–8; 17.1–11, 20–26; Acts 2.42–47; Romans 12.3–21; 1 Corinthians 3.10–11, 16–23; 10.14–17; 12.12–31a; Ephesians 1.15–23; 4.1–16; 5.21–33; Colossians 1.15–28; 2.16–19; 3.5–17; 1 Thessalonians 1.1–10; 2.1–8; 1 Peter 2.2–10; Revelation 1.4–20.

11f PRAYER OF COMMITMENT
God our Father,
it is your purpose
to bring your whole creation
into full unity in Christ.
We commit ourselves to you.
Help us to live for others
even as your love includes all;
to seek out from others
the truth they have grasped;
to trust each other
as fellow-workers
in the one community you have given us;
to obey your call
to make visible
the unity of your Church.
Come, Holy Spirit, help us. Amen.

The Promise of His Glory, p. 254

11g INTERCESSION

We pray that Christ may be seen in the life of the Church, saying, Jesus, Lord of the Church,
in your mercy hear us.

You have called us into the family of those who are children of God. May our love for our brothers and sisters in Christ be strengthened by your grace. Jesus, Lord of the Church,
in your mercy hear us.

You have called us to be a temple where the Holy Spirit can dwell. Give us clean hands and pure hearts so that our lives will reflect your holiness. Jesus, Lord of the Church,
in your mercy hear us.

You have called us to be a light to the world so that those in darkness come to you. May our lives shine as a witness to the saving grace you have given for all. Jesus, Lord of the Church,
in your mercy hear us.

You have called us members of the body of Christ, so when one suffers all suffer together. We ask for your comfort and healing power to bring hope to those in distress. Jesus, Lord of the Church,
in your mercy hear us.

You have called us to be the Bride where Christ the Lord is the Bridegroom. Prepare us for the wedding feast where we will be united with him for ever. Lord of the Church,
hear our prayer,
and make us one in heart and mind
to serve you with joy for ever. Amen.

The Promise of His Glory, p. 235

11h AT THE PEACE

Brothers and sisters, we are the body of Christ.
By one Spirit we were baptized into one body.
Keep the unity of the Spirit in the bond of peace.
Amen. We are bound by the love of Christ.

1 Corinthians 12.13; Ephesians 4.3; 2 Corinthians 5.14; *A New Zealand Prayer Book*, p. 419

11i LONGER PREFACE

Father, all-powerful and ever-living God, we do well always and everywhere to give you thanks through Jesus Christ our Lord. Through his cross and resurrection he freed us from sin and death and called us to the glory that has made us a chosen race, a royal priesthood, a holy nation, a people set apart. Everywhere we proclaim your mighty works, for you have called us out of darkness into your own wonderful light. And so, with all the choirs of angels in heaven we proclaim your glory, for ever praising you and saying/singing ...

Roman Missal*

11j AFTER COMMUNION
Lord, in this communion you have joined us to yourself, to the whole church and to the whole world, which is your creation and ours. And now we, the church and the world are mystically and wonderfully renewed. Blessed be your name for ever and ever. **Amen.**

Michael Powell, *All Year Round 1990*, p. 153

11k BLESSING
Be on your guard, stand firm in the faith, be people of courage, be strong, do everything in love; and the blessing ...

1 Corinthians 16.13, *Bible Praying*, 455*

---

12. THE CITY, INDUSTRY, THE UNEMPLOYED, WORK

See also AUTHORITY

12a OPENING RESPONSE
We have come to the city of the living God, to the heavenly Jerusalem, with thousands of angels in joyful assembly.
Alleluia!
We have come to God the judge of all, to Jesus the mediator of the new covenant.
Alleluia!

Hebrews 12.22–24, 28 (*GNB**), *Patterns for Worship*, 6A10

12b INVITATION TO CONFESS
Jesus saw the city, and wept over it, because it did not recognise the time of God's coming. We confess our part in the self-centredness, blindness and sin of the life of our city.

Luke 19.41, *Patterns for Worship*, 13B14

12c KYRIE
Lord Jesus, you wept over the sins of your city. On our city:
Lord, have mercy.

Lord, have mercy.
Lord Jesus, you heal the wounds of sin and division, jealousy
and bitterness. On us: Christ, have mercy.
Christ, have mercy.
Lord Jesus, you bring pardon and peace to the sinner. Grant us
peace: Lord, have mercy.
Lord, have mercy.

Holy Trinity Church, Wealdstone, Patterns for Worship, 13C20

12d PRAYER

God bless this city
and move our hearts with pity
lest we grow hard.
God bless this place
with silence, solitude and space
that we may pray.
God bless these days
of rough and narrow ways
lest we despair.
God bless the night
and calm the people's fright
that we may love.
God bless this land
and guide us with your hand
lest we be unjust.
God bless this earth
through pangs of death and birth
and make us whole.

Prayer in the Morning

12e SUITABLE SCRIPTURE PASSAGES

2 Samuel 5.1–5, 9–10; 6.1–5, 12b–19; Jeremiah 29.1, 4–7; Amos
7.7–15; Micah 3.5–12; Psalms 24; 48.
Luke 13.31–35; Philippians 3.17 – 4.1; Hebrews 11.8–10;
13.12–14; Revelation 21.9–14.

12f THE RIGHT ATTITUDE

Those who live in our cities and outer estates tell us:
'Do not come with compassion, but with desire.
Do not come with generosity, but with humility.
Do not come to bring light, but to find it.
Do not come to gain virtue, but to receive glory.
Do not come to bring Jesus Christ, but to embrace him.'

Church Urban Fund

12g INTERCESSION
Let us pray for humankind, as people labour to provide for
themselves, their families, their communities:
We pray for those who, no matter how hard they work, have
too little to live on. *Silence.*
We pray for those who gain great wealth from their work, and
carry a great responsibility to use it well. *Silence.*
We pray for those who have no work, who feel deprived and
belittled. *Silence.*
We pray for those in charge of other workers, who have delicate relationships to maintain. *Silence.*
We pray for those who have retired, who seek a new direction
for their lives. *Silence.*
We pray for those who are just starting work, full of excitement
and apprehension. *Silence.*
We make our prayers in the name of Jesus Christ, the carpenter,
teacher and healer who is Lord of all. **Amen.**

Companion to the Lectionary 6, p. 109

12h AT THE PEACE
The name of this city from now on shall be: 'The Lord is here.'

Ezekiel 48.35, Michael Counsell

12i PREFACE
And now we give you thanks because you call us to live in your
city, while we look for the city which is to come, designed and
built by you, with eternal foundations, to which we journey as
citizens of heaven.

Hebrews 13.14; 11.10, *Patterns for Worship*, 13N23

12j THANKSGIVING
Living God, Father of light, Hope of nations, Friend of sinners,
Builder of the city that is to come; your love is made visible in
Jesus Christ, you bring home the lost, restore the sinner and
give dignity to the despised. In the face of Jesus Christ your
light shines out, flooding lives with goodness and truth, gathering into one a divided and broken humanity. **Amen.**

Patterns for Worship, 13P18

12k BLESSING
God, who has prepared for you a city with permanent foundations, bring you to the eternal and triumphant joy of that city of
the great King. And the blessing ...

Patterns for Worship, 13T34

13. THE COMMANDMENTS, THE LAW

See also THE BIBLE, THE COVENANT, WORKS

13a OPENING RESPONSE

God does not wish us to walk in darkness; in his mercy he has revealed to us the way of life. His word is a lantern to our feet, **And a light to our paths**.

Psalm 119.105, Michael Counsell

13b INVITATION TO CONFESS

God so loved the world that he gave his only Son Jesus Christ to save us from our sins, to be our advocate in heaven, and to bring us to eternal life. Let us confess our sins, in penitence and faith, firmly resolved to keep God's commandments and to live in love and peace with our neighbours.

ASB, p. 126*

13c CONFESSION

Almighty God,
long-suffering and of great goodness:
We confess to you,
we confess with our whole heart
our neglect and forgetfulness of your commandments,
our wrong doing, speaking, and thinking;
the hurts we have done to others;
and the good we have left undone.
O God, forgive your people who have sinned against you;
and raise us to newness of life;
through Jesus Christ our Lord. Amen.

My God, My Glory*

13d ABSOLUTION

God, the Father of mercies, has reconciled the world to himself through the death and resurrection of his Son Jesus Christ, not counting our trespasses against us, but sending his Holy Spirit to shed abroad his love among us. By the ministry of reconciliation entrusted by Christ to his Church, receive his pardon and peace to stand before him in his strength alone, this day and evermore. **Amen.**

The Promise of His Glory, p. 118

13e COLLECT

Set our hearts on fire with love for you, O Christ our God, that in its flame we may love you with all our heart, with all our mind, with all our soul and with all our strength, and our neighbours as ourselves, so that keeping your commandments, we may glorify you, the giver of all good gifts. **Amen.**

A Manual of Eastern Orthodox Prayers, p. 23*

13f SUITABLE SCRIPTURE PASSAGES

Exodus 20.1–4, 7–9, 12–20; Deuteronomy 4.1–2, 6–9; 5.12–15; 6.1–9; 11.18–21, 26–28; Nehemiah 8.1–12; Jeremiah 31.31–34; Psalms 1; 19; 81.1–10; 119.1–8, or 9–16, or 33–40, or 97–104, or any other section.
Matthew 5.17–48; Mark 2.23 – 3.6; 12.28–34; John 13.31–35; 15.9–17; Romans 4.13–25; 7.15–25a; 8.1–11; 10.5–15; 13.8–14; 1 Corinthians 9.16–23; Galatians 2.15–21; 3.23–29; 1 John 3.16–24; 5.1–6.

13g CHOOSING TO OBEY

God has given you a choice between a blessing and a curse. If you will turn back to the Lord and with all your heart obey his commandments, then the Lord your God will have mercy on you. The commandment God gives you is not too difficult for you or beyond your reach. No, it is here with you. You know it and can quote it, so now obey it. God gives you a choice between good and evil, between life and death: choose life! Decide today whom you will serve.
We will serve the Lord; he is our God.

Deuteronomy 30.1–3, 11, 14, 19; Joshua 24.15, 18, Michael Counsell

13h INTERCESSION

God our Father, grant us the help of your Spirit in our prayers for the salvation of humankind. We pray for the whole church, that in faith and unity it may constantly be renewed by your Holy Spirit for mission and service. Lord, in your mercy,
hear our prayer.

We pray for the peoples of the world and the leaders of the nations, that they may seek justice, freedom and peace for all. Lord, in your mercy,
hear our prayer.

We pray for our own country and for all who have authority and influence, that they may serve in wisdom, honesty and compassion. Lord, in your mercy,
hear our prayer.

We pray for the communities in which we live and work, that there we may use your gifts to set people free from drudgery

and poverty, and together find joy in your creation. Lord, in your mercy,
hear our prayer.

We pray for those who are ill ..., for those in sorrow ..., for the anxious, the lonely, the despairing, the persecuted, and for all who suffer from cruelty, injustice or neglect, that they may find strength and hope. Lord, in your mercy,
hear our prayer.

We pray for the life and witness of this church and all its members, that we may serve you in holiness throughout our lives.
Lord, hear our prayers, in the strong name of Jesus Christ. Amen.

Editors, Prayers for the People, 28.28

13i AT THE PEACE
Great peace have those who love God's law; nothing shall cause them to stumble.

Psalm 119.165

13j PREFACE
Day and night we give you thanks because you have revealed the commandments which lead to righteousness.

Psalm 119.62, 164, Michael Counsell

13k THANKSGIVING
Almighty God,
we thank you for the gift of your holy word.
May it be a lantern to our feet,
a light to our paths,
and a strength to our lives.
Take us and use us
to love and serve
in the power of the Holy Spirit
and in the name of your Son,
Jesus Christ our Lord. Amen.

ASB, p. 105

13l BLESSING
May the almighty and eternal God sanctify and govern your hearts and bodies in the ways of his laws and the works of his commandments; that under God's protection, now and ever, you may be preserved in body and soul; and the blessing ...

BCP 1662*

14. CONFIRMATION, CONVERSION, CALL

14a CALL TO WORSHIP
Jesus said to his disciples, 'Follow me.'
They left everything and went with him.

Matthew 4.19–20

14b INVITATION TO CONFESS
Thus says the high and lofty One who inhabits eternity, whose name is Holy: 'I dwell in the high and holy place, and with those who are of a contrite and humble spirit.'

Isaiah 57.15

14c CONFESSION
Lord, because we have loved the world too much; because we would rather be successful than be useful; because we have bartered the most precious things for the cheap pleasures of the moment,
we are sorry, and we ask your forgiveness.

Lord, because we have compromised with the truth; because we have been disloyal to you and to our friends; because we have taken the easy way, and irresponsibly followed the crowd,
we are sorry, and we ask your forgiveness.

Lord, because we have been too lazy to use the opportunities you have given us; because we have been too undisciplined to resist the temptations of unlawful appetites and desires; because we have been too proud to own we were in the wrong,
we are sorry, and we ask your forgiveness.

Lord, because we have not forgiven others; because we have not accepted ourselves, though you accepted us long ago; because we have not used the means of grace which your Church so freely offers us,
we are sorry, and we ask your forgiveness.

Lord, because we have neglected to give you the worship we owe you; because we have spurned the voice of conscience and been deaf to your commands; because we have forgotten your invitation to prove ourselves worthy of eternal life with you,
we are sorry, and we ask your forgiveness.
Silence.

Services for Special Occasions, p. 103

14d ABSOLUTION

God has rescued you from the power of darkness, and brought you safe into the kingdom of his dear Son: in Christ your sins are forgiven and you are set free. **Amen.**

Colossians 1.13–14, *Bible Praying*, 158

14e COLLECT

Lord Jesus, who called your first disciples to leave all selfishness and imitate your life of love: sharpen our ears to the sound of your call to us, that henceforth we may gladly follow you as our leader. **Amen.**

Michael Counsell

14f SUITABLE SCRIPTURE PASSAGES

Exodus 3.1–15; Deuteronomy 11.18–21, 26–28; 30.15–20; Joshua 24.1–2a, 14–24; 1 Samuel 3.1–10; 15.34 – 16.13; 1 Kings 19.9–18; Proverbs 1.20–33; 8.1–4, 22–31; 9.1–6; Isaiah 6.1–8; 44.1–5; 55.1–11; Jeremiah 1.4–10; 15.15–21; 31.31–34; Ezekiel 17.22–24; Hosea 5.15 – 6.6.

Matthew 4.12–23; 11.16–19; 16.24–27; 28.16–20; Mark 1.14–20; 2.13–22; Luke 9.51–62; 14.25–33; 24.45–52; John 3.1–17; 14.15–18; 15.1–11; Acts 9.1–6; 16.16–34; Romans 5.1–8; 8.11–17; 1 Corinthians 1.1–9; 12.12–13; Galatians 1.11–24; 5.16–25; Ephesians 1.3–14; Philippians 1.21–30; 1 Thessalonians 1.1–10; 2.9–13; James 5.13–20; 1 Peter 1.17–23; 2.4–10.

14g THE DECISION

Before God and this congregation, you must affirm that you turn to Christ and reject all that is evil:

Do you turn to Christ?

I turn to Christ.

Do you repent of your sins?

I repent of my sins.

Do you reject selfish living, and all that is false and unjust?

I reject them all.

Do you renounce Satan and all evil?

I renounce all that is evil.

Will you each, by God's grace, strive to live as a disciple of Christ, loving God with your whole heart, and your neighbour as yourself, until your life's end?

I will, with God's help.

You have heard these our brothers and sisters respond to Christ. Will you support them in their calling?

We will.

A Prayer Book for Australia, p. 56

14h INTERCESSION
We pray to God the Holy Spirit, saying:
Holy Spirit, come upon us.
Come Holy Spirit, creator, and renew the earth:
Holy Spirit, come upon us.
Come Holy Spirit, counsellor, and touch our lips that we may
proclaim your word:
Holy Spirit, come upon us.
Come Holy Spirit, power from on high; make us channels of
peace and ministers of healing:
Holy Spirit, come upon us.
Come Holy Spirit, breath of God, give life to the dry bones
around us, and make us a living people, holy and free:
Holy Spirit, come upon us.
Come Holy Spirit, wisdom and truth; strengthen us to be bold
in faith:
Holy Spirit, come upon us.

Canadian *Book of Alternative Services*, p. 123

14i AT THE PEACE
The offer of Jesus is peace in our hearts here on earth, and eternal life with him. Let us claim that peace for ourselves and
share it with our neighbours.

Michael Counsell

14j LONGER PREFACE
Father, while all your creation groans with pain like the pain of
childbirth, and longs to share the freedom of the children of
God, your Spirit pleads for us in groans words cannot express.
Father in heaven:
we give you thanks and praise.

The law of the Spirit brings us life in Christ, and sets us free
from the law of sin and death. Father in heaven:
we give you thanks and praise.

Like all who are led by your Spirit, we are your children. By
your Spirit's power we cry, 'Abba, Father.' Father in heaven:
we give you thanks and praise.

The Spirit confirms that we are your children, fellow-heirs with
Christ, sharing his suffering now, that we may share his glory.
Father in heaven:
we give you thanks and praise.

51

So by your Spirit we praise you for ever and proclaim your glory with all the company of heaven, for ever praising you and saying/singing ...

Romans 8.2, 14–25, Patterns for Worship, 8P12*

14k PRAYER AFTER COMMUNION
Gracious God, in baptism you make us one family in Christ your Son, one in the sharing of his body and blood, one in the communion of his Spirit. Help us to grow in love for one another and come to the full maturity of the body of Christ. Most loving God,
you send us into the world you love.
Give us grace to go thankfully and with courage
in the power of your Spirit.

A Prayer Book for Australia, p. 68

14l BLESSING
May the Father bless you, who created all things in the beginning; may the Son of God heal you; may the Holy Spirit enlighten you, guard your bodies, save your souls, direct your thoughts, and bring you safe to the heavenly country; and the blessing of the triune God be upon you, and remain with you for ever. **Amen.**

Services for Special Occasions, p. 110*

---

15. THE COVENANT, NEW YEAR

See also SACRIFICE

15a ADORATION
Let us pray.
Let us adore the Father, the God of love. He created us; he continually preserves and sustains us; he has loved us with an everlasting love, and given us the light of the knowledge of his glory in the face of Jesus Christ.
You are God; we praise you; we acknowledge you to be the Lord.

Let us glory in the grace of our Lord Jesus Christ. Though he was rich, yet for our sakes he became poor; he was tempted in all points as we are, yet without sin; he went about doing good and preaching the gospel of the kingdom; he became obedient to death, death on the cross; he was dead and is alive for ever;

he has opened the kingdom of heaven to all who trust in him;
he sits at the right hand of God in the glory of the Father; he
will come again to be our Judge.
You, Christ, are the King of Glory.

Let us rejoice in the fellowship of the Holy Spirit, the Lord, the
Giver of life. By him we are born into the family of God, and
made members of the body of Christ; his witness confirms us;
his wisdom teaches us; his power enables us; he will do for us
far more than we ask or think.
All praise to you, Holy Spirit.
Silence.

*The Methodist Service Book**

15b CONFESSION AND ABSOLUTION
Let us humbly confess our sins to God.
God our Father, you have set forth the way of life for us in your
beloved Son: we confess with shame our slowness to learn of
him, our failure to follow him, our reluctance to bear the cross.
Have mercy on us, Lord, and forgive us.

We confess the poverty of our worship, our neglect of fellowship and of the means of grace, our hesitating witness for
Christ, our evasion of responsibilities in your service, our
imperfect stewardship of your gifts.
Have mercy on us, Lord, and forgive us.

Let each of us in silence make her or his own confession to God.
Silence.
**Have mercy on me, O God, according to your steadfast love;
according to your abundant mercy
blot out my transgressions.
Wash me thoroughly from my iniquity,
and cleanse me from my sin.
Create in me a clean heart, O God,
and put a new and right spirit within me.**

This is the message we have heard from him and proclaim to
you, that God is light and in God is no darkness at all. If we
walk in the light, as God is in the light, we have fellowship with
one another, and the blood of Jesus his Son cleanses us from all
sin. If we say we have no sin, we deceive ourselves, and the

truth is not in us. If we confess our sins, God is faithful and just, and will forgive our sins and cleanse us from all unrighteousness.
Amen. Thanks be to God.

The Methodist Service Book*

15c COLLECT
Father, you have appointed our Lord Jesus Christ as Mediator of a new covenant; give us grace to draw near with fullness of faith and join ourselves in a perpetual covenant with you, through Jesus Christ our Lord. **Amen.**

The Methodist Service Book*

15d SUITABLE SCRIPTURE PASSAGES
Genesis 8.20 – 9.17; 15.1–12, 17–18; 17.1–7, 15–16; 18.1–10a; 32.22–31; 2 Samuel 7.1–11, 16; Jeremiah 23.1–6; 31.27–34; 33.14–16; Hosea 2.14–20; Psalms 50.1–8, 22–23; 89.1–4, 15–26. Matthew 1.18–25; 26.26–29; 28.16–20; Mark 14.22–25; Luke 1.26–38, 46–55 (Magnificat); 2.21; 4.16–24; John 14.15–21; 15.1–8; Romans 4.13–25; 16.25–27; 1 Corinthians 11.23–26; 2 Corinthians 1.18–22; 3.1–6; Hebrews 5.5–10; 9.11–15; 12.18–29.

15e THE COVENANT
In the Old Covenant, God chose Israel to be his people and to obey his laws. Our Lord Jesus Christ, by his death and resurrection, has made a New Covenant with all who trust in him. We stand within this Covenant and we bear his name.
On the one side, God promises in this Covenant to give us new life in Christ. On the other side, we are pledged to live no more for ourselves but for him.
Today, therefore, we meet expressly, as generations before us have met, to renew the Covenant which bound them, and binds us, to God.
All stand.

Beloved in Christ, let us again claim for ourselves this Covenant which God has made with his people, and take the yoke of Christ upon us.
To take his yoke upon us means that we are content that he appoints us our place and work, and that he himself be our reward.
Christ has many services to be done; some are easy, some are difficult; some bring honour, others bring reproach; some are suitable to our natural inclinations and material interests, others are contrary to both. In some we may please Christ and

please ourselves, in others we cannot please Christ except by denying ourselves. Yet the power to do all these things is given us in Christ, who strengthens us.

Therefore let us make this Covenant of God our own. Let us give ourselves anew to him, trusting in his promises and relying on his grace.

The people sit or kneel.

Lord God, Holy Father, since you have called us through Christ to share in this gracious Covenant, we take upon ourselves with joy the yoke of obedience, and, for love of you, engage ourselves to seek and do your perfect will.

We are no longer our own, but yours.

I am no longer my own, but yours.

Put me to what you will, rank me with whom you will;

put me to doing, put me to suffering;

let me be employed for you or laid aside for you,

exalted for you or brought low for you;

let me be full, let me be empty;

let me have all things, let me have nothing;

I freely and wholeheartedly

yield all things to your pleasure and disposal.

And now, glorious and blessed God,

Father, Son, and Holy Spirit,

you are mine and I am yours.

So be it. And the Covenant now made on earth,

let it be ratified in heaven. Amen.

*The Methodist Service Book**

15f   AT THE PEACE

God says: 'Behold, I give you my covenant of peace for ever.'

Numbers 25.12

15g   PREFACE

You formed us in your own image: male and female you created us. When we turned away from you in sin, you did not cease to care for us, but opened a path of salvation for all people. You made a covenant with Israel, and through your servants Abraham and Sarah gave the promise of a blessing to all nations. Through Moses you led your people from bondage into freedom; through the prophets you renewed your promise of salvation.

Canadian *Book of Alternative Services*, p. 193

15h THANKSGIVING
Now praise our God:
our God is good, his mercy lasts for ever.
Step with confidence through the gate of the year.
**We will seek to love and serve our God
on each and every day. Amen.**

Michael Counsell

15I BLESSING
May God keep you in all your days.
May Christ shield you in all your ways.
May the Spirit bring you healing and peace.
May the Holy Trinity drive all darkness from you
and pour upon you blessing and light. **Amen.**

The Promise of His Glory, p. 203

---

16. THE CREATION

See also ECOLOGY, HARVEST, NATURE, SUFFERING

16a GREETING
The Lord of all creation be with you;
The Lord bless you.

Patterns for Worship, 0A8, source unknown

16b INVITATION TO CONFESS
Almighty God, we come together to thank you for the beauty
and glory of your creation; to praise you for your holiness and
grace; to acknowledge our responsibility to animals and for our
use of the created world. But, first of all, we pray for your
forgiveness because of our part in sins of thoughtlessness and
cruelty towards animal life.
Silence.

Andrew Linzey, RSPCA *Order of Service for Animal Welfare*

16c CONFESSION
**Almighty God, you have given us
temporary lordship of your beautiful creation.
But we have misused our power,
turned away from responsibility,
and marred your image in us.
Forgive us, true Lord,
especially for our callousness and cruelty to animals.
Help us to follow the way of your Son, Jesus Christ,**

who expressed power in humility
and lordship in loving service.
Enable us, by your Spirit, to walk in newness of life,
healing injury, avoiding wrong
and making peace with all your creatures.

Andrew Linzey, RSPCA Order of Service for Animal Welfare

16d ABSOLUTION

God of everlasting love, who is eternally forgiving, pardon and
restore us, and make us one with you in your new creation.
Amen.

Andrew Linzey, RSPCA Order of Service for Animal Welfare

16e COLLECT

Holy Spirit, mighty wind of God, inhabit our darkness, brood
over our abyss, and speak to our chaos; that we may breathe
with your life and share your creation in the power of Jesus
Christ. **Amen.**

All Desires Known

16f SUITABLE SCRIPTURE PASSAGES

Genesis 1.1 – 2.4a; 2.4b–9, 15–24; Job 38.1–11; Proverbs 8.1–4,
22–31.
Isaiah 5.1–7; 40.21–31; Psalms 8; 19; 33.1–12; 65; 96.1–9; 104.1–9,
24–34, 35b; 136; 147.1–11, 20c; 148.
Matthew 6.25–34; Luke 8.22–25; John 1.1–14; Romans 8.18–25; 2
Corinthians 5.6–10; Colossians 1.15–20; Hebrews 1.1–4; 2.5–12;
Revelation 4.

16g THE FAITH OF A NATIVE AMERICAN

Teach your children what we have taught our children – that
the earth is our mother. Whatever befalls the earth befalls the
sons and daughters of the earth. If men spit upon the ground,
they spit upon themselves.
This we know: the earth does not belong to us,
we belong to the earth.
This we know: all things are connected.
Like the blood which unites one family,
all things are connected.
Whatever befalls the earth
befalls the sons and daughters of the earth.
We did not weave the web of life, we are merely a strand in it.
Whatever we do to the web, we do to ourselves.

Chief Seattle, speech to the President of the USA, 1854

16h INTERCESSIONS
(*Each petition is followed by silence and then* Lord, in your mercy,
hear our prayer.)

Let us pray for the Church and for the world.
Grant, almighty God, that all who confess your name may be
united in your truth, live together in your love, and reveal your
glory in the world.

Guide the people of this land, and of all the nations, in the ways
of justice and peace; that we may honour one another and serve
the common good.

Give us all a reverence for the earth as your own creation, that
we may use its resources rightly in the service of others and to
your honour and glory.

Bless all whose lives are closely linked with ours, and grant that
we may serve Christ in them, and love one another as he loves
us.

Comfort and heal all those who suffer in body, mind or spirit;
give them courage and hope in their troubles, and bring them
the joy of your salvation.

We commend to your mercy all who have died, that your will
for them may be fulfilled; and we pray that we may share with
all your saints in your eternal kingdom.

US BCP 1979, p. 388

16i

Almighty God, in giving us dominion over things on earth, you
made us fellow workers in your creation: give us wisdom and
reverence so to use the resources of nature, that no one may suffer from our abuse of them, and that generations yet to come
may continue to praise you for your bounty; through Jesus
Christ our Lord. **Amen.**

US BCP 1979, p. 827

16j AT THE PEACE
The Creator who brought order out of chaos,
give peace to you.
The Saviour who stilled the raging storm, give peace to you.
The Spirit who broods on the deeps, give peace to you.

The Open Gate, p. 110

16k LONGER PREFACE

God of all power, Ruler of the Universe, you are worthy of glory and praise.
Glory to you for ever and ever.

At your command all things came to be: the vast expanse of interstellar space, galaxies, suns, the planets in their courses, and this fragile earth, our island home.
By your will they were created and have their being.

From the primal elements you brought forth the human race, and blessed us with memory, reason and skill. You made us the rulers of creation. But we turned against you, and betrayed your trust; and we turned against one another.
Have mercy, Lord, for we are sinners in your sight.

Again and again, you called us to return. Through prophets and sages you revealed your righteous Law. And in the fullness of time you sent your only Son, born of a woman, to fulfil your Law, to open for us the way of freedom and peace.
By his blood, he reconciled us.
By his wounds, we are healed.

And therefore we praise you, joining with the heavenly chorus, with prophets, apostles and martyrs, and with all those in every generation who have looked to you in hope, to proclaim with them your glory, in their unending hymn, for ever praising you and saying / singing ...

US BCP 1979, p. 369*

16l THANKSGIVING

Father, we give you thanks and praise for your Son, Jesus Christ our Lord. He is the image of the unseen God, the first-born of all creation. He created all things in heaven and on earth: everything visible and everything invisible, thrones, dominions, sovereignties, powers – all things were created through him and for him. Lord of all creation:
we worship and adore you.

He is the radiant light of your glory: he holds all creation together by his word of power. Lord of all creation:
we worship and adore you.

He is first to be born from the dead. All perfection is found in him, and all things were reconciled through him and for him, everything in heaven and everything on earth, when he made peace by his death on the cross. Lord of all creation: **we worship and adore you.**

The Church is his body, he is its head. He takes his place in heaven at your right hand, where we worship you with all of your creation, Creator, Redeemer, and life-giving Spirit. **Amen.**

Patterns for Worship, 10P16*

16m BLESSING
May God who clothes the lilies and feeds the birds of the sky, who leads the lambs to pasture and the deer to water, who multiplied the loaves and fishes and changed water into wine, lead us, feed us, multiply us, and change us to reflect the glory of our Creator through all eternity. And may the blessing ...

Trevor Lloyd, *Enriching the Christian Year*, 14Q1

---

17. THE CROSS, THE PASSION

See also PALM SUNDAY

17a CALL TO WORSHIP
Christ on the cross cries: 'My people, what wrong have I done to you? What good have I not done for you? Listen to me. Is it nothing to you, all you who pass by? Look and see if there is any sorrow like to my sorrow.'
We adore you, O Christ, and we bless you,
because by your holy cross you have redeemed the world.

Ancient Good Friday Liturgies*

17b INVITATION TO PENITENCE
Christ himself bore our sins in his body on the tree, that we might die to sin and live to righteousness. By his wounds we are healed. Let us confess our sins.

1 Peter 2.24, *In Penitence and Faith*, No. 11,* *Patterns for Worship*, 4B5

17c KYRIE
Our selfishness betrays you: Lord, have mercy;
Lord, have mercy.
We fail to share the pain of your suffering: Christ, have mercy;
Christ, have mercy.

We are afraid of being known to belong to you: Lord, have mercy;
Lord, have mercy.

Adapted from Michael Perry

17d ABSOLUTION
Through the cross of Christ, God have mercy on you, pardon you and set you free. Know that you are forgiven and be at peace: God strengthen you in all goodness and keep you in life eternal. **Amen.**

A New Zealand Prayer Book, p. 408

17e COLLECT
Christ our victim, whose beauty was disfigured and whose body was torn upon the cross; open wide your arms to embrace our tortured world, that we may not turn away our eyes, but abandon ourselves to your mercy. **Amen.**

All Desires Known

17f SUITABLE SCRIPTURE PASSAGES
Passion narratives: Matthew 26.14 – 27.66; Mark 14.1 – 15.47; Luke 22.14 – 23.56; John 18.1 – 19.42.
Other passages: Exodus 12.1–4, 11–14; Numbers 21.4–9; Job 14.1–14; Isaiah 42.1–9; 49.1–7; 50.4–9a; 52.13 – 53.12; Lamentations 1.1–12; 3.1–9, 19–24; Ezekiel 37.1–14; Psalms 22.1–22; 31.9–16; 36.5–11; 70; 71.1–14; 130;
Matthew 16.21–28; Mark 8.27–38; Luke 14.25–33; John 3.13–17; 11.1–45; 12.1–11, 20–36; 13.21–32; Romans 5.1–8; 8.6–11; 1 Corinthians 1.18–31; Philippians 2.5–11; Colossians 1.15–20; Hebrews 4.14–16; 5.7–9; 9.11–15; 10.1–25; 12.1–3.

17g AFFIRMATION OF FAITH
We have been crucified with Christ;
it is no longer we who live;
but Christ who lives in us.
The life we live in the body
we live by faith in the Son of God,
who loved us and gave himself for us. Amen.

Galatians 2.19–20, *Bible Praying*, 214

17h A LITANY FOR GOOD FRIDAY
Bearer of all pain, we come to share with you the burden of all this world's suffering: we stand by you in the refugee camp:
we wait and we weep.
At the door of the torture chamber:
we wait and we weep.

In the shanty town:
we wait and we weep.
On the streets among the broken children:
we wait and we weep.
In the oppressor's court:
we wait and we weep.
In the devastated city:
we wait and we weep.
On earth soaked with blood:
we wait and we weep.

Giver of life, we wait with you to bear your hope to earth's darkest places: we wait at the places where darkness is deeper than the deepest pain:
Where love is denied:
let love break through.
Where justice is destroyed:
let righteousness rule.
Where hope is crucified:
let faith persist.
Where peace is no more:
let passion live on.
Where truth is denied:
let the struggle continue.
Where laughter has dried up:
let music play on.
Where fear paralyses:
let forgiveness break through.

Merciful God, we meet each other today at this cross as the inhabitants of one world. We wait with each other as those who inflict wounds on each other:
be merciful to us.
As those who deny justice to others:
be merciful to us.
As those who seize wealth:
be merciful to us.
As those who are greedy:
be merciful to us.
As those who put others on trial:
be merciful to us.
As those who refuse to receive:
be merciful to us.

As those afraid of this world's torment:
be merciful to us.

Bearer of all pain,
have mercy.
Giver of life,
have mercy.
Merciful God,
have mercy.

Reach into this silent darkness with your love;
deepen the terror of this moment into new hope;
relieve the hideous cries with your quiet voice of peace;
that here we may know your salvation,
your glory, your future in Jesus Christ,
the crucified Lord. Amen.

Robin Green, in *Let all the World ...*

17i AT THE PEACE
Now in union with Christ Jesus you who once were far off have been brought near through the shedding of Christ's blood; for he is our peace.

Ephesians 2.13, *Lent, Holy Week and Easter*, p. 190

17j LONGER PREFACE
Blessed are you, gracious God, creator of heaven and earth; we give you thanks and praise through Jesus Christ our Lord, who for our salvation became obedient unto death. The cross which killed him is the cross of his glory, *his* life was lost there but *our* life was given back there. Behold the Man, the Saviour who will not save himself; Creator, whom the world disowns. Therefore with angels and archangels and all the heavenly chorus we cry out to proclaim the glory of your name, for ever praising you and saying/singing ...

Adapted by Michael Counsell

17k THANKSGIVING
Surely he has borne our griefs; he has carried our sorrows.
Surely he has borne our griefs; he has carried our sorrows.
He was despised; he was rejected,
a man of sorrows and acquainted with grief.
He has carried our sorrows.
He was pierced for our sins, bruised for no fault but ours.
He has carried our sorrows.

His punishment has won our peace,
and by his wounds we are healed.
He has carried our sorrows.
We had all strayed like sheep,
but the Lord has laid on him the guilt of us all.
He has carried our sorrows.
Glory to the Father, and to the Son, and to the Holy Spirit.
Surely he has borne our griefs; he has carried our sorrows.

Isaiah 53.3–6, Canadian *Book of Alternative Services*, p. 107

171 SOLEMN BLESSING
You believe that by his dying Christ destroyed death for ever.
Amen.
You have been crucified with Christ and live by faith in the Son
of God, who loved you and gave himself for you. **Amen.**
May he send you out to glory in his cross, and live no longer for
yourselves but for him, who died and was raised to life for us.
Amen.
And the blessing …

Galatians 2.20; 2 Corinthians 5.15, *Patterns for Worship*, 5T13

---

18. DEATH, THE BEREAVED, THE DEPARTED, FUNERALS, GRIEF

See also THE CROSS, LIFE, REMEMBRANCE SUNDAY,
SAINTS

18a INTROIT AT A REQUIEM
Rest eternal grant to them, O Lord, and may light perpetual
shine upon them. You, O God, are praised in Zion, and to you
the vow will be performed in Jerusalem. You hear our prayer,
everyone shall come to you. Rest eternal grant to them, O Lord,
and may light perpetual shine upon them.

Medieval

18b INVITATION TO CONFESS
God has shone in our hearts to give the light of the knowledge
of his glory in the face of Christ. But we have this treasure in
earthen vessels to show that the transcendent power belongs to
God and not to us. As we acknowledge our human frailty, we
call to mind our sins of word, deed, and omission, and confess
them before God our Father.
Silence.

2 Corinthians 4.6–7, *The Promise of His Glory*, p. 62

18c KYRIE

You raise the dead to life in the Spirit: Lord, have mercy.
Lord, have mercy.
You bring pardon and peace to the sinner: Christ, have mercy.
Christ, have mercy.
You bring light to those in darkness: Lord, have mercy.
Lord, have mercy.

Roman Missal

18d ABSOLUTION

May almighty God have mercy on us, forgive us our sins, and
bring us to everlasting life. **Amen.**

Roman Missal

18e COLLECT

O God who brought us to birth, and in whose arms we die, in
our grief and shock contain and comfort us; embrace us with
your love, give us hope in our confusion, and grace to let go
into new life, through Jesus Christ. **Amen.**

All Desires Known

18f SUITABLE SCRIPTURE PASSAGES

Passion narratives: Matthew 26.14 – 27.66; Mark 14.1 – 15.47;
Luke 22.14 – 23.56; John 18.1 – 19.42.
Other passages: Deuteronomy 34.1–12; 2 Samuel 1.1, 17–27;
18.5–9, 15, 31–33; Job 14.1–14; Isaiah 25.1–9; Ezekiel 37.1–14;
Wisdom 1.13–15; 2.23–24; Psalms 9.9–20; 16; 22.23–31; 23; 30;
49.1–12; 116.1–4, 12–19; 116.1–9; 118.1–2, 14–24; 130.
Matthew 27.57–66; John 6.37–40; 11.3–7, 17–20, 33–45; 12.1–11;
12.20–36; 14.1–14; 15.9–17; 19.38–42; Acts 7.55–60; Romans
5.5–11; 6.3–11; 2 Corinthians 4.5–12; 5.6–10, 14–17; Philippians
1.21–30; 2.5–11; 1 Thessalonians 4.13–18; 1 Peter 3.13–22; 4.1–8;
Revelation 21.1–6.

18g AFFIRMATION OF FAITH

I don't believe in death
who mocks in silent stealth;
he robs us only of a breath,
not of a lifetime's wealth.

I don't believe the tomb
imprisons us in the earth,
it's but another loving womb
preparing our new birth.

I do believe in Life
empowered from above,
till, freed from stress and worldly strife
we soar through realms of love.

I do believe that then,
in joy that never ends,
we'll meet all those we've loved, again,
and celebrate our friends!

Pauline Webb

18h LITANY

We thank you, our Father, that your Son Jesus Christ came to die for us. We thank you that you raised him from the dead. We thank you for the gift of life, and the life of *N*. Bring us, with *N*. and all your faithful people, to the fullness of life you promise to those who love you. Lord, in your mercy,
hear our prayer.

We confess that we have not loved you with our whole heart. We have not loved our neighbours as ourselves. We repent, and are sorry for all our sins. Grant us forgiveness, and assure us of your love. Lord, in your mercy,
hear our prayer.

Strengthen us to love and obey you, that we may live the rest of our lives in following your Son, and be ready when you call us to the fullness of eternal life. Lord, in your mercy,
hear our prayer.

We pray for those who mourn. Be close to them in their loss. Increase their faith in your undying love. Lord, in your mercy,
hear our prayer.

Show your mercy to the dying. Sustain them with hope, and fill them with the peace and joy of your presence. Lord, in your mercy,
hear our prayer.

We praise you, Lord God, for your faithful servants in every age. May we, with *[N. and]* all who have died in the faith of Christ, be brought to a joyful resurrection and the fulfilment of your eternal kingdom. **Amen.**

A Prayer Book for Australia, p. 720

See also the various funeral services, and index entries under 'death',
'departed' and 'dying' in anthologies such as Prayers for Sundays.

18i AT THE PEACE
Jesus says: Peace I leave with you. My peace I give to you. Not
as the world gives give I unto you. Do not let your hearts be
troubled, neither let them be afraid. The peace of the risen
Christ be always with you.

John 14.27, Roman Missal

18j PREFACE
Christ chose to die that he might free all people from dying. He
gave his life for us that we might give our lives to you for ever.
In our joy we sing to your glory with all of those to whom you
have promised eternal life.

Roman Missal*

18k THANKSGIVING
Father, we thank you for the life of *N*:
for the life we lived together,
for the love we shared,
for the truths that shaped our lives,
for the memories that remain.

Father, we thank you for Christ our Lord:
for the death he died,
for the grave in which he was laid,
for the victory he won,
for his resurrection on the third day.

Father, we thank you for what you have promised:
for the eternal life you give us,
for the heaven you have opened to *N*,
for the day we shall see each other,
for holding us together until then.

In Jesus' name.
Amen.

Michael Walker, Baptist Praise and Worship, 520

18l BLESSING
May God give to you and to all those whom you love his comfort and his peace, his light and his joy, in this world and the
next; and the blessing of God almighty, the Father, the Son, and
the Holy Spirit, be upon you and remain with you always.
Amen.

Michael Perham, The Promise of His Glory, p. 72

19. THE DEDICATION FESTIVAL OF A CHURCH, THE TEMPLE

19a OPENING RESPONSE
How awesome is this place!
This is none other than the house of God,
this is the gate of heaven.

Genesis 28.17

19b INVITATION TO CONFESS
You are the temple of the living God, and the Spirit of God
dwells in you. The temple of God is holy: you are that temple.
Let us confess our sins to almighty God.

1 Corinthians 3.16

19c CONFESSION
Let us confess our lack of love, and our need of grace:
When we lose patience,
when we are unkind,
when we are envious,
when we are rude or proud,
when we are selfish or irritable,
and when we will not forgive:
have mercy on us, O God.
Help us not to delight in evil,
but to rejoice in the truth;
help us always to protect, to trust,
to hope and to persevere
so that we may see you face to face,
and learn to love as you love us
in Jesus Christ our Lord. Amen.

1 Corinthians 13.4–5, *Bible Praying*, 317*

19d ABSOLUTION
The Lord, whose love for those who seek him is as great as the
heavens are high above the earth, removes *your* sins from *you* as
far as the east is from the west, and will remember them no
more; through Jesus Christ our Lord. **Amen.**

Psalm 103.11–13, *Bible Praying*, 122

19e COLLECT OF THE DEDICATION FESTIVAL
Almighty God, to whose glory we celebrate the dedication of
this house of prayer; we praise you for the many blessings you
have given to those who worship here; and we pray that all
who seek you in this place may find you, and being filled with

the Holy Spirit may become a living temple acceptable to you;
through Jesus Christ our Lord. **Amen.**

The Calendar and Lessons 1969, ASB, p. 824

19f SUITABLE SCRIPTURE PASSAGES

Genesis 28.11–19a; 1 Samuel 3.1–10; 2 Samuel 7.1–14a; 1 Kings
8.22–30, 41–43; 1 Chronicles 29.6–19; 2 Chronicles 5.6–11, 13 –
6.2; Isaiah 2.1–5; 25.1–9; 56.1, 6–8; Ezekiel 43.27 – 44.4; Psalms 15;
26.1–8; 27; 42 – 43; 48; 69.7–10, 16–18; 83; 84; 100; 118; 122; 138.
Matthew 21.12–16; Mark 13.1–8, 13–14; Luke 2.22–40; 2.41–52;
John 2.13–22; 4.19–24; 10.22–29; 1 Corinthians 3.9–13, 16–23;
Ephesians 2.19–22; Hebrews 4.12–16; 12.18–24; 1 Peter 2.1–10;
Revelation 21.9–14.

19g DEDICATION OF ONESELF

I give myself to you, Lord,
I give myself to you.
With my mind and its thinking,
I give myself to you.
With my hands and their working,
I give myself to you.
With my eyes and their seeing,
I give myself to you.
With my body and its actions,
I give myself to you.
With my heart and its loving,
I give myself to you.
I give myself to you Lord,
I give myself to you.

The Edge of Glory, p. 69

19h THE PRAYERS OF THE PEOPLE

For the Church universal,
of which these buildings are a visible symbol,
We thank you, Lord.
For your presence
whenever two or three have gathered in your name,
We thank you, Lord.
For this place
where we may be still and know that you are God,
We thank you, Lord.
For fulfilling our desires and petitions as you see best for us,
We thank you, Lord.
For our past and a vision of the future that lies ahead,
We thank you, Lord.

For the gift of the Holy Spirit and new life in baptism,
We thank you, Lord.
For the pardon of our sins
when we have fallen short of your glory,
We thank you, Lord.
For the holy eucharist
in which we have a foretaste of your eternal kingdom,
We thank you, Lord.
For the blessing of our vows
and the crowning of our years with your goodness,
We thank you, Lord.
For the faith of those who have gone before us
and for our encouragement by their perseverance,
We thank you, Lord.
For all the benefactors of this place who have died in the peace
of Christ and are at rest *(especially N.)*,
We thank you, Lord.
For the fellowship of all your saints
and especially for *N.*, our patron,
We thank you, Lord.
Silence.

O God, from living and chosen stones you prepare an everlasting dwelling place for your majesty. Grant that in the power of the Holy Spirit those who serve you here may always be kept within your presence. This we pray through Jesus Christ our Lord, who lives and reigns with you and the Holy Spirit, one God, now and for ever. **Amen.**

Canadian *Book of Alternative Services*, p. 671

19i AT THE PEACE
We are fellow-citizens with the saints, and of the household of God, through Christ our Lord who came and preached peace to those who were far off and those who were near.

Ephesians 2.17, 19, *ASB*, p. 170

19j LONGER PREFACE
Blessed are you, gracious God, creator of heaven and earth; heaven itself cannot contain you and your glory fills all the world. You accept our setting apart of places for your worship, and in them pour out your gifts of grace upon your faithful people. This table is a sign to us of the heavenly altar, where your saints and angels praise you. Here we have recalled the sacrifice of your Son; here we have been fed with the body and blood of your Son; here our sins have been forgiven; here we

have tasted the joys of your eternal kingdom. Grant that in these mysteries we may be united with one another and strengthened for service in your world. Therefore with angels and archangels and those who worship you in every age, we raise our voices in joyful praise to proclaim the glory of your name, for ever praising you and saying/singing ...

Canadian *Book of Alternative Services*, p. 673*

19k THANKSGIVING
O Lord our God, we thank you for those of past generations who have worshipped you here; those who in this place have taught the Christian faith to others; those whose ministries have been a source of blessing in this church; those who have faithfully borne responsibilities in this congregation. We thank you for those who minister to us, especially for ... our *minister (and his/her family)*; those who bear office in this church; those who look after the organisations and fellowship groups; those who contribute to our worship week by week. We thank you for being here together with us in worship; for the story of your love which we hear from the Bible; for the sacraments of Baptism and Holy Communion; for those special moments when we are sure of your presence. Through Jesus Christ our Lord. **Amen.**

Companion to the Lectionary 6, p. 120

19l BLESSING
May God in the plenitude of love pour upon you the torrents of grace, bless you and keep you in holy fear, prepare you for a happy eternity, and receive you at last into immortal glory; and may the blessing of God almighty, the Father, the Son and the Holy Spirit, be among you and remain with you always. **Amen.**

Coventry Cathedral*

---

20. ECOLOGY, THE ENVIRONMENT, CONSERVATION

See also THE CREATION, NATURE, HARVEST

20a CALL TO WORSHIP
Let us rejoice in the world we see around us;
Let us praise the giver of beauty and new life.

Michael Counsell

20b INVITATION TO CONFESS
We confess our sin, and the sins of our society, in the misuse of God's creation.

Adapted from Michael Perry

20c KYRIE
We have treated the world as if it were ours; Lord, have mercy,
Lord, have mercy.
We have treated our neighbours with little respect; Christ, have mercy,
Christ, have mercy.
We have treated our talents with neglect; Lord, have mercy,
Lord, have mercy.

The Open Gate, p. 57

20d ABSOLUTION
The Lord forgives all your sins and heals the sickness of society; he redeems your life from the grave, and crowns you with mercy and loving-kindness. **Amen.**

Psalm 103.4–5, Michael Counsell

20e COLLECT
Heavenly Father, your Holy Spirit gives breath to all living things; renew us by this same Spirit, that we may learn to respect what you have given and care for what you have made, through Jesus Christ your Son, our Lord. **Amen.**

Andrew Linzey, RSPCA Order of Service for Animal Welfare

20f SUITABLE SCRIPTURE PASSAGES
Genesis 1.1 – 2.4a; 2.4–9, 15–25; Psalms 8; 24; 104.
Matthew 6.24–34; 10.26–31; John 1.1–14; Colossians 1.15–20; Revelation 4.

20g AFFIRMATION OF FAITH
Do you believe that the majestic beauty and complexity of the world around us come from one who cares?
We believe and trust in God.
Do you believe that our Saviour, by taking human flesh and using bread and wine made all material things holy?
We believe and trust in Jesus.
Do you believe that God has put into our hearts the power to love the creation and to care for it as good stewards of his bounty?
We believe and trust in the Holy Spirit.
This is the faith of the Church.
This is our faith.
We believe and trust in God, Father, Son and Holy Spirit.

Michael Counsell

20h INTERCESSION

Creator God, you have formed a universe of wonder and delight, and appointed the human race to be the priests of creation, to care for it in your name and to offer it to you. We pray for all who seek to arouse the consciences of their neighbours in the need to care for our environment. Lord, in your mercy, **hear our prayer**.

Creator God, you have entrusted the oceans to our care. Guide those who make fishing policies, and stay the hand of those who pollute our seas. Lord, in your mercy, **hear our prayer**.

Creator God, you have given us pure air to breathe. Help us to control the emission of all that can poison it. Lord, in your mercy, **hear our prayer**.

Creator God, you have created a delicate balance of forests and plants. Show us ways of conserving them and not destroying them. Lord, in your mercy, **hear our prayer**.

Creator God, you have filled the world with a myriad species of moving things. Let us not take them for granted or harm them by our thoughtlessness. Lord, in your mercy, **hear our prayer**.

Creator God, you have given to human minds the skill to make new discoveries in medicine and science. Teach us to use them to heal and not to harm, that we may share in your ongoing work of creation, through Jesus Christ our Lord. **Amen.**

Michael Counsell

20i AT THE PEACE

God made the world and rested the seventh day; therefore, there remains a sabbath rest for the people and creatures of God.

Genesis 2.2; Hebrews 4.9

20j PREFACE

And now we give you thanks because all things are of your making, all times and seasons obey your laws, but you have chosen to create us in your image, setting us over the whole world in all its wonder. You have made us stewards of your creation, to praise you day by day for the marvels of your wisdom

and power: so earth unites with heaven to sing the new song of
creation …

Roman Missal, adapted in *Patterns for Worship*, 10N19

20k THE DRAMA OF CREATION

Leader	In the beginning, God made the world:
Women	Made it and mothered it,
Men	Shaped it and fathered it;
Women	Filled it with seeds and signs of fertility,
Men	Filled it with love and its folk with ability.
Leader	All that is green, blue, deep and growing,
All	**God's is the hand that created you.**
Leader	All that is tender, firm, fragrant and curious;
All	**God's is the hand that created you.**
Leader	All that crawls, flies, swims, walks or is motionless,
All	**God's is the hand that created you.**
Leader	All that speaks, sings, cries, laughs or keeps silence,
All	**God's is the hand that created you.**
Leader	All that suffers, lacks, limps or longs for an end,
All	**God's is the hand that created you.**
Leader	The world belongs to the Lord,
All	**The earth and all its people are his.**

A Wee Worship Book, p. 8

20l BLESSING

May God the Creator bless you in your care of the world
around you. May Jesus, God's Son, bless you in providing for
your children's children and all whom he loves. May God the
Holy Spirit bless you with the gift of wisdom, until all creation
is blessed through you, for ever and ever. **Amen.**

Michael Counsell

---

21. EPIPHANY, REVELATION, THE WISE MEN

See also EVANGELISM

21a GREETING

The grace of God has dawned upon the world with healing for
all people.
Thanks be to God.

Titus 2.11

21b APPROACH TO WORSHIP

King Jesus, we bring you our gold:

talents your Father gave us,
skills we have acquired,
a little money, a little power,
a little success perhaps,
and plenty of ambition.
These we offer to you,
so that you may make them really worth something
in your kingdom.

Jesus, great High Priest, we bring you our frankincense:
deep needs and longings,
which are sometimes easier to admit in church:
the need for forgiveness and peace,
the need for friendship and love,
the wish to do good
and the knowledge that we must have help
if we are to do it.
Lord, help us,
pray for us.

Jesus, crucified Saviour, we bring you our myrrh:
shadows on our path,
weakness, illness, limitations,
grief for ourselves and others,
our knowledge of parting and pain.
These we offer to you
so that what we bear
may be touched with the holiness
of what you bore for us;
and so that, by your grace,
we may have a part
in the world's redemption.

*There's a Time and a Place**

21c **CONFESSION**
Lord Jesus Christ, wise men from the East worshipped and
adored you; they brought you gifts – gold, incense, and myrrh.
We too have seen your glory, but we have often turned away.
Lord, in your mercy,
forgive us and help us.

We too have gifts, but we have not fully used them or offered
them to you. Lord, in your mercy,
forgive us and help us.

We too have acclaimed you as king, but we have not served you with all our strength. Lord, in your mercy,
forgive us and help us.

We too have acknowledged you as God, but we have not desired holiness. Lord, in your mercy,
forgive us and help us.

We too have welcomed you as Saviour, but we have failed to tell others of your grace. Lord, in your mercy,
**forgive us and help us.
Make our trust more certain,
make our love more real,
make our worship more acceptable to you;
for your glory's sake. Amen.**

Editors, *Prayers for the People*, 2.14

21d ABSOLUTION
You, who once were far away, have been brought near through the blood of Christ; he himself is your peace. **Amen.**

Ephesians 2.13–14, *Bible Praying*, 157

21e COLLECTS
O God, the source of all insight, whose coming was revealed to the nations not among men of power but in a woman's lap; give us grace to seek you where you may be found, that the wisdom of this world may be humbled and discover your unexpected joy, through Jesus Christ. **Amen.**

All Desires Known

21f SUITABLE SCRIPTURE PASSAGES
Isaiah 49.1–13; 60.1–6; 60.8–22; Jeremiah 31.7–14; Baruch 4.36 – 5.9; Psalms 71; 72.10–15; 96; 97; 98; 100; 113; 132.
Matthew 2.1–12; 16.13–20; Mark 1.21–28; John 1.29–34; 1.43–51; 2.1–11; 4.7–26; Ephesians 3.1–12.

**21g AFFIRMATION OF FAITH
We believe in God the Father,
who has revealed his loving kindness to us,
and in his mercy saved us –
not for any good deed of our own,
but because he is merciful.**

**We believe in Jesus Christ,
who gave himself up for us
to free us from our sin,**

**and set us apart for himself –
a people eager to do good.**

**We believe in the Holy Spirit,
whom God poured out on us generously
through Christ our Saviour –
so that justified by grace
we might become heirs
with the hope of eternal life. Amen.**

Titus 2.14; 3.4–7, Bible Praying, 223

21h INTERCESSION

Biddings

Let us pray to the Father through Christ
who is our Light and life.
Father, your Christ is acclaimed as the glory of Israel: look in
mercy on your Church, sharing his light. Lord, have mercy.
Christ, have mercy.

Father, your Christ in his temple brings judgement on the
world: look in mercy on the nations, who long for his justice.
Lord, have mercy.
Christ, have mercy.

Father, your Christ, who was rich, for our sakes became poor:
look in mercy on the needy, suffering with him. Lord, have
mercy.
Christ, have mercy.

Father, your Christ is the one in whom faithful servants find
their peace: look in mercy on the departed, who see your salvation. Lord, have mercy.
Christ, have mercy.

Father, your Christ is revealed as the one destined to be reject-
ed: look in mercy on us who now turn towards his passion.
Lord, have mercy.
Christ, have mercy.

Lord God, you kept faith with Simeon and Anna and showed
them the infant King. Give us grace to put all our trust in your
promises, and the patience to wait for their fulfilment; through
Jesus Christ our Lord. **Amen.**

The Promise of His Glory, p. 275

21i   AT THE PEACE
Welcome one another as Christ has welcomed you for the glory
of God.

The Promise of His Glory, p. 244

21j   PREFACE
His star, mysterious and inviting, calls us to worship the Christ
who is born. For he is Emmanuel, God revealed in human form
for all the human race; to him we offer our homage and our
gifts.

A New Zealand Prayer Book, p. 491

21k   POST-COMMUNION PRAYER
Lord God, the bright splendour of all the nations: may we who
with the Wise Men have beheld the glory of your presence discern the radiance of your Son, even Jesus Christ our Lord.
Amen.

The Promise of His Glory, p. 226

21l   SOLEMN BLESSING
May God the Father, who led the Wise Men by the shining of a
star to find the Christ, the Light from Light, lead you also in
your pilgrimage to find the Lord. **Amen.**
May God the Son, who turned water into wine at the Wedding
Feast at Cana, transform your lives and make glad your hearts.
Amen.
May God the Holy Spirit, who came upon the beloved Son at
his baptism in the River Jordan, pour out his gifts on you who
have come to the waters of new birth. **Amen.**
And the blessing …

The Promise of His Glory, p. 227

---

22. THE EUCHARIST, BREAD,
MAUNDY THURSDAY, THE VINE, WINE

22a   CALL TO WORSHIP
Come, let us celebrate with praise and thanks the Sacrament of
the New and Eternal Covenant, which proclaims the Last
Supper and declares the death and triumph of the Lord, and his
living presence in the holy mysteries of his Body and Blood, in
the midst of his people to whom the same Lord gives his word
'I am the living bread which comes down from heaven; if anyone eats of this bread he shall live for ever.'

Blessed be God: Father, Son and Holy Spirit.
Both now and for evermore.

Brazil Experimental Liturgy

22b **INVITATION TO CONFESS**
Come to this table, not because you are strong, but because you
are weak; come not because any goodness of your own gives
you a right to come, but because you need mercy and help;
come, because you love the Lord a little and would like to love
him more; come, not because you are worthy to approach him,
but because he died for sinners; come, because he loved you
and gave himself for you:
Your death, O Lord, we commemorate,
your resurrection we proclaim,
your coming again in glory we anticipate:
glory to you, living Saviour and Lord! Amen.

Editors, *Prayers for the People*, 28.57

22c **CONFESSION**
God, in this sacrament
we come to your only Son, Jesus Christ.
Sick, we approach the physician;
unclean, we approach the fountain;
blind, we approach the light;
poor, we approach the monarch of all.
In your mercy, heal us,
cleanse us, enlighten us and clothe us,
so that we may receive the bread of angels
with reverence and humility,
repentance and love,
purity and faith,
for the good of our souls.
Make us members of Christ's body,
that one day we may see face to face
him whose presence here is veiled,
and who lives and reigns with you and the Holy Spirit,
one God for ever and ever. Amen.

Adapted from St Thomas Aquinas

22d **ABSOLUTION**
This sacrament is the sign of God's loving-kindness. This shall
touch your lips, your guilt will be gone and your sins be
forgiven. **Amen.**

Isaiah 6.7, Michael Counsell

COLLECTS

22e

Lord Jesus Christ, we worship you living among us in the sacrament of your body and blood. May we offer to our Father in heaven a solemn pledge of undivided love. May we offer to our brothers and sisters a life poured out in loving service of that kingdom where you live with the Father and the Holy Spirit, one God, for ever and ever. **Amen.**

Roman Missal

22f

O God whose greeting we miss and whose departure we delay, make our hearts burn with insight on our ordinary road; that, as we grasp you in the broken bread, we may also let you go, and return to speak your word of life in the name of Christ. **Amen.**

All Desires Known

22g SUITABLE SCRIPTURE PASSAGES
Genesis 14.17–20; Exodus 12.1–14; 16.2–15; Deuteronomy 8.2–3, 14–16; 2 Kings 4.42–44; Isaiah 5.1–7; 55.1–5; Psalms 42 – 43; 78.23–29; 80.7–15; 105.1–6, 37–45; 116.1–4, 11–19; 145.10–18. Matthew 14.13–21; 15.21–28; 20.1–6; 21.33–46; 26.17–30; Mark 6.30–34, 53–56; Luke 24.13–35; John 2.1–11; 6.1–21; 6.24–35, 41–51, 51–58; 13.1–7, 31b–35; 15.1–8; 21.1–19; 1 Corinthians 10.16–17; 11.23–29.

22h AFFIRMATION OF FAITH
There is one God and Father:
from him all things come.
There is one Lord Jesus Christ:
through him we come to God.
There is one Holy Spirit:
in him we are baptized into one body.
We believe and trust in one God:
Father, Son and Holy Spirit. Amen.

1 Corinthians 8.6; 12.13, *Bible Praying*, 209

22i INTERCESSIONS FOR MAUNDY THURSDAY
Father, on this, the night he was betrayed, your Son Jesus Christ washed his disciples' feet. We commit ourselves to follow his example of love and service. Lord hear us
and humble us.

On this night, he prayed for his disciples to be one. We pray for
the unity of your Church ... Lord hear us
and unite us.

On this night, he prayed for those who were to believe through
their message. We pray for the mission of your Church ... Lord
hear us
and renew our zeal.

On this night, he commanded them to love, but suffered rejection himself. We pray for the rejected and unloved ... Lord hear
us
and fill us with your love.

On this night, he reminded them that if the world hated them it
hated him first. We pray for those who are persecuted for their
faith ... Lord hear us
and give us your peace.

Lent, Holy Week and Easter, p. 188

22j AT THE PEACE
The kingdom of God is not a matter of eating and drinking, but
of righteousness, peace and joy in the Holy Spirit.

Romans 14.17, *Patterns for Worship*, 0R25, freely available

22k PREFACE
And now we give you thanks because when his hour had
come, in his great love he gave this supper to his disciples,
that we might proclaim his death, and feast with him in his
kingdom.

ASB, p. 155

22l PRAYER AFTER COMMUNION
Eternal God, we thank you for refreshing us with these heavenly gifts: may our communion strengthen us in faith, build us up
in hope, and make us grow in love; for the sake of Jesus Christ
our Lord. **Amen.**

Danish Lutheran Rite

22m SOLEMN BLESSING
May the Father, who fed his children with bread and honey in
the wilderness, strengthen you in your pilgrimage to the
Promised Land. **Amen.**
May the Son, who gave his flesh for food and his blood for
drink, keep you in eternal life and raise you up on the last day.
Amen.

81

May the Holy Spirit, who leads us into all truth, help you discern the Lord's body and empower you to proclaim his death until he comes. **Amen.**
And the blessing …

Michael Perham, *Enriching the Christian Year*, 19F1

23. EVANGELISM, MISSION, WITNESS

See also EPIPHANY, FISH, OTHER FAITHS

23a OPENING RESPONSE
Jesus said, As the Father sent me so I send you,
To make all people my disciples.

John 20.21; Matthew 28.19, Michael Counsell

23b INVITATION TO CONFESSION
If anyone sins, we have an advocate with the Father, Jesus Christ the righteous; and he is the propitiation for our sins, and not for ours only, but also for the sins of the whole world.

1 John 2.1, *The Promise of His Glory*, p. 241

23c KYRIE
We have not held out the word of life in a dark and twisted world. Lord, have mercy.
Lord, have mercy.
We have failed to share our bread with the hungry. Christ, have mercy.
Christ, have mercy.
We have closed our hearts to the love of God. Lord, have mercy.
Lord, have mercy.

The Promise of His Glory, p. 242

23d ABSOLUTION
Hear the assurance of God's forgiveness:
In the time of his favour the Lord answers you; in the day of salvation he helps you; the Lord comforts you, he has compassion upon you; he has not forsaken you, nor has he forgotten you. Lift up your eyes and look around: the Lord is your saviour and your redeemer; in Christ you are forgiven. **Amen.**

Isaiah 49.8–26, *Bible Praying*, 146

23e COLLECT
Draw your Church together, O God, into one great company of disciples, together following our Lord Jesus Christ into every

walk of life, together serving him in his mission to the world, and together witnessing to his love on every continent and island. **Amen.**

A New Zealand Prayer Book, p. 141

23f   SUITABLE SCRIPTURE PASSAGES
1 Kings 8.22–30, 41–43; Isaiah 2.1–5; 44.6–8; 49.1–7; 56.1–8; 62.1–5; Jonah 3.1–5, 10 – 4.11; Psalms 22.23–31; 36.5–10; 40.1–11; 67; 86.1–10, 16–17; 96; 98; 138.
Matthew 4.12–23; 9.35 – 10.8; 13.1–9, 18–23; 15.21–28; 22.1–14; 28.16–20; Mark 1.9–15; 1.14–20; 1.40–45; 6.1–13; 7.24–37; Luke 3.7–18; 5.1–11; 7.1–10; 10.1–11, 16–20; 24.36b–48; 24.44–53; John 1.29–42; 15.26–27; 16.4b–15; 21.1–19; Acts 1.1–11; 2.14a, 22–32; 3.12–19; 4.5–12; 4.32–35; 5.27–32; 8.26–40; 10.34–43; 10.44–48; 11.1–18; 16.9–15; 16.16–34; 17.22–31; Romans 1.1–7; 10.5–15; 1 Corinthians 9.16–23; Galatians 1.1–12; 3.23–29; Ephesians 1.15–23; 2.11–22; 1 Peter 4.1–8.

23g   AFFIRMATION OF FAITH
Let us declare our faith in God:
We believe in God the Father,
Who, creating heaven and earth,
formed us in His own image.
We believe in God the Son,
Who, entering the world to live and die and rise again,
made us children of the Father,
inheritors together of His kingdom.
We believe in God the Holy Spirit,
Who, strengthening us to share the Son's work,
sends us out to preach the good news in all the world.
We believe in one God, Father, Son and Holy Spirit,
Glorious Trinity.

Will you proclaim by word and deed the good news of God in Christ Jesus?
With God's help, we will.
Will you live the servant life of Christ, loving your neighbour as yourself?
With God's help, we will.
Will you acknowledge Christ's authority over human society, interceding for the leaders and governments of the world?
With God's help, we will.
Will you carry forward the prophetic ministry of Christ, crying out for justice, hearing the voice of the dispossessed?
With God's help, we will.

Will you persevere in resisting evil and, when you fall into sin, repent and return to the Lord?
With God's help, we will.
Will you seek to glorify God in whatever ministry He gives you, in the places to which He calls you?
With God's help, we will.

Janet Henderson, partly based on *US BCP 1979*, p. 304

23h INTERCESSION
For a clearer vision of the work you have set before us and for a better understanding of your gospel.
Lord, direct us.
For a deeper commitment in your service and a greater love for all your children.
Lord, direct us.
For a fresh understanding of the task before us and for a sense of urgency in our proclamation.
Lord, direct us.
For a greater respect and acceptance among Christians of different traditions and for a common goal in evangelism.
Lord, direct us.

Gathering our prayers and praises into one, let us pray as Jesus taught us.
Our Father ...

Lord, you have consecrated the world by sending your Son into the midst of it and by making all things new in him. We ask you to give us gathered here today and all your people the courage, power and encouragement we need to share fully in his mission to the world and so further his kingdom, to the honour and glory of his name. **Amen.**

May God bless our work today. **Amen.**
Let us bless the Lord.
Thanks be to God.

Anglican Province of the Indian Ocean

23i AT THE PEACE
Christ came and proclaimed the gospel: peace to those who are far off, and peace to those who are near.

Ephesians 2.17, *The Promise of His Glory*, p. 244

23j PREFACE

For by water and the Holy Spirit you have made us a new people in Jesus Christ our Lord, to show forth your glory in all the world.

US BCP 1979, p. 378

23k THANKSGIVING

Lord God, we thank you for our heritage of faith:
For the vision of apostles and evangelists who brought it to us, gracious Lord,
we give you thanks and praise.
For the courage of martyrs and teachers who secured it for us, gracious Lord,
we give you thanks and praise.
For the devotion of preachers and pastors who proclaimed it to us, gracious Lord,
we give you thanks and praise.
For the love of families and friends who nourished it within us, gracious Lord,
we give you thanks and praise.
For the freedom to speak of it in the world about us, and to share it with our neighbours, gracious Lord,
we give you thanks and praise.

Lord God,
we thank you for our heritage of faith:
give us the will and the strength
to pass it on to others
for the glory of your name;
through Jesus Christ our Lord. Amen.

Editors, *Prayers for the People*, 17.70

23l BLESSING

God the Sender, send us. God the Sent, come with us. God the Strengthener of those who go, empower us, that we may go with you and find those who will call you Father, Son and Holy Spirit. **Amen.**

The Church in Wales, source unknown

24. EVENING

24a CALL TO WORSHIP

The Lord almighty grant us a peaceful night and a perfect end.
Amen.
Our help is in the Name of the Lord;
The maker of heaven and earth.

US BCP 1979, p. 127

Let our prayer be set forth in your sight as incense:
the lifting up of our hands as the evening sacrifice.

Psalm 141.2

24b CONFESSION

We confess to God almighty, the Father, the Son, and the Holy Spirit, that we have sinned in thought, word, and deed, through our own grievous fault. Wherefore we pray God to have mercy upon us.
Almighty God, have mercy upon us, forgive us all our sins and deliver us from all evil, confirm and strengthen us in all goodness, and bring us to life everlasting. Through Jesus Christ our Lord. Amen.

The Prayer Book as Proposed in 1928

24c RESPONSIVE CONFESSION

We have wounded your love:
O God, heal us.
We stumble in the darkness:
Light of the world, transfigure us.
We forget that we are your home:
Spirit of God, dwell in us.

Prayer at Night

24d ABSOLUTION

The almighty and merciful Lord grant you pardon and forgiveness of all your sins, time for amendment of life, and the grace and strength of the Holy Spirit. **Amen.**

The Prayer Book as Proposed in 1928, modified in *The Promise of His Glory*, p. 126

EVENING PRAYERS
(See also the evening prayers for each week in *Prayers for Sundays*.)

24e

God in the night
God at my right

God all the day
God with me stay
God in my heart
Never depart
God with thy might
Keep us in light
Through this dark night. **Amen.**

The Promise of His Glory, p. 144

24f

Yours is the day, O Lord, and yours is the night. Let Christ the
Sun of Righteousness abide in our hearts to drive away the
darkness of evil thoughts: for he is Lord for ever and ever.
Amen.

The Promise of His Glory, p. 144

24g

In darkness and in light,
in trouble and in joy,
help us, heavenly Father,
to trust your love,
to serve your purpose,
and to praise your name,
through Jesus Christ our Lord. Amen.

The Daily Office, adapted in *Patterns for Worship,* 0J49

24h SUITABLE SCRIPTURE PASSAGES
Psalms 4; 31.1–6; 91; 134.
Mark 1.29–39; Luke 24.13–35.

24i CONFIDENCE
Lord, now let your servant depart in peace,
according to your word.
I will lie down in peace and take my rest,
For it is you, Lord, who make me dwell in safety.
I have put my trust in you, Lord,
I have said, You are my God.
The darkness is not dark to you; the night is as clear as the day,
Darkness and light to you are both alike.
Into your hands I commend my spirit,
For you have redeemed me, Lord God of truth. Amen.

Luke 2.29; Psalms 4.8; 31.7; 139.11; 31.5

24j EVENING LITANY
We pray to the Lord, saying: in faith we pray:
we pray to you our God.

That the rest of this day may be holy, peaceful, and full of your presence; in faith we pray:
we pray to you our God.
That the work we have done and the people we have met today may bring us closer to you; in faith we pray:
we pray to you our God.
That we may be forgiven our sins and failures; in faith we pray:
we pray to you our God.
That we may hear and respond to your call to peace and justice; in faith we pray:
we pray to you our God.
That you will sustain the faith and hope of those who are lonely, oppressed and anxious; in faith we pray:
we pray to you our God.
That you will strengthen us in your service, and fill our hearts with longing for your kingdom; in faith we pray:
we pray to you our God.
God of mercy,
you know and love us
and hear our prayer:
keep us in the eternal fellowship
of Jesus Christ our Saviour. Amen.

Canadian *Book of Alternative Services*, p. 118, altered in *Patterns for Worship*, 0H23

24k AT THE PEACE
In returning and rest you shall be saved; in quietness and trust shall be your strength.

Isaiah 30.15

24l PREFACE
Jesus accepted the disciples' invitation to abide with them as evening approached, and made himself known in the breaking of bread.

Luke 24.29–31

24m THANKSGIVING
Dear God, thank you for all that is good, for our creation and our humanity, for the stewardship you have given us of this planet earth, for the gifts of life and of one another, for your Love which is unbounded and eternal. **Amen.**

Prayer at Night

BLESSINGS
24n

Be the peace of the Spirit mine this night,
Be the peace of the Son mine this night,

Be the peace of the Father mine this night,
The peace of all peace be mine this night,
Each morning and evening of my life. **Amen.**

Carmina Gadelica

24o

May the love of the Word made flesh enfold us, his joy fill our
lives, his peace be in our hearts; and the blessing of God be with
us this night and always. **Amen.**

Celebrating Common Prayer, p. 108

---

25. FAITH, ABRAHAM, ANXIETY, DOUBT, TRUST

See also CONFIDENCE, GUIDANCE, PERSEVERANCE

25a GREETING
Greetings, friends in the faith; God's grace be with you all!
Amen.

Titus 3.15, Bible Praying, 21

25b PRAYER OF APPROACH AND ABSOLUTION
Let us pray.
We have heard about you ...
We have heard about you,
God of all power.
You made the world out of kindness,
Creating order out of confusion;
You made each one of us in your own image;
Your finger print is on every soul.
So we praise you.
We praise and worship you.

We have heard about you,
Jesus Christ:
The carpenter who left his tools and trade;
The poor man who made others rich;
The healer who let himself be wounded;
The criminal on whom soldiers spat,
Not knowing they were fouling the face of God;
The saviour who died and rose again.
So we praise you.
We praise and worship you.

We have heard about you,
Holy Spirit.
You broke the bonds of race and nation,
To let God speak in every tongue;
You made disciples drunk with grace;
You converted souls and emptied pockets;
You showed how love made all things new
And opened the doors to change and freedom.
So we praise you.
We praise and worship you.

We have heard about you,
God, three-in-one.
And you, the Lord of All,
Have heard about us ...
But not through second-hand reports,
Not from the tales that others tell.
You have put your ear to our heart
Both when we prayed and when we doubted.
You know well what we fear and question,
    what we long for,
        and from whom we turn away.
And even when we become deaf to you,
You never stop listening for us.
In silence, in penitence and in confidence,
We do not repeat what you know already.
We ask to be made whole.

(A silence.)

Lord, have mercy on us.
Christ, have mercy on us.
Lord, have mercy on us.

(A silence.)

God is good.
On all whose lives are open to change
    from guilt to grace,
    from darkness to light,
God pronounces his pardon
And grants his peace.
Thanks be to God.
Amen.

A Wee Worship Book, p. 4

25c KYRIE

Father, you have entrusted the world to our care, and we have
betrayed you. Lord, have mercy.
Lord, have mercy.
Jesus, you have entrusted our neighbours to our care, and we
have betrayed you. Christ, have mercy.
Christ, have mercy.
Spirit, you have entrusted your gifts to our care, and we have
betrayed you. Lord, have mercy.
Lord, have mercy.

The Open Gate, p. 57

25d COLLECT

Risen Christ, whose absence leaves us paralysed, but whose
presence is overwhelming, breathe on us with your abundant
life; that where we cannot see we may have courage to believe
that we may be raised with you. **Amen.**

All Desires Known

25e SUITABLE SCRIPTURE PASSAGES

Genesis 12.1–9; 15.1–6; 28.10–19a; 2 Kings 5.1–14; Jeremiah
17.5–10; 32.1–3a, 6–15; Hosea 11.1–11; Psalms 121; 13; 17.1–7, 15;
19.7–14; 22.1–15; 25.1–10; 27; 33.12–22; 37.1–9; 42 – 43; 63.1–8;
85.8–13; 90.1–6, 13–17; 107.1–9, 43; 119.33–40; 130; 138.
Matthew 6.24–34; 9.9–13, 18–26; 14.22–33; 15.21–28; 16.13–20;
25.31–46; Mark 5.21–43; Luke 17.5–10; John 6.56–69; 20.19–31;
Acts 7.55–60; Romans 1.16–17; 3.22b–28; 4.1–5, 13–25; 8.14–17;
10.5–15; 1 Corinthians 15.12–20; 2 Corinthians 5.6–10, 14–17;
Galatians 2.15–21; 3.23–29; Ephesians 2.1–10; Philippians
3.4b–14; Colossians 1.1–14; 2 Timothy 1.1–14; Hebrews
10.11–14, 19–25; 11.1–3, 8–16; 11.29 – 12.2; 1 John 3.16–24; 5.9–13.

25f AFFIRMATION OF FAITH

We believe O God of all gods,
That you are the eternal maker of life:
We believe O God of all gods,
That you are the eternal maker of love.

We believe, O God and Lord of all people,
that you are the creator of the high heavens,
that you are the creator of the skies above,
that you are the creator of the oceans below.

We believe, O Lord and God of all people,
That you are the one who created our souls and set their warp,

That you are the one who created our bodies from dust and
from ashes,
That you gave to our bodies their breath
and to our souls their possession.

Lord, bless to us our bodies,
Lord, bless to us our souls,
Lord, bless to us our lives,
Lord, bless to us our belief.

A Wee Worship Book, p. 18

25g INTERCESSION
We bring *(name)* in weakness, for your strengthening.
We bring *(name)* in sickness, for your healing.
We bring *(name)* in trouble, for your calming.
We bring *(name)* who is lost, for your guidance.
We bring *(name)* who is lonely, for your love.
We bring *(name)* who is dying, for your resurrection.

The Edge of Glory, p. 72

25h AT THE PEACE
We are all one in Christ Jesus. We belong to him through faith,
heirs of the promise of the Spirit of Peace.

Galatians 3.28, *Patterns for Worship*, 12R13; freely available

25i PREFACE
He is the Word through whom you made the universe, the
Saviour you sent to redeem us. By the power of the Holy Spirit
he took flesh and was born of the Virgin Mary. For our sake he
opened his arms on the cross; he put an end to death and
revealed the resurrection. In this he fulfilled your will and won
for you a holy people.

Roman Missal

25j THANKSGIVING
Thank you, Father, for making yourself known to us and showing the way of salvation through faith in your Son. We ask you
now to teach and encourage us through your word, so that we
may be ready to serve you; for the glory of our Lord Jesus
Christ. **Amen.**

A Prayer Book for Australia, p. 36

25k BLESSING
The God of hope fill you with all joy and peace in believing,
and the blessing ...

Romans 15.13, *Prayers for the People*, 16.54

26. FAMILY, HOME, MARRIAGE

See also CHILDREN, MOTHERING SUNDAY, PARENT-
HOOD

26a OPENING SENTENCE
Jesus said, 'I give you a new commandment: love one another.
Just as I have loved you, you also must love one another. By
this love you have for one another, everyone will know that
you are my disciples.'

John 13.34

26b INVITATION TO CONFESS
Jesus said, 'Before you offer your gift, go and be reconciled.' As
brothers and sisters in God's family, we come together to ask
our Father for forgiveness.

Matthew 5.24, *Patterns for Worship*, 14B15, freely available

26c CONFESSION
**We confess to God almighty, the Creator, the sharer of our
pain, the giver of love, that we have sinned in thought, word
and deed, by yielding to temptation, through our own fault.
So we ask God to forgive us, to protect us from evil and
strengthen us in temptation, to pour divine love into our
hearts and bring us to eternal life in Christ.**

Source unknown

26d ABSOLUTION
God loves you, and pours his ample forgiveness into your
hearts, however undeserving you may be, to wash away all
guilt and fear. Believe in his love, and trust in his forgiveness.
Through the authority given me from Christ in my ordination,
I declare that God has forgiven you. Forget the past, step into
the future in faith, hope and love; and pray for each other and
for me, for we are all forgiven sinners. **Amen.**

Source unknown

26e COLLECT
God of intimacy, you surround us with friends and family to
cherish and to challenge. May we so give and receive caring in
the details of our lives that we also remain faithful to your
greater demands, through Jesus Christ. **Amen.**

All Desires Known

26f SUITABLE SCRIPTURE PASSAGES
Genesis 1.20–28; 2.18–24; 21.8–21; 24.34–38, 42–49, 58–67;
25.19–34; 29.15–28; 37.1–4, 12–28; 43.3–11, 15; 45.1–15; 50.15–21;

Family

Exodus 2.1–10; Deuteronomy 4.1–2, 6–9; 1 Samuel 1.20–28; 2 Samuel 11.1–15; Proverbs 31.10–31; Song of Solomon 2.8–13; Hosea 1.2–10; 2.14–20; Ecclesiasticus 3.2–6, 12–14; Psalms 34.11–20; 45.1–2, 6–17; 127; 128.
Matthew 2.13–15, 19–23; 5.21–37; Mark 2.13–22; 3.20–35; 9.30–37; 10.2–16; Luke 2.22–40; 2.41–52; John 2.1–11; 19.25–27; 2 Corinthians 1.3–7; Colossians 3.12–23.

26g AFFIRMATION OF FAITH
Let us declare our faith in God:
**We believe in God the Father,
from whom every family
in heaven and on earth is named.
We believe in God the Son,
who lives in our hearts through faith,
and fills us with his love.
We believe in God the Holy Spirit,
who strengthens us with power from on high.
We believe in one God;
Father, Son, and Holy Spirit. Amen.**

Ephesians 3.14–17, Bible Praying, 216

26h INTERCESSION
Sovereign Lord, your Son has revealed you as our heavenly Father, from whom every family in heaven and on earth is named. Father of all:
hear your children's prayer.

You have made your Church a spiritual family, a household of faith. Through baptism we are reborn as brothers and sisters of Christ. Deepen our unity and fellowship in him. Father of all:
hear your children's prayer.

You sent your Son to give his life as a ransom for the whole human family. Give justice, peace and racial harmony to the world he died to save. Father of all:
hear your children's prayer.

You gave your Son a share in the life of a family in Nazareth. Help us to value our families, to be thankful for them, and to live sensitively within them. Father of all:
hear your children's prayer.

Your Son drew around him a company of friends. Bring love and joy to all who are alone. Help us all to find in the brothers

and sisters of Christ a loving family. Father of all:
hear your children's prayer.

You are the God of the dead as well as the living. In confidence
we remember those of the household of faith who have gone
before us. Bring us with them to the joy of your home in heav-
en. Father of all:
hear your children's prayer.

Patterns for Worship, 14H20, source unknown

26i AT THE PEACE
Jesus said, 'Whoever does the will of God is my brother, and
sister and mother.' As we have opportunity, let us work for
good to all, especially members of the household of faith.

Mark 3.35; Galatians 6.10, *Patterns for Worship*, 14R14

26j PREFACE
It is right to thank and praise you, God our Creator, because out
of your love you made us, and in your love you made us male
and female, that in learning affection for each other we might
grasp the intensity of your longing for us. In sharing family life
we learn that forgiveness and self-sacrifice are the key to our
hearts as to yours. So, with all lovers down the ages, and with
those who share your life in eternity, we adore the holiness of
that pure love which binds together the persons of the Trinity,
for ever praising you and saying/singing ...

Michael Counsell

26k THANKSGIVING
We thank God for giving us other people to be part of our lives:
For parents, and the love which brought us to birth: we praise
you, O Lord,
and bring you thanks today.
For mothers who have cherished and nurtured us: we praise
you, O Lord,
and bring you thanks today.
For fathers who have loved and supported us: we praise you, O
Lord,
and bring you thanks today.
For brothers and sisters with whom we have shared our home:
we praise you, O Lord,
and bring you thanks today.
For children, entrusted to our care as parents: we praise you, O
Lord,
and bring you thanks today.

For other relatives and friends who have been with us in our
hopes and our joys: we praise you, O Lord,
and bring you thanks today.
For all who first spoke to us of Jesus, and have drawn us into
the family of our Father in heaven: we praise you, O Lord,
and bring you thanks today.
Help us to live
as those who belong to one another and to you,
now and always. Amen.

Editors, *Prayers for the People*, 6.59

261 BLESSING
May the Father from whom every family in earth and heaven
receives its name strengthen you with his Spirit in your inner
being, so that Christ may dwell in your hearts by faith, and
that, knowing his love, broad and long, deep and high beyond
our knowledge, you may be filled with all the fullness of God.
And the blessing ...

Ephesians 3.15–19, *Patterns for Worship*, 14T36

27. FISH, FISHERMEN, SEAMEN

See also EVANGELISM, PETER

27a CALL TO WORSHIP
Jesus calls his church to fish for people.
Come, let us adore him.

Michael Counsell

27b INVITATION TO CONFESS
When we are at our lowest, then God is with us. Let us cry out
for God's forgiveness.

Psalm 139.8, Michael Counsell

27c CONFESSION
Out of the depths, O Lord, we cry to you. O Lord, hear our
voice:
listen to our cry for mercy.
If you kept a record of our sins, who could stand before you? O
Lord, hear our voice:
listen to our cry for mercy.
But you offer forgiveness, and therefore we fear you. O Lord,
hear our voice:
listen to our cry for mercy.

We wait for you, O Lord, and in your promise we put our hope.
O Lord, hear our voice:
listen to our cry for mercy.
We long for you, O Lord, more than the sleepless long for the
morning. O Lord, hear our voice:
listen to our cry for mercy.

Psalm 130.1–6, Prayers for the People, 14.17*

27d ABSOLUTION
People of God, put your trust in the Lord, for with the Lord is
unfailing love, and with him is full redemption. Hear God's
forgiveness: The Lord himself will redeem you from all your
sins through our Saviour, Jesus Christ. **Amen.**

Psalm 130.7–8, Prayers for the People, 15.19

COLLECTS

27e

O Saviour Christ, when the wind is boisterous and our faith
weak, and we begin to sink even as we come to you, stretch
forth your hand, O Lord, as of old to your fearful disciple, and
say to the sea of our difficulties, 'Peace, be still'; for your holy
name's sake. **Amen.**

Dean Vaughan

27f

Almighty God, you led your people through the sea, and made
a path for them in deep waters: be near all those who face the
dangers of the seas; protect them from disaster, help them on
their way, and bring them safely to their desired haven with
hearts thankful for your mercy; through Jesus Christ our Lord.
Amen.

The Scottish Prayer Book, adapted in Prayers for the People, 14.19

27g SUITABLE SCRIPTURE PASSAGES
Genesis 1.20–28; Jonah 1.17 – 2.10; Psalms 65.1–7; 66.1–12;
89.1–8; 93; 107.1–3, 23–32; 114.
Matthew 4.12–23; 7.7–11; 8.23–27; 14.13–22; 14.22–33; 17.24–27;
Mark 1.14–20; 4.35–41; 6.35–44; 5.1–11; 9.12–17; 24.33–43; John
6.1–13; 21.1–19.

27h AFFIRMATION OF FAITH
Christ died for our sins
in accordance with the Scriptures;
he was buried;
he was raised to life on the third day
in accordance with the Scriptures;

afterwards he appeared to his followers,
and to all the apostles:
this we have received and this we believe. Amen.

1 Corinthians 15.3–5, Bible Praying, 211

27i INTERCESSION
We joyfully pray to Christ, who chose to build his Church on
the foundation of the apostles and prophets:
Lord, be with your people.

You called Peter from his fishing to fish for people: never cease
to call apostles, that many may be saved.
Lord, be with your people.

You prayed for Peter, that his faith should not fail: confirm your
Church in the faith.
Lord, be with your people.

You stilled the tempest at sea, when the disciples feared the
ship was sinking: protect your Church in the midst of trouble,
and give her that peace which the world cannot give.
Lord, be with your people.

After the Resurrection you gathered your scattered flock round
Peter: Good Shepherd, gather all your people now into the
unity for which you prayed.
Lord, be with your people.

You sent Paul as an apostle to all the world: make us true her-
alds of your gospel.
Lord, be with your people.

You entrusted the keys of the kingdom to your Church: open
the gates of heaven to all who have placed their trust in you.
Lord, be with your people.

In your mercy you forgave Peter his denials: forgive us all our
trespasses.
Lord, be with your people.

Additional Curates Society

27j AT THE PEACE
Jesus said to those who were fishing, 'Come and eat.' They
knew it was the Lord. So Jesus took the bread and gave it to
them, and they ate together.

John 21.12–13, Michael Counsell

27k LONGER PREFACE

Truly it is right and good to glorify you, at all times and in all places, to offer you our thanksgiving, O Lord, Holy Father, Almighty and Everlasting God. Through your living word you created all things, and pronounced them good. You made human beings in your own image, to share your life and reflect your glory. When the time had fully come, you gave Christ to us as the Way, the Truth and the Life. He accepted baptism and consecration as your Servant to announce the good news to the poor. At the last supper, Christ bequeathed to us the eucharist, that we should celebrate the memorial of the cross and resurrection, and receive his presence as food. To all the redeemed Christ gave the royal priesthood and, in loving his brothers and sisters, chooses those who share in the ministry, that they may feed the Church with your Word and enable it to live by your Sacraments. Wherefore, Lord, with the angels and all the saints, we proclaim and sing your glory, for ever praising you and saying/singing ...

*The Lima Liturgy**

27l THANKSGIVING AFTER COMMUNION

Lord God, the source of truth and love, keep us faithful to the apostles' teaching and fellowship, united in prayer and the breaking of bread, and one in joy and simplicity of heart, in Jesus Christ our Lord. **Amen.**

Westcott House, *Patterns for Worship*, 12J31

27m SOLEMN BLESSING

May the blessing of Christ our God be upon you, who revealed his wisdom to simple fisherfolk. **Amen.**
May the blessing of the Holy Spirit be upon you, whom he sent down upon them, through them catching the whole world in his net. **Amen.**
May the blessing of the Holy Trinity be upon you, who is the Lover of the human race. **Amen.**

Orthodox Troparion for Pentecost Sunday*

28. FORGIVENESS, RECONCILIATION

See also HEALING, JUDGEMENT, LENT, REPENTANCE, SALVATION

28a GREETING

The grace of our Lord Jesus Christ, and the love of God, and the fellowship of the Holy Spirit, be with you all.
And also with you.
Bless the Lord who forgives all our sins.
His mercy endures for ever.

2 Corinthians 13.13; Psalms 103.3; 136, Canadian *Book of Alternative Services*, p. 216

28b INVITATION TO CONFESS

God shows his love for us in this: while we were still sinners Christ died for us. Sure of reconciliation through the death of his Son, we confess our sins to God.

Romans 5.8, *In Penitence and Faith*, No. 4

28c CONFESSION

O God of life,
Eternity cannot hold you,
Nor can our little words catch
The magnificence of your kindness,
Yet in the space of our small hearts
And in silence
You can come close and repair us.
(Silence.)

O God of life,
Grant us your forgiveness
**for our wild thoughts,
our thoughtless deeds,
for our empty speech
and the words with which we wounded.**
(Silence.)

O God of life,
Grant us your forgiveness
**for our false desires,
for our hateful actions,
for our wastefulness
and for all we left untended.**
(Silence.)

O loving Christ,
Hanged on a tree
Yet risen in the morning,
Scatter the sin from our souls
  as the mist from the hills;

Begin what we do,
Inform what we say,
Redeem who we are.
In you we place our hope,
our great hope, our living hope,
this day and evermore.
Amen.

A Wee Worship Book, p. 17

28d KYRIE
Lord Jesus, you came to reconcile us to one another and to the Father: Lord, have mercy.
Lord, have mercy.
Lord Jesus, you heal the wounds of sin and division: Christ, have mercy.
Christ, have mercy.
Lord Jesus, you intercede for us with your Father: Lord, have mercy.
Lord, have mercy.

Roman Missal

28e ABSOLUTION
May God who pardoned David through Nathan the prophet when he confessed his sins, and Peter weeping bitterly for his denial, and the sinful woman weeping at his feet, and the publican and the prodigal son, may the same God forgive you all things, through me a sinner, both in this world and in the world to come, and set you uncondemned before his terrible judgement seat. Have no further care for the sins which you have confessed, depart in peace. **Amen.**

Orthodox prayer, *Oxford Book of Prayer*, p. 753

28f COLLECT
God of infinite love, grant that we who know your mercy may rejoice in your forgiveness and gladly forgive others for the sake of Jesus Christ our Saviour. **Amen.**

A New Zealand Prayer Book, p. 576*

28g SUITABLE SCRIPTURE PASSAGES
Genesis 18.20–32; Exodus 32.7–14; 2 Samuel 11.26 – 12.13a; Isaiah 1.1, 10–20; 43.18–25; Jeremiah 18.1–11; 31.31–34; Hosea 1.2–10; Jonah 3.1–5, 10; Psalms 19.7–14; 25.1–10; 30; 32; 51.1–17; 79.1–9; 85; 103.1–13, 22; 130.
Matthew 5.21–37; 5.38–48; 9.9–13, 18–26; 18.21–35; Mark 2.1–12; 2.13–22; Luke 7.36 – 8.3; 15.1–10; 15.1–3, 11b–32; 24.36b–53; John 8.1–11; Romans 5.1–11; 1 Corinthians 4.1–5; 2 Corinthians 5.16–21;

Ephesians 2.11–22; 4.25 – 5.2; Colossians 1.1–20; 1 Timothy 1.12–17; Philemon 1–21; Hebrews 2.10–18; 5.1–10; 9.11–14; 1 John 1.1 – 2.2; 4.7–21.

28h AFFIRMATION OF FAITH
We believe in the Lord God, the Holy One,
Father, Son and Holy Spirit;
we are his witnesses and his servants.
He alone is the Lord,
apart from him there is no saviour;
he has revealed and saved and proclaimed;
he is our creator, our redeemer and our king;
it is he who blots out our transgressions
and remembers our sins no more. Amen.

Isaiah 43.10–25, Bible Praying, 202

28i THE COVENTRY LITANY OF RECONCILIATION
All have sinned and fallen short of the glory of God.
The hatred which divides nation from nation, race from race, class from class,
Father forgive.
The covetous desires of people and nations to possess what is not their own,
Father forgive.
The greed which exploits the work of human hands, and lays waste the earth,
Father forgive.
Our envy of the welfare and happiness of others,
Father forgive.
Our indifference to the plight of the imprisoned, the homeless, the refugee,
Father forgive.
The lust which dishonours the bodies of men, women and children,
Father forgive.
The pride which leads to trust in ourselves and not in God,
Father forgive.
Be kind to one another, tender-hearted, forgiving one another, as God in Christ forgave you.

Coventry Cathedral

28j AT THE PEACE
God has entrusted to us the message of reconciliation. First be reconciled to one another.

2 Corinthians 5.18; Matthew 5.24, The Promise of His Glory, p. 244

28k PREFACE

He is coming to reconcile and to forgive. Christ is the new beginning.

A New Zealand Prayer Book, p. 491

28l THANKSGIVING

Father, in your love you have brought us from evil to good and from misery to happiness. Through your blessings give the courage of perseverance to those you have called and justified in faith. Grant this through Jesus Christ our Lord. **Amen.**

Rite of Reconciliation, *Roman Missal*

28m SOLEMN BLESSING

May the Lord guide your hearts in the way of his love and fill you with Christ-like patience. **Amen.**

May he give you strength to walk in newness of life and to please him in all things. **Amen.**

May almighty God bless you, the Father, and the Son, ✠ and the Holy Spirit. **Amen.**

The Lord has freed you from your sins. Go in peace. **Amen.**

Rite of Reconciliation, *Roman Missal*

29. GRACE, MERCY

29a GREETING

The grace of our Lord Jesus Christ, and the love of God, and the fellowship of the Holy Spirit, be with you all.

And also with you.

The Lord of mercy be with you.

The Lord bless you.

2 Corinthians 13.13, *Patterns for Worship*, 0A8, source of this version unknown

29b PENITENTIAL RITE

Coming together as God's family, with confidence let us ask the Father's forgiveness, for he is full of gentleness and compassion.

Lord, we have sinned against you. Lord, have mercy.

Lord, have mercy.

Lord, show us your mercy and love.

And grant us your salvation.

May almighty God have mercy on us, forgive us our sins, and bring us to everlasting life. **Amen.**

Roman Missal

29c COLLECT

Stir up your power, Lord, and with great might come among us; and, because we are sorely hindered by our sins, let your bountiful grace speedily help and deliver us; through Jesus Christ our Lord. **Amen.**

Gelasian Sacramentary, The Promise of His Glory, p. 346

29d SUITABLE SCRIPTURE PASSAGES

Genesis 9.8–17; Isaiah 40.21–31; Psalms 22.23–31; 25.1–10; 30; 66.1–9; 86.11–17; 103.1–13, 22; 123; 138.
Matthew 20.1–16; John 1.10–18; Romans 1.16–17; 3.22b–28; 1 Corinthians 1.1–9; 4.1–5; 2 Corinthians 4.13 – 5.1; Galatians 2.15–21; Ephesians 2.1–10; Titus 3.4–7; James 2.1–10, 14–17.

29e AFFIRMATION OF FAITH

**We believe in God who saved us
not because of good things we have done,
but because of his mercy.
God saved us by the washing of rebirth,
and renewal by the Holy Spirit,
whom he poured out on us generously
through Jesus Christ our Saviour;
so that justified by his grace
we might become heirs
with the hope of eternal life.
This is a trustworthy saying.
Amen.**

Titus 3.4–8, Bible Praying, 224

29f THE PRAYERS OF THE PEOPLE

(Each petition is followed by a response such as Let us pray to the Lord. **Lord, have mercy.***)*

For the peace from above, for the loving kindness of God,
and for the salvation of our souls ...
For the peace of the world, for the welfare of the
holy Church of God, and for the unity of all peoples ...
For [our Bishop, and for] all the clergy and people ...
For [our President, for] the leaders of the nations,
and for all in authority ...
For this city (town, village ...), for every city and community,
and for those who live in them ...
For seasonable weather,
and for an abundance of the fruits of the earth ...

For the good earth which God has given us,
and for the wisdom and will to conserve it ...
For those who travel on land, on water ...
or in the air [or through outer space] ...
For the aged and infirm, for the widowed and orphans,
and for the sick and suffering ...
For the poor and the oppressed,
for the unemployed and the destitute, for prisoners and
    captives,
and for all who remember and care for them ...
For all who have died in the hope of the resurrection,
and for all the departed ...
For deliverance from all danger, violence,
oppression and degradation ...
For the absolution and remission of our sins and offences ...
That we may end our lives in faith and hope,
without suffering and without reproach ...
That you will defend us, deliver us,
and in your compassion protect us, Lord, by your grace ...

US BCP 1979, p. 383*

29g THE PEACE

Grace and peace to you from God our Father and from the Lord
Jesus Christ:
peace be with you. Amen.

Romans 1.7, *Bible Praying*, 3*

29h LONGER PREFACE

Father, all-powerful and ever-living God, we do well always and
everywhere to give you thanks. Grace is your gift to your family
to renew us in spirit. You give us strength to purify our hearts, to
control our desires, and so to serve you in freedom. You teach us
how to live in this passing world, with our heart set on the world
that will never end. Now, with all the saints and angels, we worship you, for ever praising you and saying/singing ...

Roman Missal

29i THANKSGIVING

Thanks and praise be to you, almighty God. You justify us
through faith and give us peace in our Lord Jesus Christ.
Through faith:
we are saved by grace.

Through him you brought us by faith into this experience of
grace in which we live, where we rejoice in the hope of sharing
your glory. Through faith:
we are saved by grace.

Not only so, but we also rejoice in our sufferings, because we know that suffering produces perseverance; perseverance, character; and character, hope. Through faith:
we are saved by grace.

And hope does not disappoint us, because you have poured out your love into our hearts by the Holy Spirit. Through faith:
we are saved by grace.

You show us how much you love us: while we were helpless, Christ died for the ungodly. While we were still sinners, Christ died for us. Through faith:
we are saved by grace. Amen.

Romans 5.1–8, *Patterns for Worship*, 5P7*

29j BLESSING
Unto God's gracious mercy and protection we commit you. The Lord bless you and keep you. The Lord make his face to shine upon you, and be gracious to you. The Lord lift up the light of his countenance upon you, and give you his peace. And the blessing ...

Numbers 6.24–26

---

30. GUIDANCE

See also FAITH, THE SPIRIT, THE TRUTH

30a CALL TO WORSHIP
In the love of the Father, in the light of Christ, in the leading of the Spirit.
We place ourselves today.

The Open Gate, p. 13

30b PENITENCE
Almighty God, our Father, we come to you with humble hearts, to confess our sins:
For turning away from you, and ignoring your will for our lives: Father forgive us,
save us and help us.
For behaving just as we wish, without thinking of you: Father forgive us,
save us and help us.

For failing you – not only by what we do, but by our thoughts and words: Father forgive us,
save us and help us.
For letting ourselves be drawn away from you by temptations in the world about us: Father forgive us,
save us and help us.
For acting as if we were ashamed to belong to your dear Son Jesus: Father forgive us,
save us and help us.
Father, we have failed you often, and humbly ask your forgiveness:
help us so to live
that others may see your glory;
through Jesus Christ our Lord. Amen.

Editors, *Prayers for the People*, 4.13

30c COLLECT
Dearest Lord, be a bright flame before us, be a guiding star above us, be a smooth path beneath us, be a kindly shepherd behind us, today and for evermore. **Amen.**

St Columba, quoted in *The Open Gate*, p. 32

30d SUITABLE SCRIPTURE PASSAGES
Genesis 28.10–11a; Exodus 13.20–22; Deuteronomy 32.8–14; Isaiah 42.13–16; 58.9–11; Hosea 11.1–11; Psalms 5.1–8; 17.1–7, 15; 19.7–14; 23; 25.1–10; 32; 43; 48; 73.23–28; 107.1–9, 43; 119.105–112; 139.1–10, 23–24; 143.7–8.
Luke 1.68–79 (Benedictus); John 16.12–15; Romans 8.14–17.

30e AFFIRMATION OF FAITH
We believe in one world,
full of riches meant for everyone to enjoy.
We believe in one race,
the family of humankind,
learning to live together by the way of self-sacrifice.
We believe in one life,
exciting and positive,
which enjoys all beauty, integrity and science,
uses the disciplines of work to enrich society,
harmonises with the life of Jesus
and develops into total happiness.
We believe in one morality: love,
the holiness of sharing the sorrows and joys of others,
of bringing people together as true friends,
of working to get rid of the causes of poverty, injustice,
    ignorance and fear;

Love: the test of all our thoughts and motives.
Love: which is God forgiving us, accepting us,
and making us confident under the Holy Spirit's control.
We believe in Jesus, and the Bible's evidence about him,
whose life, death and resurrection
prove God's permanent love for the world,
who combines in himself life, love, truth, humanity,
reality and God,
saving, guiding, reforming and uniting
all people who follow the way.
We believe in the purpose of God
to unite in Christ everything, spiritual and secular,
to bring about constructive revolution in society,
individuals and nations
and to establish world government under his loving direction.

Subir Biswas, in *Liturgy of Life*, 103

30f   THE LORD'S PRAYER
Eternal Spirit, Life-giver, Pain-bearer, Love-Maker,
Source of all that is and that shall be,
Father and Mother of us all,
Loving God, in whom is heaven:
The hallowing of your name echo through the universe!
The way of your justice be followed
by the peoples of the world!
Your heavenly will be done by all created beings!
Your commonwealth of peace and freedom
sustain our hope and come on earth!
With the bread we need for today, feed us.
In the hurts we absorb from one another, forgive us.
In times of temptation and test, strengthen us.
From trials too great to endure, spare us.
From the grip of all that is evil, free us.
For you reign in the glory of the power that is love,
now and for ever. Amen.

Prayer at Night

30g   AT THE PEACE
Blessed be the Lord God of Israel, who guides our feet into the
way of peace.

Luke 1.68, 79

30h   PREFACE
Through Jesus Christ our Lord. In fulfilment of his true
promise, the Holy Spirit came down from heaven, lighting

upon the disciples, to teach them and to lead them into all truth; uniting peoples of many tongues in the confession of one faith, and giving to your Church the power to serve you as a royal priesthood, and to preach the gospel to all nations.

US BCP 1979, p. 380

30i THANKSGIVING
Almighty God, our heavenly Father, you have accepted us as your children in your beloved Son Jesus Christ our Lord, and fed us with the spiritual food of his most precious Body and Blood, giving us the forgiveness of sins and the promise of eternal life. We thank and praise you for these inestimable benefits and we offer and present ourselves entirely to you, to be a holy and living sacrifice, which is our reasonable service. Grant us grace to adapt ourselves no longer to the pattern of this present world, but let our minds be remade and our whole nature transformed that we may be able to discern your will and know what is good, acceptable and perfect; so that we may obey you here on earth, that we may at last rejoice with all your saints in your heavenly kingdom; through Jesus Christ our Lord, who lives and reigns with you and the Holy Spirit, one God, for ever. **Amen.**

West African Experimental Liturgy*

30j BLESSING
May Christ's holy, healing, enabling Spirit be with you, and guide you on your way at every change and turn. And the blessing ...

Patterns for Worship, 8T22

---

31. HARVEST, AGRICULTURE

See also THE CREATION, ECOLOGY, NATURE, POSSESSIONS, THANKS

31a OPENING RESPONSE
The land has produced a harvest,
our God has blessed us.
God has richly blessed us,
Praise him, everyone on earth.

Psalm 67.6–7, Michael Counsell

31b INVITATION TO CONFESS

The whole creation is suffering, and cries out with pain. Our sin affects the world of nature. Let us confess our sins against God and God's creation.

Romans 8.22, Michael Counsell

31c CONFESSION

God our Father, we are sorry for the times when we have used your gifts carelessly, and acted ungratefully. Hear our prayer and in your mercy;
forgive us and help us.
We enjoy the fruits of the harvest, but sometimes forget that you have given them to us; Father, in your mercy;
forgive us and help us.
We belong to a people who are full and satisfied, but ignore the cry of the hungry. Father, in your mercy;
forgive us and help us.
We are thoughtless, and do not care enough for the world you have made. Father, in your mercy;
forgive us and help us.
We store up goods for ourselves alone, as if there were no God and no heaven. Father, in your mercy;
forgive us and help us.

Adapted from Michael Perry

31d ABSOLUTION

May God, who has sown the seed of eternal life in your hearts, pluck out the weeds of sin that you have confessed, and bring forth in you the fruit of good works for the harvest of eternity.
Amen.

Michael Counsell

31e COLLECT

Creator of the fruitful earth, you have made us stewards of all things. Give us grateful hearts for your goodness, and steadfast wills to use your bounty well, that the whole human family, today and in generations to come, may with us give thanks for the riches of your creation. We ask this in the name of Jesus Christ our Lord. **Amen.**

Canadian *Book of Alternative Services*, p. 396

31f SUITABLE SCRIPTURE PASSAGES

Genesis 1.1 – 2.4a; 2.4–9, 15–25; 9.8–17; Deuteronomy 8.1–10 or 7–18; 26.1–11; Isaiah 61.1–4; Joel 2.21–27; Psalms 8; 24; 65; 66.2–3, 5, 7–8; 67; 85.8–13; 100; 104; 125.2–6; 126; 145; 147; 148; 150.

Matthew 5.1–10; 6.24–34; 10.26–31; 13.18–30; Luke 12.15–31; 17.11–19; John 1.1–14; 4.31–38; 6.25–35; 12.20–36; Acts 10.10–16; 14.13–17; 1 Corinthians 3.6–10; 2 Corinthians 9.6–15; Colossians 1.15–20; 1 Timothy 2.1–7; 6.6–10; Revelation 4; 14.14–18.

31g A STATEMENT OF FAITH

We believe that God hopes and works for a world where all shall be included in the feast of life;
and that in Christ we see how costly it is to bring that world about.
We believe that God's strategy for a new world is to put the poorest first;
and that nothing is more important than to bring the poor good news.
We believe that rich and poor can be generous, wise and creative because all are made in God's image;
and that all are made poorer when some are left out.
We confess that we use our strength to protect ourselves and order the world to benefit the rich and not the poor;
and that none of us can be trusted with too much power over others.
Yet we believe that despite the persistence of evil, now is the time when more good can be done;
and we long for that time when the meek shall inherit the earth, and all who hunger and thirst after justice shall be satisfied.

Feast for Life*

31h INTERCESSION

Let us pray to God, the Lord of the harvest, that he will bring to fruition all that he desires for his creation.
Lord of the harvest, when we lift up our eyes to perceive with Christ's eyes, we see that the fields of the world are already white for harvest: we pray for your Church, that it may be spiritually equipped to reap the harvest of souls. Lord of creation,
in your mercy hear us.

Lord of the harvest, you have created the universe by your eternal Word, and have blessed humankind in giving us dominion over the earth: we pray for your world, that we may share and conserve its resources, and live in reverence for the creation and in harmony with one another. Lord of creation,
in your mercy hear us.

Lord of the harvest, whose Son has promised that the Spirit will lead us into all truth: we pray for the community in which you have set us, for one another and for ourselves, that we may bear the harvest of the Spirit in love and joy and peace. Lord of creation,
in your mercy hear us.

Lord of the harvest, though you have given the human race a rich land, a land of streams and springs, wheat and barley, vines and oil and honey, we have made by sin a world of suffering and sorrow: we pray for those who bear the weight of affliction, that they may come to share the life of wholeness and plenty. Lord of creation,
in your mercy hear us.

Lord of the harvest, your Christ, the first-fruits of the resurrection, will put in the sickle for the harvest of the dead at the end of time: we pray for all those who have gone before us in his peace, that he will bring safely home all whom you have given him, and gather us all to share together in the banquet of the age to come. Merciful Father,
Accept these prayers for the sake of your Son our Saviour Jesus Christ. Amen.

Michael Perham, *Enriching the Christian Year*, 14C1

31i   AT THE PEACE
God satisfies you with the finest wheat, God has established peace on your borders.

Psalm 147.14

31j   PREFACE
Through Jesus Christ our Lord, the Word active in creation, who dwelling among us himself rejoiced in the beauty of the earth, giving thanks to you for the fruits of harvest and the fishes of the sea, and through his own work hallowing all human service.

The Province of the West Indies

31k   THANKSGIVING
Let us thank God for all his mercies. For the order and constancy of nature, for the beauty and the bounty of the world, for day and night, summer and winter, seedtime and harvest, for the diverse gifts of splendour and the use which each season brings, we praise God,
We thank him.

For the men and women who work upon our farms, for those who shape the farmer's tools and build his machines, for all who supply our food and sustain our lives, we praise God,
We thank him.

For our homes and the joys of home, for our friends and for all occasions of fellowship, for all the gracious ministries of human affection, we praise God,
We thank him.

For communion with God, who created us and holds us ever within the embrace of his love, for the life, death and resurrection of Jesus Christ, who shows us who God is, sets us free, and makes us one, for the Holy Spirit who touches our hearts to love and obedience, we praise God,
We thank him.

Services for Special Occasions, p. 73

311 BLESSING
May the God who binds up the brokenhearted, who proclaims freedom to those held captive by poverty, and promises justice to all who mourn its loss, bless you with beauty instead of ashes, the oil of gladness in place of grief, and instead of your spirit of despair, a garment of unending praise; through Jesus Christ our Lord. **Amen.**

Feast for Life

---

32. HEALING, COUNSELLING, MENTAL ILLNESS

See also FORGIVENESS, THE NEEDY, SALVATION, SUFFERING

32a INTRODUCTION

Leader	Everything that happens on earth happens at the time God chooses.
Women	God sets the time for birth and the time for death,
Men	the time for sorrow and the time for joy,
Women	the time for tearing and the time for mending,
Men	the time for killing and the time for healing.
Leader	Everything that happens on earth
All	**happens at the time God chooses.**

A Wee Worship Book, p. 46

32b INVITATION TO CONFESS

The grace of God has dawned upon the world with healing for all. Let us come to him, in sorrow for our sins, seeking healing and salvation.

Titus 2.11, Patterns for Worship, 8B10, freely available

32c KYRIE

Lord Jesus, you healed the sick:
Lord, have mercy.
Lord, have mercy.
Lord Jesus, you forgave sinners:
Christ, have mercy.
Christ, have mercy.
Lord Jesus, you gave yourself to heal us and bring us strength:
Lord, have mercy.
Lord, have mercy.

Ministry to the Sick, p. 29, Roman Missal

32d ABSOLUTION

God forgives you; forgive others; forgive yourself.
(*Pause.*)
Through Christ, God has put away your sin:
approach your God in peace, through Jesus your Redeemer.
Amen.

The New Zealand Eucharistic Liturgy 1984

32e COLLECT

We come to you Lord, for you alone can heal and restore us. We are not able to heal ourselves, for you alone can forgive, restore, sanctify, satisfy. We come to you Lord, for you alone can heal and restore us. **Amen.**

The Open Gate, p. 52

32f SUITABLE SCRIPTURE PASSAGES

Numbers 21.4–9; 1 Kings 17.17–24; 2 Kings 5.1–14; Isaiah 35.1–10; 40.27–31; 53.3–5; Jeremiah 8.18 – 9.1; Hosea 6.1–3; Psalms 23; 30; 34.1–8; 41; 42.1–7; 46; 91; 103.1–8; 107.1–3, 17–22; 121; 145; 146; 147.1–11, 20c.
Matthew 8.5–13; 8.14–17; 9.9–13, 18–26; 15.21–28; Mark 1.29–39; 1.40–45; 2.1–12; 2.23 – 3.6; 5.21–43; 7.24–37; 10.46–52; Luke 7.1–10; 8.26–39; 11.9–13; 13.10–17; 17.11–19; John 6.47–51; 9.1–7; 10.14–15, 27–30; 14.1–3, 27; Romans 8.31b–39; 2 Corinthians 1.3–5; 12.7–10; Ephesians 3.14–21; Philippians 1.20–26; 4.4–7; James 5.13–20; Revelation 21.10, 22 – 22.5.

32g **AFFIRMATION OF FAITH**
I believe and trust in God the Father,
who made all things.
I believe and trust in his Son Jesus Christ,
who redeemed the world.
I believe and trust in his Holy Spirit,
who gives life to the people of God.

Ministry to the Sick, p. 44, *Roman Missal*

32h **PRAYERS FOR HEALING**
O Christ our Lord,
As in times past
Not all the sick and suffering
Found their own way to your side,
But had to have their hands taken,
   or their bodies carried,
   or their names mentioned;
So we, confident of your goodness,
Bring others to you.
As in times past,
you looked at the faith of friends
And let peace and healing be known,
Look on our faith,
Even our little faith,
and let your kingdom come.

We name before you
Those for whom pain is the greatest problem;
Who are remembered more for their distress
   than for their potential;
Who at night cry, 'I wish to God it were morning,'
And in the morning cry, 'I wish to God it were night.'
(Here names may be mentioned aloud.)
Lord Jesus Christ, Lover of all,
Bring healing, bring peace
(or another similar sung or spoken response).

We name before you
Those whose problem is not physical;
Those who are haunted by the nightmares of their past
   or the spectres of their future,
Those whose minds are shackled to neuroses,
   depression and fears,
Who do not know what is wrong

115

And do not know how to pray.
(Here names may be mentioned aloud.)
Lord Jesus Christ, Lover of all,
Bring healing, bring peace.

We name before you
Those in whose experience light has turned to darkness,
As the end of a life,
Or the breaking of a relationship
Leaves them stunned in their souls
   and silent in their conversation,
Not knowing where to turn or whom to turn to
   or whether life has any purpose any more.
(Here names may be mentioned aloud.)
Lord Jesus Christ, Lover of all,
Bring healing, bring peace.

And others whose troubles we do not know,
Or whose names we would not say aloud,
We mention now in the silence which you understand.
(Silence.)
Lord Jesus Christ, Lover of all,
Bring healing, bring peace.

Lord God,
You alone are skilled to know the cure
For every sickness and every soul.
If by our lives your grace may be known,
Then in us, through us,
And, if need be, despite us,
Let your kingdom come.

On all who tend the sick,
   counsel the distressed,
   sit with the dying,
   or develop medical research
We ask your blessing,
That in caring for your people
They may meet and serve their Lord.
And for those who, in this land,
Administer the agencies of health and welfare,
We ask your guidance that in all they do
Human worth may be valued,
And the service of human need fully resourced.

This we ask in the name of him
Whose flesh and blood have made all God's children special.
Amen.

A Wee Worship Book, p. 47

32i AT THE PEACE
'Peace, peace to those who are far and to those who are near,'
says the Lord, 'and I will heal them.'

Isaiah 57.19

32j PREFACE
All thanks and praise to you, loving Father, for sending your
only Son to be our Saviour. He took upon himself our human
nature, shared our joy and our tears, bore all our sickness, and
carried all our sorrows. He brought us through death to the life
of his glorious resurrection, giving for our frailty eternal
strength, and restoring us in your perfect image.

A Prayer Book for Australia, p. 685

32k AFTER COMMUNION
Father of all mercies, for your gifts of healing and forgiveness,
for grace to love and care for one another, for your hidden
blessings, and for all you have in store for us, we give you
thanks, through Jesus Christ our Lord. **Amen.**

A Prayer Book for Australia, p. 688

32l BLESSING
May Christ, who out of defeat brings a new hope and a new
future, fill you with his new life; and the blessing ...

A New Zealand Prayer Book, p. 538*

---

33. HUMILITY, THE MIND OF CHRIST

See also JUDGEMENT

33a OPENING PRAYER
O God, our Father, for this time of worship direct and control
our thoughts that we may think only of you. Grant us reverence
as we remember your glory; penitence as we remember your
holiness; gratitude as we remember your love. So grant that we
may rise from our worship with knowledge deepened; with
love kindled; with strength to live more nearly as we ought:
through Jesus Christ our Lord. **Amen.**

Epilogues and Prayers, p. 80*

33b PENITENTIAL SECTION
Jesus said, 'There is joy among the angels of God over one sinner who repents.'
'Come to me all who labour and are heavy laden and I will give you rest.'
God has promised forgiveness to all who truly repent, turn to Christ in faith, and are themselves forgiving. In silence we call to mind our sins.
(*Silence.*)

Let us confess our sins.
Merciful God,
we have sinned
in what we have thought and said,
in the wrong we have done
and in the good we have not done.
We have sinned in ignorance:
we have sinned in weakness:
we have sinned through our own deliberate fault.
We are truly sorry.
We repent and turn to you.
Forgive us, for our Saviour Christ's sake,
and renew our lives to the glory of your name. Amen.

(*The Absolution is declared by the presiding priest:*)
Through the cross of Christ God have mercy on you, pardon you and set you free. Know that you are forgiven and be at peace. God strengthen you in all goodness and keep you in life eternal. **Amen.**

A New Zealand Prayer Book, p. 407

33c COLLECT
Incline us, O God, to think humbly of ourselves, to be saved only in the examination of our own conduct, to consider our fellow-creatures with kindness, and to judge of all they say and do with the charity which we would desire from them ourselves; through Jesus Christ our Lord. **Amen.**

Jane Austen

33d SUITABLE SCRIPTURE PASSAGES
Proverbs 25.6–7; Ecclesiasticus 10.12–18; Psalms 25.1–9; 131.
Mark 9.30–37; 10.35–45; Luke 14.1, 7–14; 18.9–14; John 13.1–7, 31b–35; Romans 11.1–2a, 29–32; 12.1–8; 2 Corinthians 5.17–21; Philippians 2.1–13.

33e AFFIRMATION OF FAITH
Jesus Christ, the Son of God,
though he was divine,
did not cling to equality with God,
but made himself nothing.
Taking the form of a slave,
he was born in human likeness.
He humbled himself,
and was obedient to death –
even the death of the cross.
Therefore God has raised him on high,
and given him the name above every name:
that at the name of Jesus
every knee should bow,
and every voice proclaim
that Jesus Christ is Lord,
to the glory of God the Father. Amen.

Philippians 2. 9–11, *Bible Praying*, 218*

33f PRAYER
O God, our Father, give us the humility which realizes its ignorance; admits its mistakes; recognizes its need; welcomes
advice; accepts rebuke. Save us from pride in our knowledge,
and make us to think of the great ocean of truth all undiscov-
ered before us. Save us from pride in our achievement, and
make us to remember all that we still have to do. Save us from
pride in our performance, and make us to remember how far
short of perfection our best must still fall. Help us in the days
ahead, to study with diligence; to learn with eagerness. And
give us a retentive memory to remember that which we have
learned; and a resolute will to put it into action. **Amen.**

Epilogues and Prayers, p. 81*

33g AT THE PEACE
Let this mind be in you, which was also in Christ Jesus. Then
the peace of God, which passes all understanding, will keep
your hearts and minds in him.

Philippians 2.5; 4.7

33h PREFACE
He not only taught his disciples that whoever wants to be great
must be the servant of all, he also set us an example of humility
in his life and his death.

Mark 9.35, Michael Counsell

33i THANKSGIVING
Blessed are you, God of all glory, through your Son the Christ.
His name is Jesus:
because he saves his people from their sins.
He will be called Emmanuel:
God is with us. Alleluia!
Let us praise the Lord, the God of Israel:
he has come to his people and set them free.
He gave up all the glory of heaven:
and took the nature of a servant.
In humility he walked the path of obedience:
to die on the cross.
God raised him to the highest place above and gave him the
name above every name:
Jesus Christ is Lord!

Holy Trinity, Wealdstone, in Patterns for Worship, 2P1

33j BLESSING
May God bless you, that in you may be found love and humility, obedience and thanksgiving, discipline, gentleness and
peace. And the blessing ...

Celebrating Common Prayer, p. 158*

---

34. JOY

34a GREETING
May Christ's grace and peace be with you.
May he fill our hearts with joy.

Source unknown

34b INVITATION TO CONFESS
God is love, and we are his children. There is no room for fear
in love: we love because he loved us first. Let us confess our
sins in penitence and faith.

Scottish Experimental Liturgy 1977

34c CONFESSION
**Most merciful God, we confess that we have sinned against
you in thought, word, and deed, by what we have done, and by
what we have left undone. We have not loved you with our
whole heart; we have not loved our neighbours as ourselves.
We are truly sorry and we humbly repent. For the sake of your
Son Jesus Christ, have mercy on us and forgive us; that we may**

delight in your will, and walk in your ways, to the glory of
your Name. Amen.

US BCP 1979, p. 79

34d ABSOLUTION
Hear the words of God's forgiveness:
The Lord hide his face from your sins and blot out all your
iniquity; the Lord create in you a pure heart, and renew within
you a steadfast spirit; the Lord comfort you by his Holy Spirit
and restore to you the joy of your salvation; through Jesus
Christ our Redeemer. **Amen.**

Psalm 51.9–12, *Bible Praying*, 114*

34e COLLECT
God of our joy and gladness, you have promised in the
Scriptures that though heaviness endure for a night, joy comes
in the morning: grant that we who mourn for a world unaware
of your presence may bring in the sheaves of your harvest with
joy, and join with all your children in the dance of the Eternal
Trinity. **Amen.**

Michael Counsell

34f SUITABLE SCRIPTURE PASSAGES
Nehemiah 8.1–3, 5–6, 8–10; Isaiah 55.10–13; Zephaniah 3.14–20;
Zechariah 9.9–12; Baruch 5.1–9; Psalms 4; 30; 65.9–13; 119.1–8;
126.
John 16.20–22; 17.6–19; Philippians 4.1–9.

34g AFFIRMATION OF FAITH
I believe, O God of all gods, that you are
The eternal Father of Life.
I believe, O God of all gods, that you are
The eternal Father of Love.
I believe, O God of all gods, that you are
The eternal Father of Peace.
I believe, O God of all gods, that you are
The eternal Father of Joy.
I believe, O God of all gods, that you are
The eternal Father of the saints.
I believe, O God of all gods, that you are
The Creator.
I believe, O God of all gods, that you are
The eternal Father, strong to save.
I believe, O God of all gods, that you are
The eternal Father of me.

The Edge of Glory, p. 64

34h PRAYER

I am weary of the dark voices crying doom;
I am weary of the fearful voices crying only for their nation;
I am weary of the disinherited voices crying in hopelessness;
let my voice sing the laughter of God;
let my voice sing good news to the poor;
let my voice sing restitution of the oppressed;
let my voice sing healing of the violated;
let my voice sing the return of the banned;
let my voice be the laughter of God. **Amen.**

Go Tell it on the Mountain

34i AT THE PEACE

Rejoice in the Lord always, and again I say rejoice, then the peace of God which passes all understanding will keep your hearts and minds through Jesus Christ our Lord.

Philippians 4.1–7

34j LONGER PREFACE

God our Father, giver of life and light, maker of all things, we praise you for earth and sea, for wind and fire. We thank you for the peoples of the world. For all the wonder of creation we praise you:
Hosanna in the highest!
You made our hearts to share your love. You know our tears and laughter. For your gift of love we praise you:
Hosanna in the highest!
Therefore with all your people of every place and age we join the saints and angels, for ever praising you and saying/ singing ...

*Additional Eucharistic Prayers**

34k THANKSGIVING AFTER COMMUNION

Loving Father, we thank you for feeding us at the supper of your Son. Sustain us with your Spirit, that we may serve you here on earth, until our joy is complete in heaven and we share the eternal banquet with Jesus Christ our Lord. **Amen.**

Lent, Holy Week and Easter, p. 194

34l BLESSING

May God give to you and to those you love his comfort and his peace, his light and his joy, in this world and the next. And the blessing ...

Patterns for Worship, OT48

35. JUDGEMENT, ANGER, THE FALL, PRIDE, SIN, SINNERS

See also ADVENT, FORGIVENESS, HUMILITY, JUSTICE

35a RESPONSIVE INTRODUCTION
We have come to the city of the living God, to the heavenly
Jerusalem, with thousands of angels in joyful assembly.
Alleluia!
We have come to God the judge of all, to Jesus the mediator of
the new covenant.
Alleluia!

Hebrews 12.22–24, 28 (*GNB**), *Patterns for Worship*, 6A10

35b INVITATION TO CONFESS
Jesus, you came to call sinners.

Mark 2.17

35c KYRIE
You were sent to heal the contrite: Lord, have mercy.
Lord, have mercy.
You came to call sinners: Christ, have mercy.
Christ, have mercy.
You plead for us at the right hand of the Father: Lord, have
mercy.
Lord, have mercy.

Roman Missal

35d ABSOLUTION
O Lord God, whose mercies are sure and full and ever new:
grant us the greatest of them all, the Spirit of your dear Son;
that in the day of judgement we may be presented to you if not
blameless, yet forgiven, if not successful, yet faithful, if not
holy, yet persevering, deserving nothing, but accepted in him
who pleads our cause and redeems our lives, even Jesus Christ
our Lord. **Amen.**

The Promise of His Glory, p. 107

35e COLLECT
Just and holy God, work in our lives by the power of your
Spirit, so that love of you, not fear of judgement, may stir us to
act justly and with compassion; that when we meet you face to
face, we may rejoice in your eternal presence: through Jesus
Christ our Lord. **Amen.**

Companion to the Lectionary 6, p. 11

35f SUITABLE SCRIPTURE PASSAGES

Exodus 32.1–14; Isaiah 65.1–9; Jeremiah 4.11–12, 22–28; 18.1–11; Amos 7.7–17; Jonah 3.10 – 4.11; Micah 3.5–12; Zephaniah 1.7, 12–18; Malachi 4.1–2a; Ecclesiasticus 10.12–18; Psalms 14; 25.1–9; 51.1–17; 106.1–6, 19–23; 149.

Matthew 5.21–37; 13.24–30, 36–43; 16.21–28; 21.23–32; 21.33–46; 22.1–14; 25.31–46; Luke 14.1, 7–14; 18.9–14; John 3.14–21; 8.2–11; 11.17–27; 12.20–33; Romans 5.1–19; 6.1b–11; 6.12–23; 7.15–25a; 14.1–12; 1 Timothy 1.12–17; Hebrews 12.18–29; 1 John 3.1–13.

35g AFFIRMATION OF FAITH

I believe, Lord,
that everything good in the world
comes from you.
I believe in your great love for all people.
I believe that, because you preached love,
freedom and justice,
you were humiliated,
tortured and killed.
I believe that you continue
to suffer in our people …
I believe that you call me
to defend your cause,
but I also believe that you accompany me
in the task of transforming this world
into a different one
where there is no suffering or weeping;
a world where there is a gigantic table
set with free food
where everyone is welcome.
I believe that you accompany us
in waiting for the dawning of a new day.
I believe that you will give us strength
so that death does not find us
without having done enough,
and that you will rise
in those who have died seeking a different world.

El Salvadorean peasant woman, Latinamerica Press

35h INTERCESSION

We pray for the coming of God's kingdom, saying: Father, by your Spirit:
bring in your kingdom.
You came in Jesus to bring good news to the poor, sight to the blind, freedom to the captives, and salvation to your people:

anoint us with your Spirit; rouse us to work in his name. Father, by your Spirit:
bring in your kingdom.
Send us to bring help to the poor and freedom to the oppressed. Father, by your Spirit:
bring in your kingdom.
Send us to tell the world the good news of your healing love. Father, by your Spirit:
bring in your kingdom.
Send us to those who mourn, to bring joy and gladness instead of grief. Father, by your Spirit:
bring in your kingdom.
Send us to proclaim that the time is here for you to save your people. Father, by your Spirit:
bring in your kingdom.
Lord of the Church:
hear our prayer
and make us one in heart and mind
to serve you with joy for ever. Amen.

Patterns for Worship, 16H22

35i AT THE PEACE
Most merciful Lord, your love compels us to come in. Our hands were unclean, our hearts were unprepared; we were not fit even to eat the crumbs from under your table. But you, Lord, are the God of our salvation, and share your bread with sinners. So cleanse and feed us with the precious body and blood of your Son, that he may live in us and we in him; and that we, with the whole company of Christ, may sit and eat in your kingdom. Amen.

ASB, p. 170

35j PREFACE
And now we give you thanks because he is the Saviour. In your mercy and faithfulness you have promised to us after the fall that his truth might instruct the ignorant, his holiness purify sinners, and his strength sustain the weak. Since the time is at hand when the one whom you sent should come, since the day of our deliverance has begun to dawn, full of confidence in your promises, we exult with joy.

The Promise of His Glory, p. 132

35k THANKSGIVING
Almighty God, by your gift the tree of life was set at the heart of the earthly paradise, and the bread of life was set at the heart of

125

your Church. Let this divine nourishment bring us, not to judgement, but to life eternal; through Jesus Christ our Lord. **Amen.**

Prayers for use at the Alternative Services

351 BLESSING

May the Lord Jesus Christ, the Son of the living God, set his passion, cross and death between his judgement and your souls, now and in the hour of your death. May he grant mercy and grace to the living, rest to the dead, to his holy Church peace and concord, and to us sinners everlasting life and glory; and may the blessing ...

Horae B.V.M.

36. JUSTICE

See also JUDGEMENT, PEACE, REMEMBRANCE SUNDAY

36a CALL TO WORSHIP

God says: My servant will bring justice to every nation,
We long for your justice, O God.
My servant will bring lasting justice to all,
Help us to serve the cause of right.

Isaiah 42.1, 3, *For the Sake of Justice**

36b INVITATION TO CONFESS

Let us confess to God the sins and shortcomings of the world; its pride, its selfishness, its greed; its evil divisions and hatreds. Let us confess our share in what is wrong, and our failure to seek and establish that peace which God wills for his children.

Service for Remembrance Sunday

36c CONFESSION

You asked for our hands, that you might use them for your purpose;
We gave them for a moment, then withdrew them, for the work was hard.
You asked for our mouths, to speak out against injustice;
We gave you a whisper, that we might not be accused.
You asked for our eyes, to see the pain of poverty;
We closed them, for we did not want to see.
You asked for our ears, that we might hear the cries of the oppressed;
We did not listen, for it was too hard.

You asked for our lives, that you might work through us;
We gave a small part, that we might not get too involved.
Forgive us for the times we have washed our hands of people,
walked away when they needed us, offered half measure;
O God, our Father and Mother, forgive us.

For the Sake of Justice

36d KYRIE

'I was hungry and you gave me no food, I was thirsty and you
have me no drink.' Lord, have mercy.
Lord, have mercy.
'I was a stranger and you did not welcome me, naked and you
did not clothe me.' Christ, have mercy.
Christ, have mercy.
'I was sick and you did not visit me, in prison, and you did not
come to me.' Lord, have mercy.
Lord, have mercy.

The Promise of His Glory, p. 242

36e ABSOLUTION

God's justice is chiefly seen in showing mercy. Though for our
sins we justly deserve to be punished, God in Christ has forgiv-
en us. **Amen.**

Michael Counsell

36f COLLECT

God whose Holy name defies our definition, but whose will is
known in freeing the oppressed, make us to be one with all
who cry for justice; that we who speak your praise may struggle for your truth, through Jesus Christ. **Amen.**

All Desires Known

36g SUITABLE SCRIPTURE PASSAGES

2 Samuel 11.26 – 12.13a; 1 Kings 21.1–10, 15–21a; Job 23.1–9,
16–17; Isaiah 9.1–6; 11.1–10; 32.15–18; 58.1–9a; 61.1–4, 8–11;
Jeremiah 2.4–13; Amos 5.6–7, 10–15; 5.18–24; 8.1–12; Habakkuk
1.1–4; 2.1–4; Ecclesiasticus 35.12–17; Psalms 5.1–8; 15; 37.1–9;
52; 71.2–4, 7–8, 12–13, 17; 72.1–7, 18–19; 81.1, 10–16; 82; 84.9–14;
98; 126; 146.5–10.
Matthew 20.1–16; Luke 1.46–55 (Magnificat); 12.49–56; 2
Thessalonians 1.1–12; 2 Timothy 1.1–14.

36h WHAT WE BELIEVE

**We believe in one God, author of life, Creator of the
  universe.
We believe in the Son, Jesus Christ our Lord,**

who came into the world to seek the lost
and to redeem the whole of creation.
**We believe in the Holy Spirit, the Giver of Life,
who renews us and helps us grow in the likeness of Christ.
We believe we are created to be faithful servants
who will not waver or be crushed,
who, by praying, working, and standing together
can bring justice and truth to the whole earth**.

For the Sake of Justice

36i INTERCESSION
We bring before God our needs and the needs of the world.
Wonderful Counsellor, give your wisdom to the rulers of the
nations: Lord, in your mercy,
hear our prayer.
Mighty God, make the whole world know that the government
is on your shoulders: Lord, in your mercy,
hear our prayer.
Everlasting Father, establish your reign of justice and righteousness for ever: Lord, in your mercy,
hear our prayer.
Prince of peace, bring in the endless kingdom of your peace:
Lord, in your mercy,
hear our prayer.
Almighty Lord,
**hear our prayer,
and fulfil your purposes in us,
as you accomplished your will
in our Lord Jesus Christ. Amen**.

The Promise of His Glory, p. 187

36j AT THE PEACE
The peace of God be with you all.
In God's justice is our peace.
Brothers and sisters, Christ calls us to live in unity.
We seek to live in the Spirit of Christ.

A New Zealand Prayerbook, p. 466

36k LONGER PREFACE
Father, all-powerful and ever-living God, we do well always and
everywhere to give you thanks. In love you created us, in justice
you condemned us, but in mercy you redeemed us, through
Jesus Christ our Lord. Through him the angels and all the choirs
of heaven worship in awe before your presence. May our voices
be one with theirs, for ever praising you and saying/singing ...

Roman Missal

361 PRAYER AFTER COMMUNION
Merciful God, we have been gathered at the table of your Son.
Hear our prayer for all our sisters and brothers in faith who
suffer for truth, justice and freedom. Strengthen their witness
and keep them, with us, under the protection of your wings.
We ask this in the name of Jesus Christ our Lord. **Amen.**

Canadian *Book of Alternative Services*, p. 418

36m BLESSING
Now may the blessing of God the Father, who made from one
every nation that occupies the earth; of God the Son, who
bought us for God from every tribe and language and people
and nation; and of God the Spirit, who brings us together in
unity, be with us and remain with us always. **Amen.**

Acts 17.26; Revelation 5.9, *Patterns for Worship*, 16T41

---

37. THE KING, CHRIST THE KING, THE KINGDOM, THE REIGN OF CHRIST

See also THE ASCENSION, AUTHORITY, PALM SUNDAY

37a INTRODUCTION
Blessed be God: Father, Son and Holy Spirit.
Blessed be God's kingdom now and for ever.

Orthodox prayer, adapted in *A Prayer Book for Australia*, p. 119

37b INVITATION TO CONFESS
Jesus says, 'Repent, for the kingdom of heaven is close at hand.'
So let us turn away from sin and turn to him, confessing our
sins in penitence and faith.

Matthew 4.17, *In Penitence and Faith*, No. 13

37c CONFESSION
O King enthroned on high,
filling the earth with your glory:
holy is your name,
Lord God almighty.
In our sinfulness we cry to you
to take our guilt away,
and to cleanse our lips to speak your word,
through Jesus Christ our Lord. Amen.

Adapted from Michael Perry

37d ABSOLUTION

Almighty God, who in Jesus Christ has given us a kingdom that cannot be destroyed, forgive us our sins, open our eyes to God's truth, strengthen us to do God's will and give us the joy of his kingdom, through Jesus Christ our Lord. **Amen.**

Bryan Spinks, *Patterns for Worship*, 0D11

37e COLLECT

**As the seed grows secretly in the earth,
as the yeast rises in the dough,
May the power of God be at work in us.
May we be like a city set on a hill,
like a lamp shining in the darkness.
May we witness together with all Christians
to the glory of God and the fulfilment of his Kingdom. Amen.**

All Year Round 1990, p. 110

37f SUITABLE SCRIPTURE PASSAGES

Exodus 19.2–8a; 1 Samuel 15.34 – 16.13; 16.1–13; 18.4–11, 16–20; 2 Samuel 7.1–14, 16; Jeremiah 23.1–6; 33.14–16; Ezekiel 34.1–2, 15–17; Daniel 7.9–10, 13–14; Psalms 20; 23; 45.1–2, 6–9; 47; 68.1–10, 32–35; 72.1–7, 18–19; 89.20–37; 93; 97; 145.8–14.
Matthew 9.35 – 10.8; 13.31–33, 44–52; 16.13–20; 21.33–46; 25.31–46; 28.16–20; Mark 4.26–34; 16.19–20; Luke 24.44–53; John 18.33–37; Acts 1.1–14; 1 Corinthians 15.20–26, 28; Ephesians 1.15–23; Revelation 1.4b–8.

37g AFFIRMATION OF FAITH

**We believe
God raised from the dead
our Lord Jesus Christ
by his mighty power,
and seated him at his right hand in heaven,
far above all rule and authority,
power and dominion,
and every title that can be given,
not only in the present age
but also in the age to come.
God placed all things under his feet
and appointed him to be head over everything
for the church, which is his body,
the fullness of him who fills everything
everywhere and always. Amen.**

Ephesians 1.20–23, *Bible Praying*, 215

37h INTERCESSION

Let us pray for the breaking in of God's kingdom
in our world today.
Lord God,
Because Jesus has taught us to trust you in all things,
We hold to his word and share his plea,
Your kingdom come, your will be done.

Where nations budget for war,
While Christ says 'Put up your sword',
Your kingdom come, your will be done.

Where countries waste food and covet fashion,
While Christ says, 'I was hungry ... I was thirsty ...',
Your kingdom come, your will be done.

Where powerful governments claim their policies are heaven
blessed,
While scripture proclaims that God has no favourites,
Your kingdom come, your will be done.

Where Christians seek the kingdom in the shape of their own
church,
As if Christ had come to build and not to break barriers,
Your kingdom come, your will be done.

Where women who speak up for their dignity
Are treated with scorn or contempt,
Your kingdom come, your will be done.

Where men try hard to be tough,
Because they're afraid to be tender:
Your kingdom come, your will be done.

Where we, obsessed with being adult,
Forget to become like children,
Your kingdom come, your will be done.

Where our prayers falter,
our faith weakens,
our light grows dim,
Your kingdom come, your will be done.

Where Jesus Christ calls us,
Your kingdom come, your will be done.

Lord God,
You have declared that your kingdom is among us.
Open our eyes to see it,
our ears to hear it,
our hearts to hold it,
our hands to serve it.
This we pray in Jesus' name.
Amen.

A Wee Worship Book, p. 9

37i AT THE PEACE
Our Saviour Christ is the Prince of Peace; of the increase of his government and of peace there shall be no end.

Isaiah 9.6

37j LONGER PREFACE
Father, all-powerful and ever-living God, we do well always and everywhere to give you thanks. You anointed Jesus Christ, your only Son, with the oil of gladness, as the eternal priest and universal King. As priest he offered his life on the altar of the cross, and redeemed the human race by this one perfect sacrifice of peace. As King he claims dominion over all creation, that he may present to you, his almighty Father, an eternal and universal kingdom: a kingdom of truth and life, a kingdom of holiness and grace, a kingdom of justice, love and peace. And so with all the choirs of angels in heaven we proclaim your glory, for ever praising you and saying / singing:

Roman Missal*

37k PRAYER AFTER COMMUNION
Lord, you give us Christ, the King of all creation, as food for everlasting life. Help us to live by his gospel and bring us to the joy of his kingdom, where he lives and reigns for ever and ever.
Amen.

Roman Missal

37l SOLEMN BLESSING
May God the Father, judge all-merciful, make us worthy of a place in his kingdom. **Amen.**
May God the Son, coming among us in power, reveal in our midst the promise of his glory. **Amen.**
May God the Holy Spirit make us steadfast in faith, joyful in hope and constant in love. **Amen.**

And the blessing of God almighty, the Father, the Son and the Holy Spirit, be among you and remain with you always. **Amen.**

The Promise of His Glory, p. 135

---

38. LENT, ASH WEDNESDAY, CONFLICT, FASTING, TEMPTATION

See also FORGIVENESS, REPENTANCE

38a GREETING
Bless the Lord who forgives all our sins;
Whose mercy endures for ever.

A Prayer Book for Australia, p. 119

38b INVITATION TO CONFESS
The sacrifice of God is a broken spirit; a broken and contrite heart he will not despise. Our sin is always before us: we acknowledge our transgressions in penitence and faith.

Psalm 51.17, *Patterns for Worship*, 4B4, freely available

38c CONFESSION
We confess that in our lives
we do not always choose the way of peace.
We spread gossip which fans the flames of hatred.
We are ready to make any sacrifice
when the world demands,
but few when God invites.
We worship the false god of security.
We hold out one hand in friendship,
but keep a weapon in the other behind our back.
We have divided your body of people
into those we trust and those we do not.
Huge problems challenge us in the world,
but our greed, fear and selfishness
prevent us from uniting to solve them.
Lord, we need your help and forgiveness,
your reconciling power.

Rev. Pat Vowles in *Let all the World ...*

38d KYRIE
Lord, we have sinned against you: Lord, have mercy;
Lord, have mercy.
Lord, show us your mercy and love: Christ, have mercy;
Christ, have mercy.

Lord, grant us your salvation: Lord, have mercy;
Lord, have mercy.

Lent, Holy Week and Easter, p. 286*

38e ABSOLUTION

The Lord have mercy on you in your distress; the Lord deliver
you from your sins and shelter you in all temptation; the Lord
make his face to shine upon you, and save you in his unfailing
love. **Amen**.

Psalm 31.9–16, *Bible Praying*, 107

38f COLLECT

Spirit of integrity, you drive us into the desert to search out our
truth. Give us clarity to know what is right, and courage to
reject what is merely strategic; that we may abandon the false
innocence of failing to choose at all, but may follow the purposes of Jesus Christ. **Amen**.

*All Desires Known**

38g SUITABLE SCRIPTURE PASSAGES

Genesis 2.15–17; 3.1–7; 9.8–17; 12.1–4a; 15.1–12, 17–18; 17.1–7,
15–16; Exodus 17.1–7; 20.1–7; Numbers 21.4–9; Deuteronomy
26.1–11; Joshua 5.9–12; 1 Samuel 16.1–13; 17.32–49; 17.57 – 18.5,
10–16; 2 Samuel 5.1–5, 9–10; Esther 7.1–6, 9–10; 9.20–22; Isaiah
50.4–9a; 55.1–9; 58.1–12; Jeremiah 11.18–20; Daniel 12.1–3; Joel
2.1–2, 12–17; Wisdom 1.16 – 2.1, 12–22; Psalms 19; 20; 22.23–31;
23; 25.1–10; 27; 32; 41; 51.1–17; 54; 63.1–8; 91.1–2, 9–16; 95; 98;
107.1–3, 17–22; 121; 124; 133.
Matthew 4.1–11; 5.38–48; 6.1–6, 16–21; 11.16–19; 16.21–28; Mark
1.9–15; 3.20–35; 8.31–38; 9.2–9; 9.38–50; 13.1–8; Luke 4.1–13;
6.27–38; 13.1–9; 13.31–35; 15.1–3, 11b–32; John 2.13–22; 3.1–21;
4.5–42; 9.1–41; Romans 4.1–5, 13–25; 5.1–11; 5.12–19; 6.12–23;
1 Corinthians 10.1–13; 2 Corinthians 5.6b – 6.10; Ephesians
5.9–14; Hebrews 4.12–16; James 1.12–15; 1 Peter 3.18–22; 1 John
5.1–6.

38h AFFIRMATION OF FAITH

Let us hold firmly to the faith we profess:
We have a high priest
able to understand our weaknesses,
who has gone into heaven –
Jesus, the Son of God.
He was tempted in every way,
just as we are,
yet without sin.
Therefore we approach

the throne of grace
with confidence;
to receive mercy
and find grace to help us
in our time of need. Amen.

Hebrews 4.14–16, *Bible Praying*, 226

38i INTERCESSION
We thank you, God, for giving us this time of Lent to prepare
for our celebration of Easter. Hear our prayers for your church
throughout the world, that by self-discipline we may be more
fit for your service. Merciful God,
forgive us and hear us.

Bring repentance for the hatreds and prejudices which divide
nation against nation, class against class and race against race.
Give your guidance to the leaders of this and every nation, and
make wars to cease in all the world. Merciful God,
forgive us and hear us.

Grant that this Lent may be a time when we learn to be more
open and loving to our friends, family and neighbours.
Merciful God,
forgive us and hear us.

As we remember how you suffered on the cross for our sake,
give us compassion for those who suffer today. May we have
the will and the wisdom to relieve their need and heal their
pain. Merciful God,
forgive us and hear us.

Strengthen us this Lent to live more confidently in your service
and to die well through your grace, that we may look forward
with gladness to sharing eternity with those we love, who have
gone before, and with the company of saints, where we may
meet you face to face and know as we are known. Merciful
God,
forgive us and hear us. Amen.

Michael Counsell

38j AT THE PEACE
Being justified by faith, we have peace with God through our
Lord Jesus Christ.

ASB, p. 170

38k PREFACE

Through Jesus Christ our Lord, who was tempted in every way as we are, yet did not sin. By his grace we are able to triumph over every evil, and to live no longer for ourselves alone, but for him who died for us and rose again.

US BCP 1979, p. 379

38l AFTER COMMUNION

Eternal God, comfort of the afflicted and healer of the broken, you have fed us this day at the table of life and hope. Teach us the ways of gentleness and peace, that all the world may acknowledge the kingdom of your Son Jesus Christ our Lord. **Amen.**

Canadian *Book of Alternative Services*, p. 399

38m SOLEMN BLESSING

May God the Father, who does not despise the broken spirit, give to you a contrite heart. **Amen.**
May Christ, who bore our sins in his body on the tree, heal you by his wounds. **Amen.**
May the Holy Spirit, who leads us into all truth, speak to you words of pardon and peace. **Amen.**
And the blessing ...

Michael Perham, *Enriching the Christian Year*, 1F1

---

39. LIFE, ETERNAL LIFE, HEAVEN

See also DEATH, RESURRECTION, SAINTS

39a CALL TO WORSHIP

Jesus said: 'Go and proclaim what you hear and see: blind people are recovering their sight; the lame are walking around; people with leprosy have been healed; deaf people can hear again; those who were dead are being raised up; and the poor are having good news preached to them. And blessed is the one who takes no offence at me.'

Matthew 11.4–6, *God of Life*

39b INVITATION AND CONFESSION

Let us acknowledge our need for God's help to change us.
We confess that we are slow to stand up straight and look you in the eye. We are afraid of what we might see if you free us from worries and troubles that keep us bent double. Forgive us, Lord. We are bent double, frozen into inaction, locked

into the habit of years. Forgive us, Lord. Touch us, Lord of
life. Heal us, so that our bonds are loosened. Heal us so that
we can rejoice when all women and men stand up straight.
Heal us, so all people can look at each other face to face. In
the name of Jesus. Amen.

God of Life

39c ABSOLUTION
Let us stand up straight.
(Stand.)
Women and men, you are freed from your infirmity:
be at peace.

God of Life

39d COLLECT
Almighty God, who through your only-begotten Son Jesus
Christ overcame death and opened to us the gate of everlasting
life: Grant that we, who celebrate with joy the day of the Lord's
resurrection, may be raised from the death of sin by your life-
giving Spirit; through Jesus Christ our Lord, who lives and
reigns with you and the Holy Spirit, one God, now and for ever.
Amen.

US BCP 1970, p. 222

39e SUITABLE SCRIPTURE PASSAGES
Deuteronomy 30.15–20; Wisdom 1.13–15; 2.23–24; Psalms 16;
23; 30; 90.1–8, 12; 118.1–2, 14–24; 133; 139.1–12, 23–24;
Luke 23.33–43; John 3.14–21; 6.24–35; 6.35, 41–51; 6.51–58;
6.56–69; 20.19–31; Romans 6.12–23; 8.6–11; 1 Corinthians
15.51–58; 2 Corinthians 4.5–12; 5.6–10, 14–17; Ephesians
1.15–23; 1 John 1.1 – 2.2; 5.9–13.

39f AFFIRMATION OF FAITH
I believe in God the Father almighty,
I believe in Jesus Christ his Son.
And I believe in the Holy Spirit,
I believe in life after death,
I believe in the resurrection.

The Book of Dimma, quoted in *The Edge of Glory*, p. 93

39g INTERCESSION
High and holy God, robed in majesty, Lord of heaven and
earth, we pray that you will bring justice, faith and salvation to
all peoples. (Especially we pray …) Lord hear us:
Lord, graciously hear us.

You chose us in Christ to be your people and to be the temple of your Holy Spirit; we pray that you will fill your Church with vision and hope. (Especially we pray ...) Lord hear us:
Lord, graciously hear us.

Your Spirit enables us to cry, 'Abba! Father!', affirms that we are fellow-heirs with Christ and pleads for us in our weakness; we pray for all who are in need or distress. (Especially we pray ...) Lord hear us:
Lord, graciously hear us.

In the baptism and birth of Jesus, you have opened heaven to us and enabled us to share in your glory: the joy of the Father, Son and Holy Spirit from before the world was made. (Especially we remember ...) May your whole church, living and departed, come to a joyful resurrection in your city of light. Lord hear us:
Lord, graciously hear us.

Source unknown, Patterns for Worship, 9H14

39h **THE PEACE**
Jesus said: 'I have come so that you may have life, and live it to the full.' The peace of the living Christ be always with you;
and also with you.

John 10.10, Michael Counsell

39i **PREFACE**
Through Jesus Christ our Lord. Out of love for sinners, he humbled himself to be born of the Virgin. By suffering on the cross he freed us from unending death, and by rising from the dead he gave us eternal life.

Roman Missal

39j **AFTER COMMUNION**
Gracious Lord, in this holy sacrament you give substance to our hope. Bring us at the last to that pure life for which we long; through Jesus Christ our Lord. **Amen.**

Memorials upon Several Occasions

39k **SOLEMN BLESSING**
May God the Father bring us to the home which his Son prepares for all who love him. **Amen.**
May God the Son give us the will to live for him each day in life eternal. **Amen.**

May God the Holy Spirit give us the assurance that our citizenship is in heaven with the blessed and beloved, and the whole company of the redeemed. **Amen.**
And the blessing …

Patterns for Worship, 15T40

40. LIGHT, CANDLEMAS, THE PRESENTATION OF CHRIST IN THE TEMPLE

See also THE AGED, THE TEMPLE

40a OPENING GREETING
Christ has brought us out of darkness,
to live in his marvellous light.

1 Peter 2.9, *The Promise of His Glory*, p. 155, freely available

40b INVITATION TO CONFESS
Jesus says, 'I am the light of the world. Those who follow me shall not walk in darkness, but will have the light of life.' Let us then bring our secret sins into his light and confess them in penitence and faith.

In Penitence and Faith, No. 10

40c CONFESSION
Heavenly and eternal Father, we confess that we have sinned against you and our neighbours. We have walked in darkness rather than light; we have called upon the name of Christ, but have not departed from our sins. Have mercy upon us, we pray you; for the sake of Jesus Christ forgive us all our sins. Cleanse us by your Holy Spirit; quicken our consciences and enable us to forgive others; lead us out from darkness to walk as children of light; through Jesus Christ our Lord. Amen.

West African Experimental Liturgy

40d ABSOLUTION
Almighty God, who pardons all who truly repent, and are themselves forgiving, have mercy upon you, pardon and deliver you from all your sins, confirm and strengthen you in all goodness, and keep you in eternal life; through Jesus Christ our Lord.
Amen. Thanks be to God.

West African Experimental Liturgy

40e COLLECT

Almighty God, you bring to light things hidden in darkness, and know the shadows of our hearts; cleanse and renew us by your Spirit, that we may walk in the light and glorify your name, through Jesus Christ, the light of the world. **Amen.**

A Kenyan Revised Liturgy

40f SUITABLE SCRIPTURE PASSAGES

Genesis 1.1–19; Exodus 13.1–16; 13.20–22; 1 Samuel 1.19b–28; Isaiah 9.1–4; 49.1–7; 51.1–6; Malachi 3.1–5; Haggai 2.1–9; Baruch 3.9–15, 32 – 4.4; Psalms 4; 24.7–10; 26; 27.1, 4–9; 42 – 43; 48; 118; 119.105–112; 119.129–136; 122; 132.

Matthew 5.13–20; Luke 2.22–40; John 1.6–8, 19–28; 2.18–22; 3.14–21; 9.1–41; Romans 12.1–5; 13.11–14; 2 Corinthians 4.5–12; Ephesians 5.8–14; Hebrews 2.14–18; 4.11–16; 1 John 1.1 – 2.2; Revelation 21.10, 22 – 22.5.

40g AFFIRMATION OF FAITH

Let us declare our faith in the Son of God:
In the beginning was the Word,
and the Word was with God,
and the Word was God.
Through him all things were made;
without him nothing was made
that has been made.
In him was life,
and that life was the light of all people.
The Word became flesh
and lived for a while among us;
we have seen his glory,
the glory of the only Son of the Father,
full of grace and truth. Amen.

John 1.1–14, Bible Praying, 204

40h INTERCESSION

O living God, we pray for your Church; for those who help us understand your teaching; for those who encourage us by their example; for those who support us through kindness and prayer. O God of life:
May we be light in the world.

O living God, we pray for the nations: for those who lead and must make difficult decisions; for those who speak out for the truth; for those who serve other people. O God of life:
May we be light in the world.

O living God, we pray for our community: for those who are sick or anxious; for those who give of their time and energy; for those who carry the burdens of others. O God of life:
May we be light in the world.

O living God, we are the fruit of your grace and the work of your hands. We live in your light, and minister only through your power at work in us. Receive our offering of praise, that your light may shine through us, this day and forever. O God of life:
May we be light in the world.

Companion to the Lectionary 6, p. 79

40i AT THE PEACE
In the tender compassion of our God the dawn from on high shall break upon us, to shine on those who dwell in darkness and the shadow of death, and to guide our feet into the way of peace.

Luke 1.78–79, ICET

40j PREFACE
And now we give you thanks because by appearing in the Temple he brings judgement on the world. The Word made flesh searches the hearts of all your people, to bring to light the brightness of your splendour.

The Promise of His Glory, p. 278

40k THANKSGIVING AFTER COMMUNION
Almighty God, our great Elder,
we have sat at your feet,
learnt from your word,
and eaten from your table.
We give you thanks and praise
for accepting us into your family.
Send us out with your blessing,
to live and to witness for you
in the power of your Spirit,
through Jesus Christ, your First Born. Amen.

A Kenyan Revised Liturgy

40l SOLEMN BLESSING
(*The people accompany their first three responses with a sweep of the arm towards the west end of the church, and their final response with a sweep towards the east end.*)
All our problems
We send to the setting sun.

141

All our difficulties
We send to the setting sun.
All the devil's works
We send to the setting sun.
All our hopes
We set on the Risen Son.

Christ the Sun of righteousness shine upon you and scatter the darkness from before your path; and the blessing of God almighty, Father, Son and Holy Spirit, be among you and remain with you always. **Amen.**

A Kenyan Revised Liturgy

40m NUNC DIMITTIS
Master, who repeated
promise of release:
all my tasks completed,
let me leave in peace.

That we've seen salvation
could not be denied:
light for every nation
and your people's pride.

Glory to the Father,
glory to the Son,
glory, Holy Spirit.
Heaven has begun! **Amen.**

Luke 2.29–32, Michael Counsell

41. LOVE, THE HEART

See also PARENTHOOD

41a GREETING
The grace of our Lord Jesus Christ, and the love of God, and the fellowship of the Holy Spirit, be with you all.
And also with you.

2 Corinthians 13.13

41b INVITATION TO CONFESS
My brothers and sisters in Christ, to prepare ourselves to celebrate this mystery of love, let us call to mind our sins and make our confession to our heavenly Father.

Source unknown

41c CONFESSION
Most merciful God,
we have sinned in thought and word and deed,
we are truly sorry and we ask you to forgive.
Help us by your Spirit
to live the new life in Christ,
loving you with all our heart,
and our neighbours as ourselves;
for Jesus Christ's sake. Amen.

Compline, *In Penitence and Faith*, No. 53

41d ABSOLUTION
May the God of love bring us back to himself, forgive us our sins, and assure us of his eternal love in Jesus Christ our Lord. **Amen.**

Stuart Thomas, in *Patterns for Worship*, 17D9

41e COLLECT
God our lover, in whose arms we are held, and by whose passion we are known; require of us also that love which is filled with longing, delights in the truth, and costs not less than everything, through Jesus Christ. **Amen.**

All Desires Known

41f SUITABLE SCRIPTURE PASSAGES
Genesis 29.15–28; Leviticus 19.1–2, 9–18; Deuteronomy 6.1–9; Song of Solomon 2.8–13; Jeremiah 31.1–6; Lamentations 3.23–33; Jonah 3.10 – 4.11; Wisdom 12.13, 16–19; Psalms 36.5–10; 62.5–12; 85.8–13; 103.8–13; 145.1–8; 145.8–14.
Matthew 5.38–48; 22.34–46; Mark 12.28–34; Luke 6.27–38; 10.25–37; John 13.31–35; 15.9–17; 17.20–26; Romans 5.1–5; 12.9–21; 13.8–14; 1 Corinthians 13.1–13; Ephesians 4.25 – 5.2; Colossians 3.12–17; 1 Thessalonians 2.1–8; 1 John 3.16–24; 4.7–21; 5.1–6.

41g AFFIRMATION OF FAITH
What can separate us from the love of God?
Can sickness or death?
No, nothing can separate us from the love of God.
Can danger or war?

No, nothing can separate us from the love of God.
Can sadness or despair?
No, nothing can separate us from the love of God.
Can the nuclear bomb or the end of the world?
No, nothing can separate us from the love of God.
Can failure or rejection?
No, nothing can separate us from the love of God.
Can loneliness or death?
No, nothing can separate us from the love of God.

The Edge of Glory, p. 78

41h INTERCESSION
With confidence and trust let us pray to the Father, saying, Lord
of compassion,
in your mercy hear us.

For the one holy catholic and apostolic Church ... let us pray to
the Father. Lord of compassion,
in your mercy hear us.

For the mission of the Church, that in faithful witness it may
preach the gospel to the ends of the earth, let us pray to the
Father. Lord of compassion,
in your mercy hear us.

For those preparing for baptism (and confirmation) ... and for
their teachers and sponsors, let us pray to the Father. Lord of
compassion,
in your mercy hear us.

For peace in the world ... that a spirit of respect and reconciliation may grow among nations and peoples, let us pray to the
Father. Lord of compassion,
in your mercy hear us.

For the poor, the persecuted, the sick and all who suffer ...; for
refugees, prisoners, and all in danger; that they may be relieved
and protected, let us pray to the Father. Lord of compassion,
in your mercy hear us.

For those whom we have injured or offended, let us pray to the
Father. Lord of compassion,
in your mercy hear us.

For grace to amend our lives and to further the reign of God, let
us pray to the Father. Lord of compassion,
in your mercy hear us.

In communion with all those who have walked the way of holiness ... let us pray to the Father. Lord of compassion,
in your mercy hear us.

Canadian *Book of Alternative Services*, p. 121, adapted in *Enriching the Christian Year*, 1C1

41i THE PEACE
Jesus said, 'A new commandment I give to you: as I have loved
you, that you also love one another.' The peace of the Lord be
always with you.
And also with you.
Let us greet one another with a sign of love.

John 15.12

41j LONGER PREFACE
Worship and praise belong to you, Father, in every place and at
all times. All power is yours. You created the heavens and
established the earth; you sustain in being all that is. In Christ
your Son our life and yours are brought together in a wonderful exchange. He made his home among us that we might for
ever dwell in you. Through your Holy Spirit you call us to new
birth in a creation restored by love. As children of your redeeming purpose we offer you our praise, with angels and
archangels and the whole company of heaven, for ever praising
you and saying/singing ...

Scottish Liturgy 1982 *

41k CONCLUDING PRAYER
May the power of your love, Lord Christ, fiery and sweet, so
absorb our hearts as to withdraw them from all that is under
heaven; grant that we may be ready to die for love of your love,
as you died for love of our love. **Amen.**

Francis of Assisi, in *Celebrating Common Prayer*, p. 145

41l BLESSING
To God the Father, who loved us first, and gave this world to be
our home: to God the Redeemer, who loves us, and by dying
and rising pioneered the way of freedom: to God the Sanctifier,
who spreads the divine love in our hearts: be praise and glory,
for time and for eternity; and may the blessing ...

Bishop Ken, *Prayer at Night*

42. MARY THE VIRGIN, THE ANNUNCIATION

See also PARENTHOOD, WOMEN

42a RESPONSIVE MAGNIFICAT
My spirit magnifies the Lord, my soul is filled with love,
for God has sent an only Son to earth from heaven above;
to earth from heaven above; so sing the birth of such a boy:
My spirit magnifies the Lord, my soul is filled with joy.

My spirit magnifies the Lord, my soul is filled with peace,
for God has sent an only Son the pris'ners to release;
the pris'ners to release; and all the tyrants to destroy:
My spirit magnifies the Lord, my soul is filled with joy.

My spirit magnifies the Lord, my soul is filled with faith,
for God has sent an only Son to break the power of death;
to break the power of death; and cleanse us all from sin's alloy:
My spirit magnifies the Lord, my soul is filled with joy.

My spirit magnifies the Lord, my soul is filled with grace,
for God has sent an only Son the wealthy to displace;
the wealthy to displace and fill the hungry they annoy:
My spirit magnifies the Lord, my soul is filled with joy.

My spirit magnifies the Lord, my soul is filled with song,
for God has sent an only Son to right all earthly wrong;
to right all earthly wrong that sinful people can deploy:
My spirit magnifies the Lord, my soul is filled with joy.

Luke 1.46–55, *The Secret Name*

42b INVITATION TO CONFESS
God says, As a mother comforts her child, so will I myself comfort you. Yet like disobedient children, we have done things to sadden God's loving heart. Let us tell God we are sorry.

Isaiah 66.13

42c KYRIE
Lord Jesus, you are mighty God and Prince of Peace: Lord, have mercy.
Lord, have mercy.
Lord Jesus, you are Son of God and Son of Mary: Christ, have mercy.
Christ, have mercy.

Lord Jesus, you are Word made flesh and splendour of the Father: Lord, have mercy.
Lord, have mercy.

Roman Missal

42d ABSOLUTION

As parents love their children, God delights to welcome back those who have strayed. At the intercession of the Mother of God, may Jesus forgive you all your sins. **Amen.**

Michael Counsell

42e COLLECT

O God, you fulfil our desire beyond what we can bear; as Mary gave her appalled assent to your intimate promise, so may we open ourselves also to contain your life within us, through Jesus Christ. **Amen.**

All Desires Known

42f SUITABLE SCRIPTURE PASSAGES

Isaiah 7.10–14; 52.7–10; Micah 5.2–4; Zechariah 2.1–10; Psalms 40; 45.10–15; 113; 131.
Luke 1.26–38a; 1.39–45; 1.46–56 (Magnificat); 2.1–19; 2.16–21; 2.22–40; 2.41–51; John 19.25–27; Galatians 4.1–7; Hebrews 10.4–10; Revelation 11.19; 12.1–6, 10; 21.1–7.

42g STATEMENT OF FAITH

O God, the source of our being, and the goal of all our longing,
we believe and trust in you.
The whole earth is alive with your glory, and all that has life is sustained by you.
We commit ourselves to cherish your world, and to seek your face.
O God, embodied in a human life,
we believe and trust in you.
Jesus our brother, born of the woman Mary, you confronted the proud and the powerful, and welcomed as your friends those of no account. Holy Wisdom of God, first-born of creation, you emptied yourself of power, and became foolishness for our sake. You laboured with us upon the cross, and have brought us forth to the hope of resurrection.
We commit ourselves to struggle against evil and to choose life.
O God, life-giving Spirit, Spirit of healing and comfort, of integrity and truth,
we believe and trust in you.

Warm-winged Spirit, brooding over creation, rushing wind and Pentecostal fire,
we commit ourselves to work with you and renew our world.

All Desires Known

42h INTERCESSION

As we pray to God, the Father of our Lord Jesus Christ, we say with Mary: Lord, have mercy on those who fear you.
Holy is your name.

Your angel declared to Mary that she was to be the mother of the Saviour. Help (... and) every Christian person to be open to your word and obedient to your will. Lord, have mercy on those who fear you.
Holy is your name.

Mary bore a son of David's line, born a king whose reign would never end. Bless (... and) all the nations of the world with Christ's gift of peace. Lord, have mercy on those who fear you.
Holy is your name.

The child Jesus grew in wisdom and stature in the home of Mary and Joseph. Strengthen our homes and families, and keep under your protection (... and) all those whom we love. Lord, have mercy on those who fear you.
Holy is your name.

At the foot of the cross of Christ stood his mother, and from the cross she received the lifeless body in her arms. Give comfort and healing to (... and) all who suffer and all who watch the suffering of those they love. Lord, have mercy on those who fear you.
Holy is your name.

Bring us with (... and) all those who have died in the faith of Christ to share the joy of heaven with Mary and all the saints. Lord, have mercy on those who fear you.
Holy is your name.

Michael Perham for St George's Church, Oakdale, *Enriching the Christian Year*, 11C1*

42i AT THE PEACE

Unto us a child is born, unto us a Son is given, and his name is called the Prince of Peace.

Isaiah 9.6, *The Promise of His Glory*, p. 179

42j LONGER PREFACE

O Eternal Wisdom, we praise you and give you thanks, because you emptied yourself of power and became foolishness for our sake; for (on this night) you were delivered as one of us, a baby needy and naked, wrapped in a woman's blood; born into poverty and exile, to proclaim the good news to the poor, and to let the broken victims go free. Therefore, with the woman who gave you birth, the women who befriended you and fed you, who argued with you and touched you, the woman who anointed you for death, the women who met you, risen from the dead, and with all your lovers throughout the ages, we magnify you, for ever praising you and saying/singing ...

All Desires Known*

42k THANKSGIVING

Blessed are you, Lord our God, King of the universe: to you be glory and praise for ever! In the greatness of your mercy you chose the Virgin Mary to be the mother of your only Son. In her obedience the day of our redemption dawned, when by the overshadowing of your Holy Spirit he took our flesh and dwelt in the darkness of her womb. In her your glory shines as in the burning bush, and so we call her blessed with every generation. With her we rejoice in your salvation, and ponder in our hearts the mystery of your love. May we bear with her the piercing sword of sorrow in hope that we like her may share the joy of heaven. As we now join our praise with hers, blessed among all women, create in us a heart of love obedient to your will, for you are Lord and you are our God for ever. **Amen.**

The Promise of His Glory, p. 17

42l SOLEMN BLESSING

May God the Father, who loved the world so much that he sent his only Son, give you grace to prepare for life eternal. **Amen.**
May God the Son, who comes to us as Redeemer and Judge, reveal to you the path from darkness to light. **Amen.**
May God the Holy Spirit, by whose working the Virgin Mary conceived the Christ, help you bear the fruits of holiness. **Amen.**
And the blessing ...

Michael Perham, *The Promise of His Glory*, p. 101

43. MINISTRY, ORDINATION, VOCATION

See also PETER

43a OPENING RESPONSES
In God's Church there are many different gifts,
but only one Spirit who gives them.
There are many ways of serving,
but only one Lord whom we serve.
People are busy about many things,
but the same God is at work in everyone.

1 Corinthians 12.4–6

43b INVITATION TO CONFESS
We are called to bear witness to the good news of God's love.
Let us confess our failure to live up to that calling.

Michael Counsell

43c KYRIE
Lord Jesus, you are the Good Shepherd. You rescue us and save
us: Lord, have mercy.
Lord, have mercy.
Lord Jesus, we follow your voice and not a stranger's. You lead
us in and out to pasture: Christ, have mercy.
Christ, have mercy.
Lord Jesus, when we are attacked you do not abandon us. You
lay down your life for your sheep: Lord, have mercy.
Lord, have mercy.

Trevor Lloyd, *Enriching the Christian Year*, 20B1

43d ABSOLUTION
Our Lord Jesus Christ, who has left power to his Church to
absolve all sinners who truly repent and believe in him, of his
great mercy forgive you all your offences; and by his authority
committed to me, I absolve you from all your sins: In the name
of the Father, and of the Son, and of the Holy Spirit. **Amen.**

US BCP 1979, p. 448

43e COLLECT
O true light, you lighten every one coming into the world; in
your mercy inflame the hearts and enlighten the understanding
of all whom you call to the service of your Church, that they may
cheerfully acknowledge and readily obey all that you would
have them believe and practise, to the benefit of your people and
to the glory of your holy name: for you are alive and reign, with
the Father and the Holy Spirit, one God for ever and ever. **Amen.**

Henry Parry Liddon*

43f SUITABLE SCRIPTURE PASSAGES

Exodus 3.1–15; 19.2–8a; 1 Samuel 3.1–10; 15.34 – 16.13; 1 Kings 19.9–18; Proverbs 1.20–33; 8.1–4, 22–31; 9.1–6; Isaiah 6.1–8; 55.1–11; Jeremiah 1.4–10; 15.15–21; Ezekiel 17.22–24.

Matthew 4.12–23; 9.35 – 10.8; 11.16–19; Mark 2.13–22; 6.1–13; Luke 5.1–11; 9.51–62; 10.1–11, 16–20; 14.25–33; John 10.1–16; Acts 1.15–17, 21–26; 1 Corinthians 1.1–9; 2 Corinthians 4.5–12; 5.20b – 6.10; 6.1–13; Galatians 1.11–24; Ephesians 1.3–14; Philippians 1.21–30; 1 Thessalonians 2.9–13; Hebrews 4.14–16; 5.7–9; 5.1–10; 7.23–28; 10.16–25.

43g AN ORDINATION CHARGE

We are not ordaining you to ministry; that happened at your baptism.

We are not ordaining you to be a caring person; you are already called to that.

We are not ordaining you to serve the Church in committees, activities, organisations; that is already implied in your membership.

We are not ordaining you to become involved in social issues, ecology, race, politics, revolution, for that is laid upon every Christian.

We are ordaining you to something smaller and less spectacular: to read and interpret those sacred stories of our community, so that they speak a word to people today; to remember and practise those rituals and rites of meaning that in their poetry address people at the level where change operates; to foster in community through word and sacrament that encounter with truth which will set men and women free to minister as the body of Christ.

We are ordaining you to the ministry of the word and sacraments and pastoral care.

God grant you grace not to betray but to uphold it, not to deny but affirm it, through Jesus Christ our Lord.

Methodist Church in Singapore*

43h INTERCESSION

We pray for the use of God's gifts to his Church, saying, Jesus, Lord of the Church,
in your mercy hear us.

God our Father, you give us gifts that we may work together in the service of your Son:
Bless those who lead, that they may be firm in faith, yet humble before you: Jesus, Lord of your Church,
in your mercy hear us.

Bless those who teach, that they may increase our understanding, and be open to your word to them: Jesus, Lord of your Church,
in your mercy hear us.

Bless those who minister healing, that they may bring wholeness to others, yet know your healing in themselves: Jesus, Lord of your Church,
in your mercy hear us.

Bless those through whom you speak, that they may proclaim your word in power, yet open their ears to your gentle whisper: Jesus, Lord of your Church,
in your mercy hear us.

Bless those who work in your world today, that in the complexity of their daily lives they may live for you, fulfil your purposes, and seek your kingdom first: Jesus, Lord of your Church,
in your mercy hear us.

Bless those who feel they have no gifts or value and those who are powerless in this world's eyes, that they may share their experience of the work of your Spirit: Jesus, Lord of your Church,
hear our prayer,
and make us one in heart and mind
to serve you with joy for ever. Amen.

Adapted from Michael Perry

43i   AT THE PEACE
God has reconciled us to himself through Christ and given us the ministry of reconciliation.

2 Corinthians 5.18, *Patterns for Worship*, 16R17, freely available

43j   LONGER PREFACE
Blessed are you, gracious God, creator of heaven and earth; we give you thanks and praise through Jesus Christ our Lord, who came not to be served, but to serve, and to give his life a ransom for many. He calls his faithful servants to lead your holy people in love, nourishing them by your word and sacraments. Now with all creation we raise our voices to proclaim the glory of your name, for ever praising you and saying/singing …

Canadian *Book of Alternative Services*, p. 226*

43k AFTER COMMUNION
Almighty Father, we thank you for feeding us with the holy
food of the Body and Blood of your Son, and for uniting us
through him in the fellowship of your Holy Spirit. We thank
you for raising up among us faithful servants for the ministry
of your Word and Sacraments. We pray that they may be to us
an effective example in word and action, in love and patience,
and in holiness of life. Grant that we, with them, may serve you
now, and always rejoice in your glory; through Jesus Christ
your Son our Lord, who lives and reigns with you and the Holy
Spirit, one God, now and for ever. **Amen.**

US BCP 1976, p. 523

43l BLESSING
Almighty God, who for the salvation of the world gives to his
people many gifts and ministries to the advancement of his
glory, stir up in you the gifts of his grace, sustain each one of
you in your own ministry; and the blessing ...

ASB, p. 396*

---

44. MOTHERING SUNDAY

See also CHILDREN, FAMILY, PARENTHOOD

44a INTRODUCTORY SENTENCE
Looking at those who sat round him Jesus said, 'These are my
mother and my brothers. Whoever does the will of God is my
brother or sister or mother.'

Mark 4.34–35

44b INVITATION TO CONFESS
God says, 'When I called, no one answered, when I spoke, they
did not listen; but they did what was evil in my sight, and
chose what did not please me. For I know their works and their
thoughts.' So let us come and confess to God.

Isaiah 66.4, 18

44c KYRIE
As parents are tender towards their children, so God is tender
to those who trust: Lord, have mercy.
Lord, have mercy.
God will not always rebuke us, nor will God's displeasure last
for ever: Christ, have mercy.
Christ, have mercy.

I have calmed and quieted my soul, my soul is like a child upon its mother's breast: Lord, have mercy.
Lord, have mercy.

Psalms 103.9, 13; 131.3

44d ABSOLUTION

God says, As a mother comforts her child, so will I myself comfort you. Your sins are forgiven: rest on God as on your mother's breast. **Amen.**

Isaiah 66.13

44e COLLECT

Ever-loving God, your care for us is greater even than a mother's love for her child; teach us to value a mother's love and see in it an expression of your grace, that we may ever feel more deeply your love for us in Christ Jesus our Saviour. **Amen.**

A New Zealand Prayer Book, p. 690

44f SUITABLE SCRIPTURE PASSAGES

Exodus 2.1–10; 1 Samuel 1.20–28; Proverbs 4.1–9; 31.10–31; Isaiah 49.8–16a; 66.10–14; Micah 4.1–5; Psalms 27.1–7; 34.11–20; 84; 87; 122; 127.1–4; 139.1–18.
Mark 10.13–16; Luke 2.33–35; 2.41–52; John 19.23–27; 2 Corinthians 1.3–7; Colossians 3.12–17; 2 Timothy 1.3–10; 1 Peter 2.1–10.

44g AFFIRMATION OF FAITH

We believe in God who loves us
and wants us to love each other.
This is our God.
We believe in Jesus,
who cared about children and held them in his arms.
He wanted a world where everyone
could live together in peace.
This is Jesus Christ.
We believe in the Holy Spirit
who keeps working with us
until everything is good and true.
This is the Holy Spirit.
We can be the Church which reminds people of God
because we love each other.
This we believe.

Prepared by children for the World Council of Churches Assembly in Canberra, 1991

44h INTERCESSION
For all our mothers and fathers,
Lord, receive our thanks and prayer.
For the security of homes and family life,
Lord, receive our thanks and prayer.
For the joy of all loving human relationships,
Lord, receive our thanks and prayer.
For your holy catholic Church, the mother of us all,
Lord, receive our thanks and prayer.
For your family in this place, and our life together,
Lord, receive our thanks and prayer.
For all the members of our families who have died,
Lord, receive our thanks and prayer.
For Mary, the Mother of Jesus, and for all who seek to follow
her example of motherhood,
Lord, receive our thanks and prayer.

Michael Perham, for St George's Church, Oakdale, *Enriching the Christian Year*, 2C2

44i THE BLESSING OF FLOWERS
O God, bless these flowers, bless us, and bless our mothers.
May the flowers remind us how much our mothers have done
for us; may they remind our mothers how much we love them;
and may they remind us all that God cares for us better than
any mother ever could. Amen.

Prayers for Sundays

44j PREFACE
And now we give you thanks because in his earthly childhood
you entrusted him to the care of a human family. In Mary and
Joseph you give us an example of love and devotion to him,
and also a pattern of family life.

ASB, p. 155

44k AFTER COMMUNION
Loving God, as a mother feeds her children at the breast, you
feed us in this sacrament with the food and drink of eternal life:
help us who have tasted your goodness to grow in grace within the household of faith; through Jesus Christ our Lord. **Amen.**

Michael Perham, *Enriching the Christian Year*, 2L2

44l THANKSGIVING
O God, as truly as you are our father, so just as truly you are our
mother. We thank you, God our Father, for your strength and
goodness. We thank you, God our Mother, for the closeness of
your caring. O God, we thank you for the great love you have
for each one of us. **Amen.**

Mother Julian of Norwich (c. 1342–1415)

44m SOLEMN BLESSING
When the Word became flesh, earth was joined to heaven in the
womb of Mary; may the love and obedience of Mary be your
example. **Amen.**
May the peace of Christ rule in your hearts and homes. **Amen.**
May you be filled with the joy of the Spirit and the gifts of your
eternal home. **Amen.**
And the blessing of God, our Maker, Friend and Inspiration, be
upon you and those you love, and remain with you always.
Amen.

Patterns for Worship, 2T8*

45. NATURE, ANIMALS, FLOWER FESTIVALS

See also THE CREATION, ECOLOGY, HARVEST

45a OPENING RESPONSES
Thanks be to you O God, that we have risen this day
To the rising of this life itself.
Be the purpose of God between us and each purpose,
The hand of God between us and each hand.
The pain of Christ between us and each pain,
The love of Christ between us and each love.
O God of the waifs, O God of the naked,
Draw us to the Shelter-house of the Saviour of the poor.

A Wee Worship Book, p. 17

45b INVITATION TO CONFESSION
'How often have I longed to gather your children, as a hen
gathers her brood under her wings,' says the Lord, 'but you
would not let me.' As wayward children we return to God and
confess our sins.

John Townend, Matthew 23.37, *Enriching the Christian Year*, 7A2

45c KYRIE
Father, you enfold us with wings of love, as a bird protects her
young. In our sin we have spurned your love. Lord, have
mercy.
Lord, have mercy.
Jesus, you gather us around you that we may learn your ways.
In our sin we have strayed from your presence. Christ, have
mercy.
Christ, have mercy.
Holy Spirit, you feed us with the seed of your holy word: In our

sin we have chosen the chaff. Lord, have mercy.
Lord, have mercy.

John Townend, Matthew 23.37, *Enriching the Christian Year*, 7B3

45d CONFESSION

Holy God, maker of the skies above,
Lowly Christ, born amidst the growing earth,
Spirit of life, wind over the flowing waters,
In earth, sea and sky,
You are there.
O hidden mystery,
Sun behind all suns,
Soul behind all souls,
In everything we touch,
In everyone we meet,
Your presence is round us,
And we give you thanks.
But when we have not touched, but trampled you in creation,
When we have not met but missed you in one another,
When we have not received but rejected you in the poor,
Forgive us,
And hear now our plea for mercy.

Iona Community Worship Book, p. 65

45e ABSOLUTION

May almighty God cleanse us from sin and make us worthy of
the kingdom of his glory. **Amen.**

The Promise of His Glory, p. 249

45f COLLECT

Lord God, may we love your creation, all the earth and every
grain of sand in it. May we love every leaf, every ray of your
light. May we love the animals. Let us not trouble them; let us
not harass them, let us not deprive them of their well-being, let
us not work against your intent. We acknowledge that to you
all is like an ocean, all is flowing and blending, and that to
withhold love from anything in your universe is to withhold
that same love from you. **Amen.**

Adapted from Feodor Dostoevsky

45g SUITABLE SCRIPTURE PASSAGES

Genesis 1.1–28; 9.8–17; Song of Solomon 2.8–13; Isaiah 11.6–9;
35.1–7; 55.10–13; Psalms 8; 19; 65.9–13; 98; 148.
Matthew 6.24–34; 10.29–31; Luke 8.22–25; 12.6–7; 12.22–31;
13.10–19; Romans 8.18–25; Revelation 4.

45h AFFIRMATION OF FAITH
We believe in God above us,
Maker and Sustainer of all life,
of sun and moon,
of water and earth,
of male and female.
We believe in God beside us,
Jesus Christ, the Word made flesh,
born of a woman's womb, servant of the poor.
He was tortured and nailed to a tree.
A man of sorrows, he died forsaken.
He descended into the earth to the place of death.
On the third day he rose from the tomb.
He ascended into heaven to be everywhere present,
and his Kingdom will come on earth.
We believe in God within us,
the Holy Spirit of Pentecostal fire,
Life-giving breath of the Church,
Spirit of healing and forgiveness,
Source of resurrection and life everlasting.
Amen.

Iona Community Worship Book, p. 22

45i INTERCESSION
It is in this mystery of communion with Christ
That we pray for the Church throughout the world,
Praying in particular for ...
We are embodied with them, now.
We pray for the people and communities of faith
From whom we have come
and to whom we shall return ...
We are embodied with them, now.
We pray for the sick, the bereaved, the oppressed
And the homeless,
praying in particular for ...
We are embodied with them, now.
We pray for the broken and torn fabric of the earth
As it yearns for healing,
praying in particular for ...
We are embodied with Christ in creation, now.
And because you are one with us, O Christ,
Enable us to share your life with the world by
Sharing our own lives with the world,
And teach us now to pray together,
Our Father ...

Iona Community Worship Book, p. 68

45j THE SIGN OF PEACE
Many grains were gathered together to make this bread,
Many grapes were mixed to make this wine.
So we who are many,
And come from many places,
Are one in Christ.
May the peace of Christ be with you.
And also with you.

Iona Community Worship Book, p. 68, based on The Didache 9.4

45k THE PRAYER OF THANKSGIVING, OR LONGER PREFACE
We offer you praise, dear God,
And hearts lifted high,
For in the communion of your love
Christ comes close to us
And we come close to Christ.
Therefore with the whole realm of nature around us,
With earth, sea and sky,
We sing to you.
With the angels of light who envelop us,
With Michael and the host of heaven,
With all the saints before and beside us,
With ... (*here may be added the names of special saints to be
    commemorated*),
With brothers and sisters, east and west,
We sing to you.
And with our loved ones,
Separate from us now,
Who yet in this mystery are close to us,
we join in the song of your unending greatness ...
(*here may be added, to lead into the Sanctus, words such as:*)
for ever praising you and saying/singing ...

Iona Community Worship Book, p. 67*

45l MEDITATION: THE SEASONS
Our lives are sometimes like winter,
when all seems cold, dreary and dead.
We, like creation, need to rest and wait.
Our lives are sometimes like spring,
where there is so much new budding
and new flowering bursting out
that we can hardly contain it,
bringing to birth that which has lain dormant for so long.
Our lives are sometimes like high summer,
relaxed, carefree and warm:

a riot of colours everywhere,
bringing with it laughter and happiness.
Our lives are sometimes like the autumn:
glorious, golden maturity,
fruitfulness that can only come about through time,
yet with a hint of death and dying.
That is the pathway to a new-found spring.

Sally Munns

45m BLESSING
May the everlasting God shield you,
east and west and wherever you go.
And the blessing of God be upon us,
The blessing of the God of life.
The blessing of Christ be upon us,
The blessing of the Christ of love.
The blessing of the Spirit be upon us,
The blessing of the Spirit of grace.
The blessing of the Trinity be upon us now and for evermore.
Amen.

Source unknown

---

46. THE NEEDY, CHARITIES, NEIGHBOURS, THE POOR

See also HEALING, RIGHTEOUSNESS, SUFFERING, THE WORLD

46a GREETING
In the name of God: Creator, Redeemer and Giver of life.
Amen.

A New Zealand Prayer Book, p. 456

46b INVITATION TO CONFESS
Jesus said, 'Inasmuch as you have not done it to the least, you have not done it to me.' Let us confess our failure to help the needy.

Matthew 25.45

46c KYRIE
Forgive us, Lord, that we live in a world where so often the starving go unfed, the thirsty remain parched, and strangers are not befriended. Lord, have mercy:
Lord, have mercy.

Forgive us, Lord, that we live in communities where so often
the sick go untended, the naked remain exposed, and prisoners
are not visited. Christ, have mercy:
Christ, have mercy.
Forgive us, Lord, that so often we are content that it be so. Lord,
have mercy:
Lord, have mercy.

Companion to the Lectionary 6, p. 10

46d ABSOLUTION
You are a warrior for justice, and we quake before your fierce
anger. You are faithful and true, and we throw ourselves upon
your mercy; it is our only hope, but it is enough. **Amen.**

Companion to the Lectionary 6, p. 11

46e COLLECT
Blessed are you, Lord God, creator of all peoples, giver of life
and health and love. Help us to see you in the world's needs, to
see your presence in the poor, to serve you in serving others,
Father, Son and Holy Spirit. **Amen.**

The Open Gate, p. 27

46f SUITABLE SCRIPTURE PASSAGES
Leviticus 19.1–2, 9–18; Deuteronomy 24.17–22; 1 Kings 17.8–16;
Proverbs 22.1–2, 8–9, 22–23; Isaiah 25.1–9; 58.1–14; Amos 5.6–7,
10–15; 8.1–12; Ecclesiasticus 35.12–17; Psalms 14; 22.25–31; 41;
52; 112; 113; 146.
Matthew 10.40–42; 12.28–34; 20.1–16; 22.34–46; 25.31–46; Luke
6.17–26; 7.11–17; 10.25–37; 14.12–14; 16.1–13; 16.19–31; Acts
4.32–35; 2 Corinthians 8.17–15; 1 Timothy 6.6–19; James 2.1–10,
14–17; 1 John 3.16–24.

46g AFFIRMATION OF FAITH
We believe in the God of life
who did not create death.
We are followers of a God
who loves and defends life;
who gives over his life to all
to show us love;
a God who endures suffering and death;
a God who is risen;
the Way, the Truth, and the Life;
a God who still invites us
to overcome all that is evil,
all that brings pain, suffering and injustice,
and to celebrate the life

**that God desires, in abundance,
for us all**.

God of Life

46h INTERCESSION

We cry to the Lord when in trouble:
Deliver them in their distress.
For those who have lost their way in life,
and those who find no home to dwell in:
We cry to the Lord when in trouble:
Deliver them in their distress.
For the sick, that God's word will deliver them,
and those whose heart is heavy:
We cry to the Lord when in trouble:
Deliver them in their distress.
For bereaved folk and those who are dying, who live in the
shadow of death: We cry to the Lord when in trouble:
Deliver them in their distress.
For those who go down to the sea in ships,
for travellers by land or by air:
We cry to the Lord when in trouble:
Deliver them in their distress.
For the starving, who dwell in a barren land,
and those in fear of floods:
We cry to the Lord when in trouble:
Deliver them in their distress.
For those oppressed by tyrants,
and all who live in dread of their enemies:
We cry to the Lord when in trouble:
Deliver them in their distress.
Give thanks to the Lord, who is gracious,
understand the loving-kindness of the Lord:
For we cried to the Lord when in trouble:
God delivered us in our distress. Alleluia! Amen.

Michael Counsell, from Psalm 107

46i AT THE PEACE

The wisdom from above produces a harvest of good deeds
from the seeds planted by the peacemakers.

James 3.17–18

46j PREFACE

To the poor he proclaimed the good news of salvation, to
prisoners, freedom, and to those in sorrow, joy.

Roman Missal

46k THANKSGIVING
Almighty God, you give seed for us to sow, and bread for us to eat; make us thankful for what we have received; make us able to do those generous things which supply your people's needs; so all the world may give you thanks and glory. **Amen.**

A New Zealand Prayer Book, p. 141

46l BLESSING
May God the Father of our Lord Jesus Christ, who is the source of all goodness and growth, pour his blessing upon all things created, and upon you his children, that you may use them to his glory and the welfare of all peoples. And the blessing ...

Sarum Rite, Prayers for use at the Alternative Services, No. 210

---

47. OBEDIENCE, ADAM, DISOBEDIENCE

47a INTRODUCTORY SENTENCE
As by Adam's disobedience many were made sinners, so by Christ's obedience many will be made righteous.

Romans 5.19

47b INVITATION TO CONFESS
Dear friends in Christ, God is steadfast in love and infinite in mercy; he welcomes sinners and invites them to his table. Let us confess our sins, confident in God's forgiveness.

Canadian *Book of Alternative Services*, p. 191

47c CONFESSION
Lord Jesus, forgive us when we fail to follow your teaching and example. When we have taken revenge and retaliated instead of offering the other cheek: Lord, forgive us:
Lord, forgive us.
When we have begrudged giving small things instead of offering more than was asked: Lord, forgive us:
Lord, forgive us.
When we have resented going out of our way for people instead of cheerfully going the extra mile: Lord, forgive us:
Lord, forgive us.
When we have flatly refused to do what was asked of us even when we knew you wanted us to do it: Lord, forgive us:
Lord, forgive us.
When we have not loved our enemies or prayed for those who persecute us: Lord, forgive us:
Lord, forgive us.

Give us strength Lord, to do what you ask and to follow your example, for we long to do your will. **Amen.**

Companion to the Lectionary 6, p. 8

47d ABSOLUTION

Almighty God have mercy upon you, pardon and deliver you from all your sins, confirm and strengthen you in all goodness, and keep you in eternal life; through Jesus Christ our Lord. **Amen.**

Canadian *Book of Alternative Services*, p. 191, source unknown

47e COLLECT

Heavenly Father, whose blessed Son was revealed that he might destroy the works of the devil, and make us children of God and heirs of eternal life: grant that we, having this hope, may purify ourselves even as he is pure; that when he shall appear in power and great glory we may be like him in his eternal and glorious kingdom; where he is alive and reigns with you and the Holy Spirit, one God, now and for ever. **Amen.**

ASB, p. 403,* *BCP 1662*

47f SUITABLE SCRIPTURE PASSAGES

Genesis 2.5–25; 3; Deuteronomy 4.1–2, 6–9; 11.18–21, 26–28; Isaiah 1.1, 10–20; Ezekiel 2.1–5; Psalm 123.
Matthew 7.21–27; 21.23–32; Mark 3.20–35; 6.1–13; Luke 17.5–10; Romans 5.12–19; 1 Corinthians 15.20–28, 45–49; Philippians 2.5–11.

47g A NEW CREED

I believe in a world meant for everyone
to live together happily in.
I believe in living a life of love,
sharing, and making friends.
I believe this is the way of Jesus,
who makes me see my faults and my sin,
forgives me and helps me
to let him make me pure.
I believe he died for me and rose again
for me, and for the whole world,
and he calls me
to join the people who follow him now.
I believe he can use even me
to carry on his work in this world.
So I give myself to him.

John Hastings

47h INTERCESSION

Almighty God, your Son Jesus Christ has promised that you will hear us when we ask in faith: receive the prayers we offer.

For the nations
We give thanks for ... We pray for ...
Guide with your wisdom and power the leaders of the nations, so that everyone may live in peace and mutual trust, sharing with justice the resources of the earth. Give the people of this land a spirit of unselfishness, compassion, and fairness in public and private life. Father, hear our prayer
through Jesus Christ our Lord.

For the Church
We give thanks for ... We pray for ...
Send out the light and truth of your gospel and bring people everywhere to know and love you. Enable those who minister among us to commend your truth by their example and teaching. May we gladly receive and obey your word. Father, hear our prayer
through Jesus Christ our Lord.

For those in need
We give thanks for ... We pray for ...
We commend to your fatherly care, merciful God, all who are in sorrow, sickness, discouragement or any other trouble. Give them patience and a firm trust in your goodness. Help those who care for them, and bring us all into the joy of your salvation. Father, hear our prayer
through Jesus Christ our Lord.

Thanksgiving for the faithful departed
We give thanks for the life and work of ...
We praise you for all your servants whose lives have honoured Christ. Encourage us by their example, so that we may run with perseverance the race that lies before us, and share with them the fullness of joy in your kingdom. Hear us, Father, through Jesus Christ our Lord,
who lives and reigns with you
in the unity of the Holy Spirit,
one God, now and for ever. Amen.

A Prayer Book for Australia, p. 172

47i AT THE PEACE
Great peace have those who love God's law; nothing shall
cause them to stumble.

Psalm 119.165

47j PREFACE
So great was your love that you gave us your Son as our
redeemer. You sent him as one like ourselves, though free from
sin, that you might see and love in us what you see and love in
Christ. Your gifts of grace, lost by disobedience, are now
restored by the obedience of your Son.

Roman Missal

47k THANKSGIVING
Eternal God, we thank you for the prophets who delivered
your word and declared your will. We thank you for Jesus, the
greatest of prophets, your Living Word, and your perfect will.
We thank you for the Holy Spirit who strengthens us to proclaim your word and do your will. All praise and thanks be to
you for ever and ever. **Amen.**

Companion to the Lectionary 6, p. 9

47l BLESSING
You have listened to God's word; now God sends you out to
obey his will, and to love others for his sake in the power of his
grace; so may the blessing ...

Michael Counsell

---

48. OTHER FAITHS, INTER-FAITH
RELATIONS, JEWS

See also EVANGELISM, RACE

48a OPENING RESPONSE
The same God whom all folk worship without fully knowing;
That God it is that we proclaim!

Michael Counsell, from Acts 17.23

48b INVITATION TO CONFESS
It is written: All have sinned and fallen short of the perfect love
of God. We confess that none of us lives up to what we profess.

Michael Counsell, Romans 3.23

48c CONFESSION
Let us pray that we will be joined together in working for rec-
onciliation, and the healing of our ancient land and its peoples.
Forgive us for remaining silent and bound by fear.
Give us the courage to speak and act with justice.
Forgive us for our arrogance in closing our eyes to other peo-
ples and cultures.
Enable us to know your redeeming love.
Forgive us for disfiguring the earth and despoiling its bounty.
Come, Holy Spirit, renew the whole creation.
Forgive us for despising the cultures of others, and taking away
their self-respect.
Give us grace to bind one another's wounds.
Forgive us for not listening to the griefs of all who are
oppressed in this land, especially ... *(Particular prayers for for-
giveness will often be appropriate.)*
Draw us together as one people.
Forgive us for our prejudice and indifference towards those
whose ways differ from our ways.
**Strengthen us to live with respect and compassion for one
another.**

The Koori Commission of the Anglican Diocese of Canberra and Goulburn, in
A Prayer Book for Australia, p. 199

48d ABSOLUTION
God says: If you are concerned about merely material comfort,
do you not think that I am concerned for those who know me
by another name, and forgive them when they repent? **Amen.**

Michael Counsell, from Jonah 4.10–11; 3.10

COLLECTS
48e

God of all the world, Jesus of Nazareth was born a Jew; so have
mercy, we pray, on your ancient people, that they may continue
to grow in the love of your name and in faithfulness to your
covenant. Fetch us all home to your fold, so that we become
one flock under the shepherd of Israel. **Amen.**

Adapted from *A New Zealand Prayer Book*, p. 588

48f

Let us pray for those who do not believe the Gospel of Christ –
for those who follow other faiths and creeds; for those who
have not heard the message of salvation; that God will open the
hearts of each one of us to the truth wherever it may be found,
and lead us to faith and obedience.
(Silence.)

Lord, hear us.
Lord, graciously hear us.
Merciful God, creator of all the people of the earth, have compassion on all who do not know you as you are revealed in Jesus of Nazareth, and by the preaching of your Gospel with grace and power, gather them into the one fold of the one Shepherd, Christ our Lord. **Amen.**

Lent, Holy Week and Easter, p. 214*

48g SUITABLE SCRIPTURE PASSAGES
2 Kings 5.1–14.
Matthew 25.31–46; Acts 17.16–31; Romans 8.1–17; 9.1–5; 11.1–2a, 13–32; 1 Corinthians 9.16–23; Ephesians 2.11–22; 1 Peter 3.13–22.

48h AFFIRMATION OF FAITH
We believe that God,
who made the world and everything in it,
is Lord of heaven and earth.
God is too great to be contained
by any human construct.
God gives life and breath to everyone.
He has made all races to be brothers and sisters,
so that we should look for God,
and find the One whom we are seeking.
Yet God is not far from each one of us:
in God we live and move,
and all of us are God's children.
This we believe,
and this we proclaim! Amen.

Michael Counsell, from Acts 17.24–28

INTERCESSIONS
48i

Lord and Father, nothing and no one is strange to you. Give us the will and the words to go to those who are strange to us bearing your love, to find that you have been there before us, and to speak your name at your moment. Give us the grace and the privilege of making you known in Jesus. **Amen.**

Christopher Lamb

48j

Pray not for Arab or Jew, for Palestinian or Israeli, but pray rather for yourselves, that you may not divide them in your prayers but keep them both together in your hearts.

A Palestinian Christian

48k

O Christ, my Way to the God of all salvation, people of other faiths believe they have their own salvation faith. Be with them, dear Lord, to encourage them on their way to their own Jerusalem, so that we all find ourselves with the spirits of just people made perfect, with the saints of every age and faith, in the presence of the eternal God, the God of many names, Creator, Lover, Saviour of us all. **Amen.**

Archbishop George Appleton in *The Oxford Book of Prayer*, 11150

48l

Eternal God, whose image lies in the hearts of all people, we live among peoples whose ways are different from ours, whose faiths are foreign to us, whose tongues are unintelligible to us. Help us to remember that you love all people with your great love, that all religion is an attempt to respond to you, that the yearnings of other hearts are much like our own and are known to you. Help us to recognize you in the words of truth, the things of beauty, the actions of love about us. We pray through Christ, who is a stranger to no land more than another, and to every land no less than to another. **Amen.**

Jesus Christ, the Life of the World, based upon *A Traveller's Prayer Book*

48m

We pray for all humanity: though divided into nations and races, yet all people are your children, drawing from you their life and being, commanded by you to obey your laws, each in accordance with the power to know and understand them. Cause hatred and strife to vanish, that abiding peace may fill the earth, and humanity everywhere be blessed with the fruit of peace. So shall the spirit of family among people show forth their faith that you are Father of all. **Amen.**

The Liberal Jewish Prayer Book

48n AT THE PEACE
Peace! *Shalom! Namaste! Ping An! Jambo! Salaam!* etc.

48o PREFACE
And now we give you thanks that Christ's body was broken and his blood shed not for us only, but for the whole human race, and he is the true light who enlightens everyone coming into the world.

Michael Counsell

48p THE BLESSING OF AARON
The Lord bless us and watch over us; the Lord make his face shine upon us and be gracious to us, the Lord look kindly on us and give us peace. **Amen.**

Numbers 6.24–26, Celebrating Common Prayer, p. 183

---

49. PALM SUNDAY

See also THE CROSS, KING

49a THE LITURGY OF THE PALMS
Blessed is the King who comes in the name of the Lord:
Peace in heaven and glory in the highest.

Luke 19.38

Let us pray.
Assist us mercifully with your help, O Lord God of our salvation, that we may enter with joy upon the contemplation of those mighty acts, whereby you have given us life and immortality; through Jesus Christ our Lord. **Amen.**

(Reading: Matthew 21.1–11; Mark 11.1–10; or Luke 19.29–40.)

The Lord be with you.
And also with you.
Let us give thanks to the Lord our God.
It is right to give him thanks and praise.

It is right to praise you, Almighty God, for the acts of love by which you have redeemed us through your Son Jesus Christ our Lord. On this day he entered the holy city of Jerusalem in triumph, and was proclaimed as King of kings by those who spread their garments and branches of palm along his way. Let these branches be for us signs of his victory, and grant that we who bear them in his name may ever hail him as our King, and follow him in the way that leads to eternal life; who lives and reigns in glory with you and the Holy Spirit, now and for ever. **Amen.**
Blessed is he who comes in the name of the Lord.
Hosanna in the highest.
Let us go forth in peace;
In the name of Christ. Amen.

US BCP 1979, p. 270

Procession with palms, singing 'All glory, laud and honour' or Psalm 118.19–29. At a suitable place the procession halts and this collect is said:

Almighty God, whose most dear Son went not up to joy but first he suffered pain, and entered not into glory before he was crucified: mercifully grant that we, walking in the way of the cross, may find it none other than the way of life and peace; through Jesus Christ our Lord. **Amen.**

William Reed Huntington*

49b COLLECT
Almighty and everliving God, in your tender love for the human race you sent your Son our Saviour Jesus Christ to take upon him our nature, and to suffer death upon the cross, giving us the example of his great humility: Mercifully grant that we may walk in the way of his suffering, and also share in his resurrection; through Jesus Christ our Lord, who lives and reigns with you and the Holy Spirit, one God, for ever and ever. **Amen.**

US BCP 1979, p. 219, *Gelasian Sacramentary*

49c SUITABLE SCRIPTURE PASSAGES
Isaiah 50.4–9a; Zechariah 9.9–11; Psalms 69.1–3, 7–9, 21–23; 118.1–2, 19–29; 31.9–16.
Matthew 21.1–11; Mark 11.1–10; Luke 19.29–40; Philippians 2.5–11.

49d AFFIRMATION OF FAITH
When tanks roll by and trumpets play
some people cheer and shout 'Hooray'
but Jesus chose another way
parading on a donkey.

He set out to impress them all …
a horse would make him proud and tall
and save him from the risk of fall …
but he rode on a donkey.

No soldier he, but King of Love!
The way he chose was well above
all hawkish ways, and as a Dove
he rode upon a donkey.

Folk must have laughed to see the sight,
a conqueror who would not fight

171

with what is wrong for what is right ...
and riding on a donkey.

He had to show that he was brave
and that he only came to save,
Less like a king, more like a slave,
for he rode on a donkey.

No matter if the world despise
this Jesus-way of sacrifice;
for love lives on when all else dies;
and he rode on a donkey.

God offered love, not pomp and show,
so people everywhere would know
the way his kingdom has to grow;
so Jesus rode on a donkey.

Who cares about the tyrant's pride?
Today Palm Sunday is world-wide
and millions stand with us, beside
the king who rode a donkey.

David J. Harding, in *Liturgy of Life*, 147

49e INTERCESSION
We stand with Christ in his suffering.
For forgiveness for the many times we have denied Jesus, let us
pray to the Lord.
Lord, have mercy.
For grace to seek out those habits of sin which mean spiritual
death, and by prayer and self-discipline to overcome them, let
us pray to the Lord.
Lord, have mercy.
For Christian people, that through the suffering of disunity
there may grow a rich union in Christ, let us pray to the Lord.
Lord, have mercy.
For those who make laws, interpret them, and administer
them, that our common life may be ordered in justice and
mercy, let us pray to the Lord.
Lord, have mercy.
For those who still make Jerusalem a battleground, let us pray
to the Lord.
Lord, have mercy.

For those who have the courage and honesty to work openly
for justice and peace, let us pray to the Lord.
Lord, have mercy.
For those in the darkness and agony of isolation, that they may
find support and encouragement, let us pray to the Lord.
Lord, have mercy.
For those who, weighed down with hardship, failure, or sor-
row, feel that God is far from them, let us pray to the Lord.
Lord, have mercy.
For those who are tempted to give up the way of the cross, let
us pray to the Lord.
Lord, have mercy.
That we, with those who have died in faith, may find mercy in
the day of Christ, let us pray to the Lord.
Lord, have mercy.

(Then, in place of the prayers of penitence, the Trisagion:)

Holy God,
holy and strong,
holy and immortal,
have mercy on us.

Lent, Holy Week and Easter, p. 83

49f AT THE PEACE
Christ is our peace. He has reconciled us to God in one body by
the cross. We meet in his name and share his peace.

Ephesians 2.14, 16; Matthew 18.20–21; 1 Thessalonians 5.13, *ASB*, p. 128

49g PREFACE
Hosanna to the Son of David! He challenges the power and the
sword; the gentle rider of a humble beast, the Servant King.

A New Zealand Prayer Book, p. 492

49h POST-COMMUNION PRAYER
We thank you that at your mystical supper, Son of God, you
have today received us as partakers; we will not speak of the
mystery to your enemies; we will not let our lips touch your
body with a Judas-kiss; but like the thief we will acknowledge
you: Remember us when you come in your kingdom, O Jesus
Christ our Lord. **Amen.**

Orthodox prayer, adapted from *The Liturgy of St John Chrysostom*

49i BLESSING
May the cross of the Son of God, who is mightier than all the
powers of evil, abide with you in your going out and your

coming in! From the wrath of evil people, from the temptations of the devil, from all low passions that beguile the soul and body, may it guard, protect and deliver you: and may the blessing ...

BCP, Church of India, Pakistan, Burma and Ceylon*

50. PARENTHOOD

See also LOVE, MARY THE VIRGIN, THE TRINITY

50a GREETING
The grace and peace of God our Father and the Lord Jesus Christ be with you.
Blessed be God, the Father of our Lord Jesus Christ.

Roman Missal

50b PRAYER OF PENITENCE
(All standing.)

Leader   God says:
When Israel was a boy, I loved him.
I called my children out of Egypt,
But the more I called, the further they went from me.
I was the one who taught them to walk;
I was the one who had taken them in my arms;
But they did not remember
That I had looked after them,
That I had led them in bonds of love,
That I had lifted them like a little child to my cheek,
That I had bent down to feed them.

(A silence ... during which we remember how we forget God.)

Cantor   Jesus Christ, Son of God, have mercy upon us.
All   **Jesus Christ, Son of God, have mercy upon us.**

(This response is sung repeatedly while everyone sits down quietly. Alternatively, the leader might say the Cantor's lines and all say the response.)

Leader   If we have forgotten you, forgotten that you made, feed and love us,
All   **Jesus Christ, Son of God, have mercy upon us** *(sung or spoken).*

Leader	If we have forgotten you, and in your place imagined a God made in our image,
All	**Jesus Christ, Son of God, have mercy upon us** *(sung or spoken)*.
Leader	If we have forgotten that you smile, and thought only that you frown,
All	**Jesus Christ, Son of God, have mercy upon us** *(sung or spoken)*.
Leader	If we have forgotten the range of your friends, and have kept you safe within our familiar circle,
All	**Jesus Christ, Son of God, have mercy upon us** *(sung or spoken)*.
Leader	If we have forgotten that we were made in your mould, and have not loved ourselves in the right way,
All	**Jesus Christ, Son of God, have mercy upon us** *(sung or spoken)*.

(A silence ... during which we ask God's forgiveness.)

Leader	God says,
	How can I give you up?
	How can I abandon you?
	My heart will not let me do it,
	My love for you is too strong.
	For I am God and not a man.
	I, the Holy One, am with you.
All	**Our Father ...**

A Wee Worship Book, p. 23

50c ABSOLUTION

The Lord, merciful and gracious, slow to be angry and full of love, will not accuse you for ever, or be angry with you always; he does not treat you as your sins deserve, nor repay you according to your wrongdoing: he has compassion on you as a father has compassion on his children, and forgives you your sins; through Jesus Christ our Lord. **Amen.**

Psalm 103.8–13, *Bible Praying*, 120

COLLECTS

50d

Christ our true mother, you have carried us within you, laboured with us, and brought us forth to bliss. Enclose us in your care, that in stumbling we may not fall, nor be overcome by evil, but know that all shall be well. **Amen.**

All Desires Known, based on the writings of Julian of Norwich

175

50e

Lord, if this day you have to correct us, put us right not out of anger, but with a mother and father's love. So may we, your children, be kept free from falseness and foolishness. **Amen.**

Mexican, source unknown

50f SUITABLE SCRIPTURE PASSAGES

Isaiah 49.8–16a; 66.10–14; Hosea 11.1–11; Psalm 103.1–13, 22.
Luke 15.1–3, 11b–32; John 10.22–30; 14.23–29; 16.12–13; 17.1–11;
2 Corinthians 13.11–13; Ephesians 3.14–21.

50g PRAYER OF FAITH

Mother of all mothers, Father of all fathers, Lover of all, we your creature creation bend to adore the beauty of your earth. Mother of all mothers, Father of all fathers, Lover of all, we your creature creation tend to ignore the beauty of your earth. Mother of all mothers, Father of all fathers, Lover of all, we your creature creation need to unite, not to fight, to conserve the fair beauty of your earth. **Amen.**

Anonymous

50h INTERCESSION

God, parent of all, we pray for those who are parents.
We pray for parents who carry the responsibilities of bringing up children alone. In the bright times and the dark:
God, be there for them.
We pray for parents wanting to do all they should for every young child, yet wondering whether they are succeeding. In the bright times and the dark:
God, be there for them.
We pray for parents delighting that the potential of growing and teenage children is being fulfilled, yet anxious about the temptations they face. In the bright times and the dark:
God, be there for them.
We pray for parents sharing the delight and pain of children who have started their own families, yet needing to keep a difficult distance. In the bright times and the dark:
God, be there for them.
We pray for all parents, that they may always be open to learn from their children, and from their own special experiences. In the bright times and the dark:
God, be there for them.

Companion to the Lectionary 6, p. 149

50i AT THE PEACE
Peace to our sisters and brothers, and love with faith from God
the Father and the Lord Jesus Christ.

Ephesians 6.23, *Bible Praying*, 14*

50j PREFACE
And now we give you thanks because, as a mother tenderly
gathers her children, you embraced a people as your own, that
with all the powers of heaven we may find a voice to sing your
praise.

Patterns for Worship, 0N30

50k THANKSGIVING
Father of all, the child born for us is the Saviour of the world.
May he who has made us your children welcome us into your
kingdom, where he is alive and reigns with you now and for
ever. **Amen.**

Canadian *Book of Alternative Services*, p. 276

50l BLESSING
It has been good for us to be in our Father's house. Go out now,
to love and serve him. And the blessing ...

Companion to the Lectionary 6, p. 149

---

51. PEACE, WAR

See also JUSTICE, REMEMBRANCE SUNDAY, THE WORLD

51a OPENING SENTENCE
Strive for perfection; work together in harmony; live in peace,
and may the God of love and peace be with you.
And also with you.

2 Corinthians 13.11, Michael Counsell

51b INVITATION TO CONFESS
Let us confess our breach of God's peace.

Michael Counsell

51c CONFESSION
We repent the wrongs we have done:
our blindness to human need and suffering;
our indifference to injustice and cruelty;
our false judgements, petty thoughts, and contempt;
our waste and pollution of the earth and oceans;

our lack of concern for those who come after us;
our complicity in the making of weapons of mass
destruction,
and our threatening of their use.

Prayer at Night

51d KYRIE

Jesus, our deliverer, we take your freedom from others. Lord, have mercy.
Lord, have mercy.
Jesus, our hope, we deprive others of hope. Christ, have mercy.
Christ, have mercy.
Jesus, God's peace, we distort your peace. Lord, have mercy.
Lord, have mercy.

A New Zealand Prayer Book, p. 459*

51e ABSOLUTION

Eternal Spirit, living God, in whom we live and move and have our being, all that we are, have been, and shall be is known to you, to the very secrets of our hearts and all that rises to trouble us. Living flame, burn into us: cleansing wind, blow through us: fountain of water, well up within us: that we may love and praise in deed and in truth. **Amen.**

Prayer at Night

51f COLLECT

God, the God of eternal peace, whose reward is the gift of peace, and whose children are the peacemakers; pour your peace into our hearts, that conflict and discord may vanish, and our love and desire be always for your peace; through Jesus Christ our Lord. **Amen.**

Mozarabic, *The Promise of His Glory*, p. 364

51g SUITABLE SCRIPTURE PASSAGES

2 Samuel 7.1–11, 16; Isaiah 2.1–5; 9.1–6; 52.7–10; Jeremiah 22.1–14; Amos 7.7–15; Micah 4.1–4; Psalms 34.9–14; 46; 84.9–14; 85.8–13; 120; 122; 147.
Matthew 5.1–12; 5.38–48; Luke 1.68–79; 2.8–14; John 14.23–29; 20.19–31; Galatians 5.1, 13–25; Philippians 4.1–9; Colossians 1.15–20; 3.12–15; James 3.13–18; 4.1–10.

51h AFFIRMATION OF FAITH

**These things shall be! The human race,
with loftier dreams and hopes, shall rise
with flame of freedom in their souls
and light of justice in their eyes.**

They shall be gentle, brave and strong,
to spill no drop of blood, but care
for all that shares the common life
of field and forest, sea and air.

Nation with nation, land with land
in God shall live as comrades free;
in every heart and brain shall throb
the pulse of one community.

Adapted from J. Addington Symonds

51i LITANY FOR PEACE
In peace let us pray to the Lord saying, 'Lord, have mercy.'
For peace from on high and for our salvation, let us pray to the Lord,
Lord, have mercy.
For the peace of the whole world, for the welfare of the holy Church of God, let us pray to the Lord,
Lord, have mercy.
For peace among our bishops, clergy and people, let us pray to the Lord,
Lord, have mercy.
For peace among the [leaders of the] nations, and those in authority, let us pray to the Lord,
Lord, have mercy.
For the peace of this city [town, place], for every city and community, and for those who live in them in faith, let us pray to the Lord,
Lord, have mercy.
For our deliverance from all evil, strife, and need, let us pray to the Lord,
Lord, have mercy.

Based on an Orthodox prayer, *A Prayer Book for Australia*, p. 194

51j AT THE PEACE
Blessed are those who make peace: they shall be called sons and daughters of God. We meet in the name of Christ and share his peace.

Matthew 5.9, *Patterns for Worship*, 0R23

51k PREFACE
And now we give you thanks because your will is to enfold the people of the whole world in your arms, as a hen gathers her chickens, and show us the way to peace.

Matthew 23.37; Luke 19.42

51l PRAYER OF SELF-OFFERING
Take our hatreds, make them into handshakes.
Take our prejudices, make them into peace-offerings.
Take our misunderstandings; make them into music.
Take our divisions; turn them into dances.
Take our helplessness; make us hope,
for you never withdraw the forces of your love.

Kate Compton, Christian Aid

51m BLESSING
Deep peace of the running water to you,
Deep peace of the flowing air to you,
Deep peace of the quiet earth to you,
Deep peace of the shining stars to you,
Deep peace of the Son of Peace to you.
And the blessing ...

Celtic Blessing

---

52. PERSEVERANCE, ENDURANCE, PATIENCE

52a INTRODUCTORY SENTENCE
Be steadfast, immovable, always abounding in the work of the
Lord.

1 Corinthians 15.58

52b PENITENTIAL SECTION
In the light of the Spirit and in union with Christ we acknowledge our failures before God. Lord, your ways are not our
ways, your thoughts are not our thoughts: what seems like
eternity is only a moment to you. In the face of eternity, help us
to be humble.
Lord, have mercy upon us.
If we have been singing praises with our voices and kept the
joy out of our hearts; if we have prayed only for what was possible and hoped only for what we could see;
Lord, have mercy upon us.
If we have taken your grace for granted and expected instant
answers to immediate requests; if we have allowed waiting on
your Spirit to slip into laziness and waiting on the Kingdom to
be replaced by apathy; if we have only thought of us waiting on
you and never pondered how you wait on us:
Lord, have mercy upon us.

Listen, for this is the true word of God: blessed are all who wait
for the Lord. God is merciful, and God's love is sure and strong.
Amen.

World Council of Churches Canberra Assembly 1991

COLLECTS
52c

God of compassion, you have willed that the gate of mercy
should always stand open for your people. Look upon us with
your mercy, that we who are following the path of your will
may continue in it to the end of our lives; through Jesus Christ
our Lord. **Amen.**

Leonine Sacramentary, The Promise of His Glory, p. 365

52d

O Lord God, when you give to your servants to endeavour any
great matter, grant us also to know that it is not the beginning,
but the continuing of the same until it be thoroughly finished,
which yields the true glory; through him who for the finishing
of your work laid down his life, our Redeemer, Jesus Christ.
Amen.

Sir Francis Drake*

52e SUITABLE SCRIPTURE PASSAGES
Genesis 32.22–31; Daniel 3.13–26; Habakkuk 1.1–4; 2.1–4;
Psalms 37.35–40; 121.
Matthew 7.13–27; 13.24–30, 36–43; Mark 13.7–13; Luke 9.51–62;
18.1–8; 21.5–19; Romans 8.18–25; 1 Corinthians 9.19–27;
Ephesians 6.10–20; Philippians 3.4b–14; 3.17 – 4.1; Colossians
1.1–14; 2 Thessalonians 2.1–5, 13–17; 3.6–13; 2 Timothy 2.8–15;
4.6–8, 16–18; Hebrews 11.29 – 12.3; James 5.7–10.

52f AFFIRMATION OF FAITH
We believe in God the Father,
who loved us
and by his grace gave us
eternal encouragement and good hope.
We believe in God the Son,
who strengthens us,
and protects us from the evil one.
We believe in God the Holy Spirit,
who leads us to God the Father's love
and to the endurance
which is the gift of Christ.
We believe in one God,
Father, Son and Holy Spirit. Amen.

2 Thessalonians 2.16; 3.3–5, Bible Praying, 221

52g INTERCESSION
In a world of change and hope, of fear and adventure,
faithful God,
glorify your name.
In human rebellion and obedience,
in our seeking and our finding, faithful God,
glorify your name.
In the common life of our society, in prosperity and need,
faithful God,
glorify your name.
As your Church proclaims your goodness
in words and actions, faithful God,
glorify your name.
Among our friends and in our homes, faithful God,
glorify your name.
In our times of joy, in our days of sorrow, faithful God,
glorify your name.
In our strengths and triumphs,
in our weakness and at our death, faithful God,
glorify your name.
In your saints in glory and on the day of Christ's coming,
faithful God,
glorify your name.

The Promise of His Glory, p. 202

52h AT THE PEACE
If you do as God commands you, then you will be able to
endure, and reach your destination in peace.

Exodus 18.23

52i PREFACE
Because in the patient endurance of your saints you have given
us an example of obedience to you, and in their eternal joy a
glorious pledge of the hope of our calling.

US BCP 1979, p. 380*

52j AFTER COMMUNION
Living God, in this holy meal you fill us with new hope. May
the power of your love, which we have known in word and
sacrament, continue your saving work among us, give us
courage for our pilgrimage, and bring us to the joys you
promise. **Amen.**

A Prayer Book for Australia, p. 143

52k BLESSING

May God the Father give you grace to run with patience the
race that is set before you, looking to Jesus the author and fin-
isher of our faith, in the power of his Holy Spirit, and may the
blessing of the Holy Trinity be with you now and until the end.
Amen.

Adapted from Hebrews 12.1

---

53. PETER, THE APOSTLES

See also FISH, MINISTRY, SAINTS

53a GREETING

Greetings to God's people:
may you have abundant grace and peace.
Blessed be the God and Father of our Lord Jesus Christ!
In his mercy he gave us new birth into a living hope,
through the resurrection of Jesus Christ from the dead.

1 Peter 1.1–3

53b INVITATION TO CONFESS

Jesus said to his apostles, 'You are my friends if you obey my
commands.' Let us now confess our disobedience to him.

David Silk, *Enriching the Christian Year*, 12A2

53c CONFESSION

Loving God, you spoke to us and we did not listen.
'I am sending you,' said God. We looked around to see who
would go, then as realisation dawned, we made off in the oppo-
site direction. So we pray:
Forgive us, and send us.
'I need workers,' said God. We looked around to see who
would respond, then, making our excuses, we tried to tiptoe
gently away. So we pray:
Forgive us, and empower us.
'You must be wise as serpents,' said Jesus. We looked around,
startled and amazed. We did not expect to bring intelligence
into reading the gospel! So we pray:
Forgive us, and embolden us.
'Be innocent as doves,' said Jesus. We looked around at those
we must face – challenged to be accepting, gentle, peaceful. So
we pray:
Forgive us, and inspire us.

Companion to the Lectionary 6, p. 92

53d KYRIE

Lord Jesus, in your love you invite us to be your friends: Lord, have mercy.
Lord, have mercy.
Lord Jesus, in your joy you choose us to go out and bear fruit: Christ, have mercy.
Christ, have mercy.
Lord Jesus, in your power you send us to be your faithful witnesses: Lord, have mercy.
Lord, have mercy.

David Silk, *Enriching the Christian Year*, 12B2

53e ABSOLUTION

God hears our prayers and forgives our sins. **Amen.**

Companion to the Lectionary 6, p. 93

53f COLLECT

Almighty God, you have built your Church upon the foundation of the apostles and prophets with Jesus Christ himself as the chief corner-stone. So join us together in unity of spirit by their doctrine, that we may be made an holy temple acceptable to you; through Jesus Christ our Lord. **Amen.**

ASB, p. 807

53g SUITABLE SCRIPTURE PASSAGES

Ezekiel 3.4–11; Psalms 18.33–37; 33; 125.
Matthew 16.13–20; Mark 14.66–72; Luke 5.1–11; John 1.29–42; 21.1–14; 21.15–19; Acts 2.14a, 22–32; 2.14a, 36–41; 4.5–12; 5.27–32; 9.36–43; 10.34–43; 12.1–11; 2 Corinthians 5.20b–6.13; 1 Peter 2.19–25; 2 Peter 1.16–21.

53h THE 'APOSTLES' CREED'

I believe in God, the Father almighty,
creator of heaven and earth.
I believe in Jesus Christ, his only Son, our Lord.
He was conceived by the power of the Holy Spirit
and born of the Virgin Mary.
He suffered under Pontius Pilate,
was crucified, died, and was buried.
He descended to the dead.
On the third day he rose again.
He ascended into heaven,
and is seated at the right hand of the Father.
He will come again to judge the living and the dead.
I believe in the Holy Sprit,
the holy catholic Church,

the communion of saints,
the forgiveness of sins,
the resurrection of the body,
and the life everlasting. Amen.

ICET

53i INTERCESSION

O God, our Father, through Jesus Christ you called Peter to care for the flock of your Church. Bless all those who are pastors and preachers and leaders for your people.

Help them to be diligent in their study and their preparation; earnest in their prayer and their devotion; faithful and loving in their visitation; sincere and honest in their preaching.

Help them to be wise in administration; loving and forgiving in their dealings with others, especially with those who are difficult; honest in their thinking so that others may respect them; clear in their speaking so that simple folk may hear them gladly. Bless all the members of your Church. Grant that they may come to church with expectation; they may worship in truth and sincerity; they may listen with humility. Give them minds which are eager to learn, and memories that are retentive to remember, and grant that they may go out into the world to practise what they have heard, and to live what they have learned.

And so grant that pastors and people may be united in love for each other, in service of others, and in witness for you; through Jesus Christ our Lord. **Amen.**

Prayers for the Christian Year, p. 160

53j AT THE PEACE

We are fellow-citizens with the saints and of the household of God, through Christ our Lord who came and preached peace to those who were far off and those who were near.

ASB, p. 170

53k PREFACE

And now we give you thanks because your Son Jesus Christ after his resurrection sent forth his apostles and evangelists to preach the gospel to all nations and to teach us the way of truth.

ASB, p. 157

531 AFTER COMMUNION
Heavenly Father, renew the life of your Church by the power of
this sacrament. May the breaking of bread and the teaching of
the apostles keep us united in your love, in the name of Jesus
Christ our Lord. **Amen.**

Canadian Book of Alternative Services, p. 412

53m SOLEMN BLESSING
May God, who has given you in the lives of the saints patterns
of holy living and victorious dying, strengthen you to follow
them in the way of holiness. **Amen.**
May God, who has kindled the fire of his love in the hearts of
the saints, pour upon you the riches of his grace. **Amen.**
May God, who calls you no longer strangers and aliens but fellow-citizens with all the saints, bring you to your home in
heaven. **Amen.**
And the blessing ...

Colossians 1.12; Ephesians 1.17–18; 2.14, Patterns for Worship, 15T37

---

54. POSSESSIONS, STEWARDSHIP

See also HARVEST, THE NEEDY

54a CALL TO WORSHIP
I appeal to you to present your bodies as a living sacrifice, holy
and acceptable to God.

Romans 12.1

54b INVITATION TO CONFESS
Do not be anxious about your life, what you shall eat or what
you shall drink. Seek first God's kingdom and his righteousness.

Matthew 6.25, 33, The Promise of his Glory, p. 241

54c CONFESSION
Let us pray to God, admitting our faults and asking for
forgiveness. Gracious and holy God: when we love our
possessions and money more than you
Forgive us.
When we turn the talents and gifts you have given us into
idols
Forgive us.

When we put things before people
Forgive us.
When we spend all our time and resources on ourselves
Forgive us.
When we speak and act as if you are not our God
Forgive us.

Companion to the Lectionary 6, p. 4

54d KYRIE
We have failed to be good stewards of your creation. Lord, have mercy.
Lord, have mercy.
We have failed to be good stewards of your gospel. Christ, have mercy.
Christ, have mercy.
We have failed to be good stewards of your gifts. Lord, have mercy.
Lord, have mercy.

The Open Gate, p. 56

54e ABSOLUTION
It is God's nature to forgive those who are truly sorry. The One True God never despairs of our fickle human nature, the One True God is always ready to help us begin again. So hear the word of pardon: through God in Jesus Christ, your sins are forgiven. **Amen.**

Companion to the Lectionary 6, p. 4

54f COLLECT
Heavenly Father, you taught us by your Son Jesus Christ that all our possessions come from you. Help us to be faithful stewards of our time, our talents and our wealth, and to consecrate gladly to your service a due proportion of all that you have given us. Take us and make us your own; for Jesus Christ's sake. **Amen.**

Church of England Central Board of Finance, Stewardship Section

54g SUITABLE SCRIPTURE PASSAGES
1 Chronicles 29.6–19; Job 31.16–20, 24–25, 31–32; Amos 6.1a, 4–7; Psalms 111.1–9; 128. Matthew 6.1–4; 6.24–34; Mark 10.17–31; Luke 12.13–21; 12.32–40; 16.1–13; 16.19–31; Acts 11.27–30; 1 Corinthians 16.1–4; 2 Corinthians 8.1–5, 9–15; 9.6–15; 1 Timothy 6.6–19; James 5.1–6.

54h AFFIRMATION OF FAITH
We believe that all our money comes from the state,
and it is right to return some of it to the state.

And we believe that all we possess and all we are
comes from God,
for each of us is an image of God,
however defaced and damaged,
and we are called by God's name.
So we believe that in gratitude to God
we should return to God a proportion
of what God has lent to us,
for everything belongs to God. **Amen**.

Michael Counsell, based on Mark 12.17

STEWARDSHIP PRAYERS

54i

Creator God, we offer all we have and are in the service of your
needy children ... You are so generous, Lord, in your daily creative dealings with us. You have formed an atmosphere, oceans
and soil in which life can multiply, and pour your sunshine and
rain abundantly upon us. As you have been so bountiful and
open-hearted to us, make us equally generous in sharing what
you have lent to us with those in need. We offer our lives to
you, as Jesus gave his life for us. **Amen.**

Michael Counsell, in *Prayers for Sundays*

54j

Almighty God, as we stand at the foot of the cross of your Son,
help us to see and know your love for us, so that in humility,
love and joy we may place at his feet all that we have and all
that we are, through Jesus Christ our Saviour. **Amen.**

Celebrating Common Prayer, p. 158

54k AT THE PEACE
If God will be with us, so that we go in peace, then the Lord
shall be our God; and of all that God gives us we will give to
him.

Adapted from Genesis 28.20–22

54l PREFACE
And now we give you thanks for the time, talents and wealth
which you have lent to us, and for accepting our offering, in
this sacrament, of a portion of them, as a token of the offering of
our whole lives to you in union with the sacrifice of our Lord
Jesus Christ on the cross.

Michael Counsell, in *Prayers for Sundays*

54m THANKSGIVING

All things come from you, O Lord!
And of your own do we give you!
Glory to the Father, and to the Son, and to the Holy Spirit;
As it was in the beginning, is now, and shall be for ever.
Amen.
For the gift of his Spirit,
Blessed be Christ.
For the catholic Church,
Blessed be Christ.
For the means of grace,
Blessed be Christ.
For the hope of glory,
Blessed be Christ.
For the triumphs of his gospel,
Blessed be Christ.
In joy and in sorrow,
Blessed be Christ.
In life and in death,
Blessed be Christ.
Now and to the end of the ages,
Blessed be Christ.

Services for Special Occasions, p. 88*

54n BLESSING

Go out into the world; enjoy what God has given you; use all
you can in God's service and for the relief of need; and the
blessing ...

Michael Counsell

55. PRAYER

55a RESPONSIVE INTRODUCTION

O Lord, open our lips.
and our mouth shall show forth your praise.
O God, make speed to save us.
O Lord, make haste to help us.

Psalms 51.15; 70.1

55b INVITATION TO CONFESS

The intellect cannot penetrate the cloud of unknowing which separates us from God; only the arrows of love can do that. But first we must tread down all that is of self beneath the cloud of forgetting.

Adapted from *The Cloud of Unknowing*

55c CONFESSION

It is sad to consider the weakness of the strongest devotions in time of prayer. I throw myself down in my room, and I invite God and his angels, and when they are there, I neglect God and his angels for the smallest noise. I talk on as though I prayed to God; and if God or his angels should ask me when I last thought of God in that prayer, I cannot tell. So certainly there is nothing, nothing in spiritual things, perfect in this world. **Amen.**

John Donne

55d ABSOLUTION

God is always more ready to hear than we are to pray. God's forgiveness is only waiting for us to claim it. Know then that Jesus died that you might be forgiven, and his death shall not be in vain. **Amen.**

Michael Counsell

55e COLLECT

Almighty God, the fountain of all wisdom, you know our needs before we ask, and our ignorance in asking; have compassion on our weakness, and give us those things which for our unworthiness we dare not, and for our blindness we cannot ask, for the sake of your Son, Jesus Christ our Lord. **Amen.**

ASB, p. 106, *BCP 1549*

55f SUITABLE SCRIPTURE PASSAGES

Genesis 18.20–32; 32.22–31; Exodus 32.1–14; 1 Kings 3.5–12; 8.22–30, 41–43; 18.20–21, 30–39; 19.9–18; Isaiah 56.1, 6–8; Jeremiah 20.7–13; Jonah 3.10 – 4.11; Psalms 9.1–6, 13–17; 17.1–9; 34.1–8; 51.1–10; 70; 79.1–9; 99; 138; 145.8–21.
Matthew 6.5–15; 18.15–20; Luke 10.38–42; 11.1–13; 18.1–8; 18.9–14; John 12.1–8; Romans 8.22–27; Ephesians 3.14–21; Colossians 1.1–14; 1 Thessalonians 3.9–13; Hebrews 7.23–28; James 5.13–20.

55g AFFIRMATION OF FAITH

I believe that God can and will bring good out of evil, even out of the greatest evil. For that purpose he needs men who make the best use of everything. I believe that God will give us all the strength we need to help us to resist in all times of distress. But he never gives it in advance, lest we should rely on ourselves and not on him alone. A faith such as this should allay all our fears for the future. I believe that even our mistakes and short-comings are turned to good account, and that it is no harder for God to deal with them than with our supposedly good deeds. I believe that God is no timeless fate, but that he waits for and answers sincere prayer and responsible actions.

Dietrich Bonhoeffer

55h INTERCESSION

I ask your prayers for God's people throughout the world; for our Bishop(s) *N.*; for this gathering; and for all ministers and people.
Pray for the Church.
(*Silence.*)
I ask your prayers for peace; for goodwill among nations; and for the well-being of all people.
Pray for justice and peace.
(*Silence.*)
I ask your prayers for the poor, the sick, the hungry, the oppressed, and those in prison.
Pray for those in any need or trouble.
(*Silence.*)
I ask your prayers for all who seek God, or a deeper knowledge of him.
Pray that they may find and be found by him.
(*Silence.*)
I ask your prayers for the departed [especially ...].
Pray for those who have died.
(*Silence.*)
(*Members of the congregation may ask the prayers or the thanksgivings of those present:*)
I ask your prayers for ...
I ask your thanksgiving for ...
(*Silence.*)
Praise God for those in every generation in whom Christ has been honoured [especially ... whom we remember today].
Pray that we may have grace to glorify Christ in our own day.
(*Silence.*)
Lord, hear the prayers of your people; and what we have asked faithfully, grant that we may obtain effectually, to the glory of your name; through Jesus Christ. **Amen.**

US BCP 1979, pp. 385, 394 (*BCP* 1549)

55i AT THE PEACE

Blessed be God the Father of our Lord Jesus Christ, the merciful
Father and God of all consolation, who strengthens us in all our
troubles, so that we may be able to console others with the
same consolation.

2 Corinthians 1.3–4

55j PREFACE

And now, God, we praise you that Jesus is close to you in eternity; he understands our weakness, because he has been tempted as we are; so that we may approach you with confidence
through him, to receive mercy and help when it is most needed.

Hebrews 1.3; 4.15–16

55k THANKSGIVING

Let us give thanks to God, saying, 'we thank you, Lord.'
For the beauty and wonder of creation,
we thank you, Lord.
For all that is gracious in the lives of men and women,
we thank you, Lord.
For daily food, for homes and families and friends,
we thank you, Lord.
For minds to think, hearts to love, and imagination to wonder,
we thank you, Lord.
For health, strength, and skill to work, and for leisure to rest
and play,
we thank you, Lord.
For patience in suffering,
for courage and faithfulness in difficult times,
we thank you, Lord.
For all who pursue justice and truth,
we thank you, Lord.
[Today we give thanks especially for ...
we thank you, Lord.]
For [... and] all the saints whose lives have reflected the light
of Christ,
we thank you, Lord.

A Prayer Book for Australia, p. 219

55l BLESSING

May God's love surround us, God's joy fill our lives, God's
peace be in our hearts, and God's blessing be with us this
day/night and always. **Amen.**

Celebrating Common Prayer, p. 132

56. PROVIDENCE, THE ARMOUR OF GOD, PROTECTION

See also ASSURANCE

56a GREETING
The grace and mercy of our Lord Jesus Christ be with you.
And also with you.

Patterns for Worship, 0A2, freely available

56b INVITATION TO CONFESS
Like a master architect, God has marked his plans for us on the palm of his hand. Yet time and time again we have frustrated those plans by following our way rather than God's. Let us bring our lives back into line with God's providence.

Michael Counsell, Isaiah 49.16

56c CONFESSION
God our Father,
long-suffering, full of grace and truth.
You create us from nothing and give us life.
You redeem us and make us your children
in the water of baptism.
You do not turn your face from us,
nor cast us aside.
We confess that we have sinned
against you and our neighbour.
We have wounded your love
and marred your image in us.
Restore us for the sake of your Son,
and bring us to heavenly joy,
in Jesus Christ our Lord. Amen.

Bryan D. Spinks, *Patterns for Worship*, 0C11

56d ABSOLUTION
The Lord enrich you with his grace, and nourish you with his blessing; the Lord defend you in trouble and keep you from all evil; the Lord accept your prayers, and graciously absolve you from your offences, for the sake of Jesus Christ, our Saviour.
Amen.

In Penitence and Faith, No. 57*

56e COLLECT
Be with us, Lord, in all our prayers, and direct our way toward the attainment of salvation; that among the changes and

chances of this mortal life, we may always be defended by your gracious help; through Jesus Christ our Lord. **Amen.**

ASB, p. 106, *Gelasian Sacramentary*

56f SUITABLE SCRIPTURE PASSAGES
Genesis 50.15–21; Exodus 1.8 – 2.10; 16.2–15; 1 Samuel 17.32–49; 1 Kings 17.8–16; 19.4–8; 2 Kings 4.42–44; Isaiah 25.1–9; 49.8–16a; Psalms 4; 9.9–20; 23; 27; 31.1–5, 19–24; 34.1–8; 34.9–14; 36.5–11; 41; 46; 48; 63.1–8; 66.1–12; 71.1–6; 90.1–6, 13–17; 91.1–6, 9–16; 107.23–32; 121; 124; 145.8–21; 147.1–11, 20c.
Matthew 6.24–34; 10.24–29; Mark 4.35–41; 6.30–34, 53–56; John 6.1–21; 17.6–19; Romans 8.26–39; 2 Corinthians 6.1–13; Ephesians 3.14–21; 2 Timothy 4.6–8, 16–18.

56g AFFIRMATION OF FAITH
You, O God our Father, created this world with your power
and watch over it with your compassion.
You are always before us to guide us,
about us to protect us,
and underneath are the everlasting arms.
You, Jesus, Son of God,
came to earth to reveal divine love,
and laid down your life that we might not perish,
but have everlasting life.
You showed us the way to live
and promised your presence till the end of the age.
You, O Holy Spirit of God,
reveal yourself in the inmost places of our hearts.
You guide and empower us to live life to the full.
You, O Holy Trinity,
surround us with your providential care.
We rejoice in you. Amen.

Michael Counsell

56h INTERCESSION
Hear our prayers, O Lord our God.
Hear us, good Lord.
Govern and direct your Holy Church;
fill it with love and truth;
and grant it that unity which is your will.
Hear us, good Lord.
Give us boldness to preach the gospel in all the world,
and to make disciples of all the nations.
Hear us, good Lord.
Bring into the way of truth

all who have erred and are deceived.
Hear us, good Lord.
Strengthen those who stand;
comfort and help the faint-hearted; raise up the fallen;
and finally beat down Satan under our feet.
Hear us, good Lord.
Guide the leaders of the nations
into the ways of peace and justice.
Hear us, good Lord.
Bless those who administer the law,
that they may uphold justice, honesty and truth.
Hear us, good Lord.
Teach us to use the fruits of the earth to your glory,
and for the good of all.
Hear us, good Lord.
Bless and keep all your people.
Hear us, good Lord.

ASB, p. 100*

56i AT THE PEACE
You are loved by God the Father and kept by Jesus Christ:
mercy, peace and love be yours for ever. **Amen.**

Jude 1–2, *Bible Praying*, 28

56j PREFACE
At the dawn of time you wrought from nothing a universe of
beauty and splendour, bringing light from darkness and order
from chaos. You formed us, male and female, in your image,
and endowed us with creative power. We turned away from
you but you did not abandon us. You called us by name and
searched us out, making a covenant of mercy, giving the law,
and teaching justice by the prophets.

A Prayer Book for Australia, p. 130

56k ENDING
The Lord almighty is our Father:
he loves us and tenderly cares for us.
The Lord Jesus Christ is our Saviour:
he has redeemed us and will defend us to the end.
The Lord, the Holy Spirit is among us:
he will lead us in God's holy way.
To God almighty, Father, Son and Holy Spirit,
be praise and glory today and for ever. Amen.

Liturgy and Death

561 BLESSING
Blessed are you, Creator and giver of peace. Peace be upon us; peace be upon this place; peace be upon this day. The deep, deep peace of God, which the world cannot give, be upon us and remain with us always. **Amen.**

The Open Gate, p. 29

---

57. RACE, TOLERANCE

See also OTHER FAITHS

57a OPENING RESPONSE
We stand before the throne of God with countless crowds from every nation and race, tribe and language.
Salvation belongs to our God! Alleluia!

Revelation 7.9, *Patterns for Worship*, 15A12, freely available

57b INVITATION TO CONFESSION
Use the petitions here in any order, and add your own. The response is: **Lord, have mercy.**

Lord, forgive us for the silence that
condones injustice
withholds forgiveness
disguises anger
prolongs quarrels
breeds misunderstandings
shows contempt
permits ignorance
kills love
expresses indifference
increases fear
makes barriers

St Barnabas' Church, Dulwich, source unknown

57c KYRIE
For the racism which denies dignity to those who are different, Lord, forgive us;
Lord, have mercy.
For the racism which recognises prejudice in others and never in ourselves, Christ, forgive us:
Christ, have mercy.

For the racism which will not recognize the work of your Spirit in other cultures, Lord, forgive us:
Lord, have mercy.

Michael Counsell

57d MUTUAL ABSOLUTION
I ask your forgiveness for what my people and I have done to you and yours, and I forgive you for what your ancestors did to my ancestors. Will you do the same for me?

We ask your forgiveness for what our people and we have done to you and yours, and we forgive you for what your ancestors did to our ancestors.

Now God has forgiven our sins, and torn the heavy veil of guilt, suspicion and bitterness which divided us. We are all children of God; we are sisters and brothers in God's family of love. **Amen.**

Michael Counsell

57e COLLECT
God, you are doing a new thing in our world, leading us along new paths of mutual discovery, joint learning, exchange and encounter, calling us to cross barriers of prejudice, fear, anxiety. Lead us on into your new world as the new people of God, with Jesus Christ, our partner and pioneer. **Amen.**

Robin Green, *A Still Place of Light*

57f SUITABLE SCRIPTURE PASSAGES
Genesis 11.1–9; 21.8–21; Deuteronomy 23.7–8; 2 Kings 5.1–14; Psalm 67.
Matthew 8.5–11; Mark 7.24–30; Luke 7.1–10; 10.25–37; Acts 2.1–21; 8.26–40; 10.44–48; 17.26–28; Romans 14.1–12; Ephesians 2.11–22; Revelation 7.9–17.

57g PRAYER OF COMMITMENT
God, we believe that you have called us together to broaden our experience of you and of each other.
We believe that we have been called to help in healing the many wounds of society and in reconciling people to each other and to God.
Help us as individuals or together, to work, in love, for peace, and never to lose heart.
We commit ourselves to each other – in joy and sorrow.
We commit ourselves to all who share our belief in reconciliation – to support and stand by them.

We commit ourselves to the way of justice and peace – in
thought and deed.
We commit ourselves to you – as our guide and friend.

The Corrymeela Community*

57h PRAYER FOR ASYLUM SEEKERS

Lord Jesus, you were a refugee in Egypt when your family fled
for fear of death. Move us by your Spirit so to welcome the
stranger who seeks asylum in our midst, that our nation may
be filled with your justice and peace, and no one in need is
denied. **Amen.**

Michael Counsell, London Ecumenical Conference, Epiphany 1996

57i ENDING FOR INTERCESSION

Hasten, Lord, the day when people will come from east and
west, from north and south, and sit at table in your kingdom
and we shall see your Son in his glory. Merciful Father,
accept these prayers
for the sake of your Son
our Saviour Jesus Christ. Amen.

Luke 13.29, *Intercessions in the Eucharist*

57j NAMING OUR MEETING (AT THE PEACE)

(*All standing.*)
Many traditions and many cultures are ours.
We stand among each other
with different histories and beliefs.
A common earth and an essential kinship are also ours.
We stand among each other.
We share our planet.
We share birth, death, hunger and love.
Let us celebrate our unity:
Our love unites us,
our struggles unite us,
we seek joy in many ways,
we are human together
in our ambiguity, our fear and our hope.

Pitt Street Uniting Church

57k LONGER PREFACE

Blessed are you, Lord God of creation, giver of all that is good,
God of peace, God of justice. Bless us and this bread, that we
may be one in heart and mind, a sign of your peace on earth.
Just as this bread which we break, once scattered as grain upon
the hills, has been gathered and made one, so gather your
children together and make us one, that we may join with that

multitude of every tribe and tongue which no one can number, for ever praising you and singing/saying ...

CAFOD, taken from the Liturgy notes for the 'Witness the Kingdom' event*

571 THANKSGIVING FOR OUR UNITY IN DIVERSITY
Lord, we thank you for our world – for its infinite varieties of people, colours, races and cultures, for the endless opportunities of making new relationships, venturing across new frontiers, creating new things, discovering new truths, healing the hurt and the broken. Forgive us for our narrowness of vision which sees only the clouds and misses the rainbow. **Amen.**

Women's World Day of Prayer 1993

57m BLESSING
The blessing of the Lord rest and remain upon all his people, in every land, of every tongue; the Lord meet in mercy all that seek him; the Lord comfort all who suffer and mourn; the Lord hasten his coming, and give us, his people, the blessing of peace. **Amen.**

With All God's People – The New Ecumenical Prayer Cycle, World Council of Churches

58. READINESS, JOHN THE BAPTIST

See also ADVENT

58a CALL TO WORSHIP
It is time for us to wake out of sleep, for deliverance is nearer to us now than it was when we first believed. It is far on in the night; day is near. Let us therefore cast off the deeds of darkness and put on our armour as soldiers of light.

Romans 13.11–12

58b INVITATION TO CONFESS
Lord God, we come to you with sorrow for our sins, and we ask for your help and strength. Help us to know ourselves and to accept our weakness. Strengthen us with your forgiving love, so that we may more courageously follow and obey your Son.

The Promise of His Glory, p. 125

58c CONFESSION
My God, for love of you
I desire to hate and forsake all sins
by which I have ever displeased you;
and I resolve, by the help of your grace,

to commit them no more;
and to avoid all opportunities of sin.
Help me to do this,
through Jesus Christ our Lord. Amen.

In Penitence and Faith, No. 81

58d ABSOLUTION USING WATER

Lord God almighty, creator of all life, of body and soul, accept this water; as we use it in faith, recalling our baptism, forgive our sins and save us from the power of evil. Lord, in your mercy give us living water, always springing up as a fountain of salvation: free us, body and soul, from all that may harm us, and welcome us into your presence in purity of heart. Grant this through Christ our Lord. **Amen.**

(*The president and people are sprinkled with water. Meanwhile suitable anthems, especially the Advent Prose, may be sung. The president concludes*:)

May almighty God cleanse us from sin and make us worthy of the kingdom of his glory. **Amen.**

In Penitence and Faith, Nos. 108, 111, 112,* *The Promise of His Glory*, p. 126

58e COLLECT

Almighty and everlasting God, whose servant and prophet John the Baptist bore witness to the truth as a burning and shining lamp: Lead us to bear witness to your Son, who is the eternal light and truth, and lives and reigns with you and the Holy Spirit, now and for ever. **Amen.**

The Promise of His Glory, p. 25

58f SUITABLE SCRIPTURE PASSAGES

Isaiah 40.1–11; 62.6–12; Malachi 3.1–4; Psalm 25.1–10.
Matthew 3.1–12; 11.2–11; 11.16–19; 21.23–32; 24.36–44; 25.1–13; 25.14–30; Mark 1.1–8; 6.14–29; 13.24–37; Luke 1.5–25; 1.57–66, 80; 1.68–79 (Benedictus); 3.1–18; 12.32–40; John 1.6–8, 19–28; Acts 13.22–26; 1 Thessalonians 5.1–11; 5.16–24; 2 Peter 3.8–15a.

58g AFFIRMATION OF FAITH

We believe in one God,
who made and loves all that is.
We believe in Jesus Christ,
God's only Son, our Lord,
who was born, lived, died and rose again,
and is coming to call all to account.
We believe in the Holy Spirit,
who calls, equips and sends out God's people,
and brings all things to their true end.

This is our faith, the faith of the Church:
We believe in one God,
Father, Son and Holy Spirit. Amen.

A Prayer Book for Australia, p. 37

58h INTERCESSION
Everlasting peace:
Soon, Lord, soon.
Nations walking in your way:
Soon, Lord, soon.
Disputes settled according to your will:
Soon, Lord, soon.
Swords becoming ploughs:
Soon, Lord, soon.
Neighbours caring for each other as for themselves:
Soon, Lord, soon.
Your will being done on earth as it is in heaven:
Soon, Lord, soon. Amen.

Companion to the Lectionary 6, p. 13

58i AT THE PEACE
In the tender compassion of our God the dawn from on high
shall break upon us, to shine on those who dwell in darkness
and the shadow of death, and to guide our feet into the way of
peace.

Luke 1.78–79, ICET

58j PREFACE OF ADVENT
And now we give you thanks because his future coming was
proclaimed by all the prophets. The virgin mother bore him in
her womb with love beyond all telling. John the Baptist was his
herald and made him known when at last he came. In his love
Christ has filled us with joy as we prepare to celebrate his birth,
so that when he comes he may find us watching in prayer, our
hearts filled with wonder and praise.

The Promise of His Glory, p. 133

58k THANKSGIVING TO JOHN THE BAPTIST
As the lover of the Spirit, the swallow that promises the summer of grace, the herald who runs in front of the procession,
you have clearly made known to us all the kindness of the
King, who shone out brightly from a pure Virgin to restore the
world to the realm of light. You banish the dominion of dark
and evil ways, and guide towards eternal life the hearts of
those baptized in repentance, blessed Prophet inspired by God!
Amen.

Vespers of St John the Forerunner, Orthodox

201

581 SOLEMN BLESSING
May God the Father, judge all-merciful, make us worthy of a place in his kingdom. **Amen.**
May God the Son, coming among us in power, reveal in our midst the promise of his glory. **Amen.**
May God the Holy Spirit make us steadfast in faith, joyful in hope and constant in love. **Amen.**
And the blessing ...

The Promise of His Glory, p. 119

59. REMEMBRANCE SUNDAY, THE ARMED FORCES, THE NATION

See also AUTHORITY, JUSTICE, PEACE

59a INTRODUCTION
We are here to worship almighty God, whose purposes are good; whose power sustains the world he has made; who loves us, though we have failed in his service; who gave Jesus Christ for the life of the world; who by his Holy Spirit leads us in his way.
As we give thanks for his great works, we remember those who have lived and died in his service and in the service of others; we pray for all who suffer through war and are in need; we ask for his help and blessing that we may do his will, and that the whole world may acknowledge him as Lord and King.

Service for Remembrance Sunday

59b INVITATION TO CONFESS
Let us confess to God the sins and shortcomings of the world; its pride, its selfishness, its greed; its evil divisions and hatreds. Let us confess our share in what is wrong, and our failure to seek and establish that peace which God wills for his children.

Service for Remembrance Sunday

59c CONFESSION
O Christ, in whose body was named all the violence of the world, and in whose memory is contained our profoundest grief, we lay open to you: the violence done to us in time before memory; the unremembered wounds that have misshaped our lives; the injuries we cannot forget and have not forgiven. The remembrance of them is grievous to us;
the burden of them is intolerable.

We lay open to you: the violence done in our name in time before memory; the unremembered wounds we have inflicted; the injuries we cannot forget and for which we have not been forgiven. The remembrance of them is grievous to us;
the burden of them is intolerable.

We lay open to you: those who have pursued a violent knowledge the world cannot forget; those caught up in violence they have refused to name; those who have enacted violence which they have not repented. The remembrance of them is grievous to us;
the burden of them is intolerable.

We lay open to you: the victims of violence whose only memorial is our anger; those whose suffering was sustained on our behalf; those whose continued oppression provides the ground we stand on. The remembrance of them is grievous to us;
the burden of them is intolerable.

Hear what comfortable words our Saviour Christ says to all who truly turn to God: Come to me, all you who labour and are heavy-laden, and I will give you rest. Take my yoke upon you, and learn from me, for I am gentle and lowly in heart, and you will find rest for your souls. For my yoke is easy, and my burden is light.

All Desires Known

59d **ABSOLUTION**
Almighty God, have mercy upon *us,* pardon and deliver *us* from all *our* sins, confirm and strengthen *us* in all goodness, and keep *us* in life eternal; through Jesus Christ our Lord. **Amen.**

Service for Remembrance Sunday

59e **COLLECT**
Grant us, O God, a vision of our nation as she could become: where justice would be available to all; where each receives according to their needs and all offer according to their abilities; where all are treated as individuals of equal worth and none are stereotyped in the minds of others; where fear is forgotten because none threatens the wellbeing of others; where all are united in a common love for their land and generosity to other nations. Then give us, O God, your grace to bring these things to be. **Amen.**

Michael Counsell

59f SUITABLE SCRIPTURE PASSAGES

Job 19.23–27a; Isaiah 2.1–5; 10.33 – 11.9; Jeremiah 8.18 – 9.1; Lamentations 1.1–6; Ezekiel 37.1–14; Amos 5.18–24; Jonah 3.1–5, 10; Wisdom 3.1–9; 6.12–16; 6.17–20; Psalms 17.1–9; 46; 47; 62.5–12; 70; 93; 126; 130.
Matthew 5.1–12; Luke 20.27–38; John 15.9–17; Romans 8.31–39; 1 Thessalonians 4.13–18; 2 Thessalonians 2.1–5, 13–17; Hebrews 9.24–28; 1 Timothy 2.1–7; Revelation 21.1–7.

59g ACT OF REMEMBRANCE

Let us remember before God all who have died as a result of war, oppression and tyranny.
From the Kohima Epitaph:
When you go home, tell them of us and say:
For your tomorrow we gave our today.
Last Post and Silence.
Lament and/or Reveille.

Epitaph in Kohima, Nagaland, India 1944

59h INTERCESSIONS

We pray for all who suffer as a result of war: For the injured and the disabled, for the mentally distressed and for those whose faith in God and in other people has been weakened or destroyed, we lift our hearts to you:
O Lord of mercy, hear our prayer.
For the homeless and refugees, for those who are hungry, and for all who have lost their livelihood and security, we lift our hearts to you:
O Lord of mercy, hear our prayer.
For those who mourn their dead; for those who have lost husband, wife, children or parents, and especially for those who have no hope in Christ to sustain them in their grief, we lift our hearts to you:
O Lord of mercy, hear our prayer.
(*Silence.*)
O Lord, hear our prayer:
for the sake of our Saviour, Jesus Christ. Amen.

Editors, *Prayers for the People*, 29.27

59i AT THE PEACE

The righteous perish, and no one understands that they are taken away from calamity and enter into peace.

Isaiah 57.1–2

59j PREFACE

And now we give you thanks because our Lord Jesus Christ laid down his life for his friends, setting us an example of sacrificial love which we remember in this sacrament. We thank you, Lord, for your many blessings on our nation, unworthy as we are; for all those whose sacrifice has given to us the freedom and peace we now enjoy, and for your promise that when a seed falls to the ground, it springs forth to a rich harvest of eternal life. Therefore we come before you in the company of saints and angels and of all those whom we remember this day, for ever praising you and saying/singing ...

Michael Counsell

59k THANKSGIVING AND PRAISE

Almighty and eternal God, from whose love in Christ we cannot be parted, either by death or life: Hear our prayers and thanksgivings for all whom we remember this day; fulfil in them the purpose of your love; and bring us all, with them, to your eternal joy; through Jesus Christ our Lord. **Amen.**

Service for Remembrance Sunday

59l BLESSING

God grant to the living, grace; to the departed, rest; to the people of every faith and nation, peace and concord; and to us and all the servants of God, life everlasting; and may the blessing ...

King's College, Cambridge *

---

60. REPENTANCE, CONFESSION, PENITENCE, RESPONSIBILITY

See also FORGIVENESS, LENT

60a CALL TO WORSHIP

May the light and peace of Jesus Christ our Lord be with you.
The Lord bless you.

The Promise of His Glory, p. 283, freely available

60b INVITATION TO CONFESS BEFORE COMMUNION

Brothers and sisters in Christ, we who come to receive the holy communion of the body and blood of our Saviour Christ can come only because of his great love for us. For, although we are completely undeserving of his love, yet in order to raise us from the darkness of death to everlasting life as God's sons and daughters, our Saviour Christ humbled himself to share our life and to die for us on the cross. In remembrance of his death, and as a pledge of his love, he has instituted this holy sacrament which we are now to share.

But those who would eat the bread and drink the cup of the Lord must examine themselves, and amend their lives. They must come with a penitent heart and a steadfast faith. Above all they must give thanks to God for his love towards us in Christ Jesus.

You, then, who truly and earnestly repent of your sins, and are in love and charity with your neighbours, and intend to lead a new life, following the commandments of God and walking in his holy ways, draw near with faith, and take this holy sacrament to strengthen and comfort you. But first, let us make a humble confession of our sins to Almighty God.

A Prayer Book for Australia, p. 108

60c CONFESSION AND ABSOLUTION

Brothers and sisters, in the presence of the God of glory, we need to confess our true human condition. In the light of Christ's self-giving life, his way of the Cross, we see the darkness in our lives.

(Silence as we reflect on the life of the individual.)

As we think of the evil and oppression in the world of which we are a part, we need to repent together with all our brothers and sisters.

(Silence as we reflect on the world's life.)

As members of a people called to follow Christ and live in his new righteousness, we need to repent for the evil in the Church's life.

(Silence as we reflect on the life of the Church.)

The Saviour of the world, the Refuge of the repentant, forgives and strengthens all who truly seek his grace. He accepts you as his sons and daughters, and sets you free from the bondage of your past. For Christ died and rose to new life that we might all share his wholeness and abundant life. **Amen.**

Church of South India

60d COLLECT

Grant us, Lord, the wisdom and the grace to use aright the time that is left to us here on earth. Lead us to repent of our sins, the evil we have done and the good we have not done; and strengthen us to follow the steps of your Son, in the way that leads to the fullness of eternal life; through Jesus Christ our Lord. **Amen.**

ASB, p. 314, from *Prayer and the Departed 1973*

60e SUITABLE SCRIPTURE PASSAGES
2 Samuel 11.26 – 12.15; Job 42.1–6, 10–17; Isaiah 55.1–5; 64.1–9;
Jeremiah 14.7–10, 19–22; Ezekiel 18.1–4, 25–32; 33.7–11; Hosea
5.15 – 6.6; Joel 2.1–2, 12–17; Psalms 14; 25.1–9; 32; 80.1–7;
106.1–6, 19–23; 119.33–40.
Matthew 3.1–12; Mark 1.9–15; Luke 7.36–50; 24.36b–48; Acts
3.12–19; James 5.13–20.

60f AFFIRMATION OF FAITH
This is the message we have heard and proclaim:
God is light;
there is no darkness in God.
If we say we know God
while walking in darkness,
we are living a lie;
but if we walk in the light –
as God is in the light –
we are a family of friends,
and the blood of Jesus makes us clean from sin.
If we deny that we have sinned,
we are fooling ourselves;
there is no truth in us.
If we confess our sins,
God who is trustworthy and fair will forgive us
and wash away whatever is wrong.
Michael Counsell, from 1 John 1.5–9

60g INTERCESSION
For the wounds still inflicted on your children, Lord, forgive
us and help us.
For infants who cry for food and get none; for the making of
orphans and widows, Lord, forgive us:
forgive us and help us.
For those who mourn and are not comforted, for those who
are guilty and are not convicted of sin, Lord, forgive us:
forgive us and help us.
For those who are lost and have no good news proclaimed to
them, but are left to think you have rejected them, Lord,
forgive us:
forgive us and help us.
Through the cross of Jesus
reconcile us to yourself
and to each other;
so that war may cease,
nation may speak peace to nation,

your will be done on earth
and your name honoured everywhere and for ever. **Amen.**

Alan Gaunt

60h AT THE PEACE
We have this in common, that we are all forgiven sinners. From
that humility, and to that dignity, let us greet one another.

Michael Counsell

60i PREFACE
Because you are always ready to forgive and now you call your
people to turn back to you, and be renewed in Christ your Son.

Scottish Experimental Liturgy 1977

60j CLOSING PRAYER
Jesus, Son of God, our true and only Saviour: you died like a
criminal on a cross; but you are God who forgives. Once
broken, helpless and in pain, you are God in whom there is
hope. You have shown us a love beyond words: give us your
forgiveness, hope and love. **Amen.**

A New Zealand Prayer Book, p. 535, adapted in *Patterns for Worship*, 5J16

60k BLESSING
Bow your heads and pray for God's blessing.
Lord, you care for your people even when they stray. Grant us
a complete change of heart, so that we may follow you with
greater fidelity. Grant this through Christ our Lord. **Amen.**
May almighty God bless you, the Father, and the Son, ✠ and the
Holy Spirit. **Amen.**

Roman Missal

---

61. THE RESURRECTION, EASTER

See also LIFE

61a GREETING
Alleluia! Christ is risen.
He is risen indeed. Alleluia!

Orthodox

61b INVITATION TO CONFESSION
Christ our passover lamb has been offered for us. Let us then
rejoice by putting away all malice and evil and confessing our
sins with a sincere and true heart.

1 Corinthians 5.7–8, *In Penitence and Faith*, No. 5

61c PENITENTIAL KYRIE

You raise the dead to life in the Spirit: Lord, have mercy;
Lord, have mercy.
You bring pardon and peace to the sinner: Christ, have mercy;
Christ, have mercy.
You bring light to those in darkness: Lord, have mercy;
Lord, have mercy.

Lent, Holy Week and Easter, p. 286

61d ABSOLUTION

God forgives us; be at peace.
(Silence.)
Rejoice and be glad, for Christ is resurrection, reconciliation
for all the human race. **Amen.**

A New Zealand Prayer Book, p. 479

61e COLLECT

God of terror and joy, you arise to shake the earth. Open our
graves and give us back the past; so that all that has been
buried may be freed and forgiven, and our lives may return to
you through the risen Christ. **Amen.**

All Desires Known

61f SUITABLE SCRIPTURE PASSAGES

1 Kings 17.17–24; Job 14.1–14; 19.23–27a; Ezekiel 36.24–28;
Daniel 12.1–3; Psalms 16; 23; 30; 31.1–4, 15–16; 66.8–20; 116.1–4,
12–19; 118.1–2, 14–24; 133; 143.
Matthew 28.1–10; Luke 7.11–17; 20.27–38; 24.13–35; 24.36b–48;
John 10.1–10; 10.11–18; 11.1–45; 12.20–36; 14.1–14; 20.1–18;
20.19–31; Acts 2.1–14a, 22–32; 3.12–19; 4.5–12; 4.32–35; 5.27–32;
7.55–60; 9.1–6; 9.36–43; 10.34–43; 17.22–31; Romans 6.3–11; 1
Corinthians 15.1–11; 15.12–20; 15.35–38, 42–50; 15.51–58; 2
Corinthians 4.13 – 5.1; Colossians 2.6–15; 3.1–4; 1 Thessalonians
4.13–18; 1 Peter 1.3–9; 1.17–23; 2.19–25; 3.13–22; 4.1–8;
Revelation 1.4–8; 5.11–14; 21.1–6.

61g AFFIRMATION OF FAITH

Jesus says to you: I am the resurrection and the life; do you
believe this?
Yes, Lord; I believe.
Jesus says to you: Those who believe in me, though they die,
yet shall they live; do you believe this?
Yes, Lord; I believe.
Jesus says to you: Whoever is alive and believes in me will
never die; do you believe this?
Yes, Lord; I believe.

**I believe that you are the Messiah,
the Son of God entering this world,
and leading us into the world to come. Alleluia! Amen.**

Adapted from John 11.25–27, Michael Counsell

61h INTERCESSION

We pray to Jesus who is present with us to eternity, saying,
Jesus, Lord of life:
in your mercy, hear us.
Jesus, light of the world, bring the light and peace of your
gospel to the nations ... Jesus, Lord of life:
in your mercy, hear us.
Jesus, bread of life, give food to the hungry ... and nourish us
all with your word. Jesus, Lord of life:
in your mercy, hear us.
Jesus, our way, our truth, our life, be with us and all who follow
you in the way ... deepen our appreciation of your truth and
fill us with your life. Jesus, Lord of life:
in your mercy, hear us.
Jesus, Good Shepherd who gave your life for the sheep, recover
the straggler, bind up the injured, strengthen the sick and lead
the healthy and strong to play. Jesus, Lord of life:
in your mercy, hear us.
Jesus, the resurrection and the life, we give you thanks for all
who have lived and believed in you ... raise us with them to
eternal life. Jesus, Lord of life:
**in your mercy, hear us, accept our prayers, and be with us
always. Amen.**

Patterns for Worship, 6H8

61i THE PEACE

The risen Christ came and stood among his disciples and said,
'Peace be with you!' Then were they glad when they saw the
Lord.
Alleluia! The peace of the risen Christ be always with you,
and also with you. Alleluia!
(*All may exchange a sign of peace, greeting one another with these
words:*) The Lord is risen.
Answer: He is risen indeed.

John 20.19–20, *Lent, Holy Week and Easter*, p. 236

61j PREFACE

Christ is risen from the dead. Love is come again. Christ is
sovereign over space and time.

A New Zealand Prayer Book, p. 492

61k EUCHARISTIC PRAYER

O Eternal Wisdom, we praise you and give you thanks, because the beauty of death could not contain you. You broke forth from the comfort of the grave; before the stone was moved, and the tomb of our world was opened wide. For on this day you were raised in power and revealed yourself to women as a beloved stranger, offering for the rituals of the dead the terror of new life and of desire fulfilled.

Therefore we join with the woman who gave you birth, the women who befriended you and fed you, who argued with you and touched you, the woman who anointed you for death, the women who met you, risen from the dead, and with all your lovers throughout the ages, for ever praising you and saying/singing:
Holy ...

Blessed is our brother Jesus, who walks with us the road of our grief, and is known again in the breaking of bread; who, on the night that he was handed over, took bread, gave thanks, broke it, and said: 'This is my body which is for you. Do this to remember me.' In the same way also the cup, after supper, saying: 'This cup is the new covenant in my blood. Do this, whenever you drink it, to remember me.'
Christ has died. Christ is risen. Christ will come again.

Come now, disturbing Spirit of our God, breathe on these bodily things and make us one body in Christ. Open our graves, unbind our eyes, and name us here; touch and heal all that has been buried in us, that we need not cling to our pain, but may go forth with power to release resurrection in the world. **Amen.**

All Desires Known*

611 EASTER SONG OF THANKS

On this *day/night* we sing to Jesus, the true Lamb of God,
who makes death to pass over all who're marked with his
    blood.
Alleluia, Christ is risen, let the heavens make it known!
Alleluia, all creation rejoice round God's throne,
alleluia, let the trumpet of peace now be blown!

On this *day/night* God leads us out by the power of his hand
out of slav'ry into freedom in his long-promised land.
Alleluia, Christ is risen, let the earth now be bright!
Alleluia, sin is powerless, God brings us his light,
alleluia, sing to Jesus, who conquers death's night!

On this *day/night* the earth and heaven are wedded again –
may our candle shine for Jesus till he comes here to reign.
Alleluia, Christ is risen, Mother Church, sing his praise!
Alleluia, may he shine on our lives with his rays,
alleluia, serving Christ for the rest of our days.

Michael Counsell, based on the Exultet (may be sung to the 'Sans Day Carol')

61m BLESSING
The Lord of the empty tomb, the conqueror of gloom,
come to you.
The Lord in the garden walking, the Lord to Mary talking,
come to you.
The Lord in the upper room, dispelling fear and doom,
come to you.
The Lord on the road to Emmaus,
the Lord giving hope to Thomas, come to you.
The Lord appearing on the shore, giving us life for evermore,
come to you.
And the blessing ...

The Edge of Glory, p. 56

---

62. RIGHTEOUSNESS, JUSTIFICATION, WORKS

See also FAITH, THE NEEDY

62a OPENING PRAYER
Living Lord,
fill us with your life-giving,
joy-giving, peace-giving presence,
that we may praise you now with our lips
and all the day long with our lives,
through Jesus Christ our Lord. Amen.

For the Family

62b PENITENCE
Let us confess our sins to almighty God.
Almighty God,
Creator of the living and the non-living,

you marvellously made us in your image;
but we have corrupted ourselves
and damaged your likeness,
by rejecting your love
and hurting our neighbour.
We are desperately sorry
and heartily repent of our sins.
Cleanse us and forgive us
by the sacrifice of your Son;
Remake us and lead us
by your Spirit, the Comforter.
We only dare to ask this
through Jesus Christ our Lord. Amen.

Almighty God, whose steadfast love is as great as the heavens are high above the earth, remove our sins from us, as far as the east is from the west, strengthen our life in his kingdom and keep us upright until the last day; through Jesus Christ our merciful high priest.

Amen. Thank you, Father, for forgiveness.
We come to your table as your children,
not presuming but assured,
not trusting ourselves but your Word:
we hunger and thirst for righteousness,
and ask for our hearts to be satisfied
with the body and blood of your Son,
Jesus Christ the Righteous. Amen.

A Kenyan Revised Liturgy

62c COLLECT

O God, before whose face we are not made righteous even by being right; free us from the need to justify ourselves by our own anxious striving, that we may be abandoned to faith in you alone, through Jesus Christ. **Amen.**

All Desires Known

62d SUITABLE SCRIPTURE PASSAGES

Proverbs 31.10–31; Isaiah 1.1, 10–20; 5.1–7; Jeremiah 17.5–10; 23.1–6; Wisdom 12.13, 16–19; Ecclesiasticus 27.4–7; Psalms 1; 4; 15; 17.1–7; 19; 26.1–8; 34.9–20; 85.8–13; 92.1–4, 12–15; 112; 125. Matthew 5.13–20; 10.40–42; Mark 7.1–8, 14–15, 21–23; Luke 6.39–49; 10.38–42; 13.1–9; 18.9–14a; John 12.1–8; Romans 1.16–17; 3.22b–28; 4.1–5, 13–17; 6.1b–11; 6.12–23; 10.5–15; 12.9–21; 13.11–14; Galatians 6.7–16; Ephesians 2.1–10; 4.25 – 5.2; 5.15–20; Philippians 1.21–30; 3.4b–14; Colossians 1.1–14; 3.1–11;

1 Thessalonians 2.9–13; 2 Thessalonians 3.6–13; Hebrews 13.1–8, 15–16; James 1.17–24; 2.1–10, 14–17; 3.1–12; 3.13 – 4.3, 7–8a.

62e AFFIRMATION OF FAITH
Jesus is Lord;
God has raised him from the dead.
By our faith we are put right with God,
and by our confession we are saved:
this we believe and this we proclaim. Amen.

Romans 10.8–10, *Bible Praying*, 207

62f INTERCESSION
O God, the Father of our Lord Jesus Christ, you came to bring good news to the poor, sight to the blind, freedom to the oppressed, and salvation to your people. Come to us now by your Holy Spirit and break down the barriers which divide, that we may truly love one another:

Persecuted minorities, all oppressed by sectarian or cold religious attitudes, all oppressed by racist politics and government, all oppressed by force or by intimidation; our God and Father,
these we bring before you.

Those who seek to remove oppression by patience, persuasion, courage and love: our God and Father,
for these we ask your grace.

All who feel compelled to turn to violence to oppose violence – that they may not be corrupted or oppressive themselves: our God and Father,
for these we pray.

All who are not whole – the hungry, the diseased, the homeless, those in poverty, depression, degradation, all who cannot find community: our God and Father,
for these we shout aloud.

Those who give their lives to bring to others wholeness and salvation: our God and Father,
for these we ask your strength.
Lord Jesus,
make us one in heart and mind,
give us a spirit of service
and true faith in Jesus Christ our Lord. Amen.

Source unknown, adapted by the Editors in *Prayers for the People*, 2.25

62g AT THE PEACE
Let love be genuine. Never pay back evil for evil. As far as it lies with you, live at peace with everyone.

Romans 12.9, 17–18, Patterns for Worship, 17R20, freely available

62h PREFACE
And now we give you thanks because you have anointed your Son as the Messiah, the light of the nations, and revealed him as the hope of all who thirst for righteousness and peace.

The Promise of His Glory, p. 238

62i THANKSGIVING
Gracious God, we humbly thank you for all your gifts so freely bestowed on us, for life and health and safety, for freedom to work and leisure to rest, and for all that is beautiful in creation and in human life. But, above all, we thank you for our Saviour, Jesus Christ, for his death and resurrection, for the gift of your Spirit, and for the hope of glory. Fill our hearts with all joy and peace in believing; through Jesus Christ our Lord. **Amen.**

A Prayer Book for Australia, p. 218

62j BLESSING
May the risen Lord Jesus watch over us and renew us as he renews the whole of his creation. May our hearts and lives echo his love. And may the blessing ...

Celebrating Common Prayer, p. 38

63. THE SABBATH, SUNDAY, PILGRIMAGE, TRAVELLERS, HOLIDAYS

63a GREETING
This is the day which the Lord has made.
Let us rejoice and be glad in it.

Psalm 118.24

63b INVITATION TO CONFESS
The Lord has commanded a holy day of rest, dedicated to him. But we have put our own pleasure and convenience before the family gathering in the house of our heavenly Father. Let us tell him we are sorry.

Michael Counsell, from Exodus 16.23

63c CONFESSION
To you, Lord, all hearts are open.
Forgive our secret sins,

forgive our habitual sins,
forgive our unnoticed sins,
our sins of thought, word and deed.
All that we have left undone;
our sins against ourselves;
our sins against others;
our sins against you.
All where we have fallen short of your glory,
and not done what you have called us to do.

The Open Gate, p. 55

63d ABSOLUTION

Late one Sunday evening, Jesus stood among his disciples and said, If you forgive people's sins, they are forgiven. The authority to declare God's forgiveness is with us today, and we share God's mercy with each other when we meet together. **Amen.**

Michael Counsell, from John 20.19–23

63e COLLECT FOR SUNDAY OBSERVANCE

O God, give your people grace to use aright your holy day; that it may be a day of mercy to the heavy-laden, a day of resurrection to newness and fullness of life; a day to worship you in the fellowship of the faithful; through Jesus Christ our Lord. **Amen.**

The Daily Service*

63f COLLECT FOR PILGRIMS

Almighty God, whose kingdom is for the poor in spirit, and whose best provision for your chosen people is a tent and a pilgrim staff; grant that we look not for permanence in the work of human hands, nor seek safety other than in the company of that Wayfarer who had nowhere to lay his head, even your Son Jesus Christ our Lord. **Amen.**

© The Church Mission Society

63g SUITABLE SCRIPTURE PASSAGES

Genesis 12.1–9; 47.1–12; Deuteronomy 5.12–15; 16.13–17; Joshua 5.9–12; 2 Samuel 6.1–5, 12b–19; Psalms 67; 81.1–10; 96; 122; 148; 149; 150.
Mark 2.23 – 3.6; Luke 13.10–17; John 10.22–29; Ephesians 1.3–14; Hebrews 11.8–16; 1 Peter 2.9–12.

63h AFFIRMATION OF FAITH

We believe in God,
who is gracious and compassionate,
slow to anger and rich in love.

We believe in God,
whose kingdom is everlasting,
whose dominion endures for ever.
We believe in God,
who is faithful to all his promises
and loving towards all he has made.
We believe in God,
who opens his hand
and satisfies the needs
of everything living.

Psalm 145.13–16, Bible Praying, 201

63i INTERCESSION
Be mindful, O Lord, of your people here before you, and of those who are absent through age, sickness or infirmity. Care for the infants, guide the young, support the aged, encourage the fainthearted, collect the scattered, and bring back the wandering to your fold. Travel with the voyagers, defend the widows, shield the orphans, deliver the captives, heal the sick. Succour all who are in tribulation, necessity or distress. Remember for good all those who love us, and those who hate us, and those who have desired us, unworthy as we are, to pray for them. And those whom we have forgotten, Lord, remember. Grant unto each according to your merciful loving-kindness, and your eternal love; through Jesus Christ our Lord. **Amen.**

Orthodox, Intercession at Great Complines

63j AT THE PEACE
God rested from his labours, when he created the heavens and the earth, and promised that we might enter into his rest. The God of peace be with you all.

Michael Counsell, from Genesis 2.2; Hebrews 4.1; Romans 15.33

63k PILGRIMS' EUCHARISTIC PRAYER
Sursum Corda
It is indeed right, always and everywhere, to praise you O God. You created the beauty of the world through which we travel. We thank you for sending your Son to be born at Bethlehem. He preached the good news of your forgiveness from boats and in the synagogues; and healed those who came to him in Galilee. He was transfigured that the disciples might see his glory on the holy mountain. He cleansed the Temple in Jerusalem, was arrested in Gethsemane, and carried his cross to Calvary, where he gave his life that we might be reconciled to you, Father, and live in peace for evermore. We praise you for

his glorious resurrection and ascension, and for sending your Holy Spirit to dwell in our hearts always, to the ends of the world. Surrounded by an invisible cloud of saints and angels we join in their praises as we say:

Holy, thrice holy God, heaven and earth are beautiful with your glory. 'Save us now' is sung in highest heaven. We bless you for Jesus who came in the name of his Father. Save us now and evermore.

In the upper room Jesus washed the disciples' feet, then shared a meal with them. He took bread, gave thanks, broke it and gave it to them saying, 'This is my body, sacrificed for you. Eat it to remind you I am with you.' After the meal he took a cup of wine and said, 'This is my blood, poured out for you. Through this all the wrong you have done will be forgiven.'

So we offer to you, Father, the sacrifice of our whole lives. Take us and make us part of the sacrifice of Jesus; we hold nothing back. Send your Holy Spirit on the Body of your Son in this place, enabling us to serve you all the days of our pilgrimage here on earth, and to live with you in eternity. **Amen.**

Michael Counsell

631 THANKSGIVING
We thank God for the wonderful world he has given to us, and for all his love and care.
For the warmth of the sun, O God of love,
we give you thanks and praise.
For the rain which makes things grow, O God of love,
we give you thanks and praise.
For the woods and the fields, O God of love,
we give you thanks and praise.
For the sea and the sky, O God of love,
we give you thanks and praise.
For the flowers and the animals, O God of love,
we give you thanks and praise.
For families and holidays, O God of love,
we give you thanks and praise.
For all your gifts, O God of love,
we give you thanks and praise.
Everything around us rejoices:
therefore give us joyful hearts to praise you in your glory;
through Jesus Christ our Lord. Amen.

Editors, *Prayers for the People*, 14.34

63m HOLY LAND BLESSING
May God the Father, who sent his Son to be born in Bethlehem,
bless you. May Jesus, who preached in Galilee and died for you
at Calvary, bless you. May God the Holy Spirit, who after the
resurrection came upon the apostles in Jerusalem, bless you.
And may the blessing of the holy and undivided Trinity be
upon you and upon the worldwide people of God, in your jour-
neying and in your rest, now and to eternity. **Amen.**

Michael Counsell

---

64. SACRIFICE

See also SALVATION

64a CALL TO WORSHIP
Jesus suffered outside the city to make us holy through his
blood. Let us come to him, looking for the city which is to come.
Through him we offer our sacrifice of praise to God. Lord, open
our lips:
and our mouth shall proclaim you praise.

Hebrews 13.12, 15, *Patterns for Worship*, 13A11

64b INVITATION TO CONFESS
Jesus Christ is just; he is the sacrifice that takes away our sins,
and not only ours, but those of the whole world. Let us confess
what we have done wrong, acknowledging our share in the
sins of the world, and ask for God's healing grace.

The Living Word

64c KYRIE
You were sent to preach the good news of light in the darkness
of the world: Lord, have mercy.
Lord, have mercy.
You were sent to plant in our hearts the seed of eternal life:
Christ, have mercy.
Christ, have mercy.
You were sent to reconcile us to yourself by the shedding of
your blood: Lord, have mercy.
Lord, have mercy.

David Silk

64d ABSOLUTION
God the Creator brings you new life, forgives and redeems you. Take hold of this forgiveness and live your life in the Spirit of Jesus. **Amen.**

A New Zealand Prayer Book, p. 460

64e COLLECT
Fearful God, you require of our love appalling sacrifice; and your lasting promise is contained in contradiction. May we so lay on your altar our dearest desires that we may receive them back from you as unaccountable gift, through Jesus Christ. **Amen.**

All Desires Known

64f SUITABLE SCRIPTURE PASSAGES
Genesis 22.1–14; Exodus 12.1–14; Leviticus 16.20–22; Isaiah 53.1–8; Psalms 4; 50.7–15; 116.
Mark 10.35–45; Romans 12.1–8; Hebrews 9.11–15; 1 Peter 2.1–5; 1 John 1.1 – 2.2.

64g AFFIRMATION OF FAITH
We believe in God almighty,
the Lord, the first and the last,
who is, who was and who is to come.
We believe in Jesus Christ,
the faithful witness,
the first to be raised from death,
the ruler of the kings of the earth:
who loves us,
and by his sacrificial death
has freed us from our sins
and made us a kingdom of priests
to serve our God and Father. Amen.

Revelation 1.5–8, Bible Praying, 230

64h INTERCESSION
Gracious God, fountain of all wisdom, we pray for all Christian people; for *Bishop N.*, and for those who teach and guard the faith … May the word of Christ dwell richly in our hearts, and knit us together in the bond of your love. Hear us:
hear us, good Lord.
We pray for the leaders of the nations, and for those in authority under them … Give them the gift of your wisdom, and a right discernment in all things. Hear us:
hear us, good Lord.

We pray for our ... *(city/town/village/community)*; for those who live and work here, and for those who visit this place ... Speak your word of peace in our midst, and help us to serve one another as Christ has served us. Hear us:
hear us, good Lord.
We pray for those who do not believe, and yet who long to know you, the very Word of life ... Open their ears to hear your voice, and open their hearts to the knowledge of your love in Christ. Hear us:
hear us, good Lord.
We pray for those bowed down with grief, fear or sickness, especially ... May your living Word bring comfort and healing to all those in need. Hear us:
hear us, good Lord.
We give thanks for all those who have died in the faith of Christ and we rejoice with *(N. and)* all your saints, trusting in the promise of your word fulfilled. Lord of the Church:
hear our prayer,
and make us one in heart and mind
to serve you with joy for ever. Amen.

From Psalm 119, *Patterns for Worship*, 11H16

64i AT THE PEACE
Grace and peace be with you from God our Father and the Lord Jesus Christ, who gave himself for our sins according to the will of our God and Father; to whom be glory for ever and ever. **Amen.**

Galatians 1.3–5, *Bible Praying*, 10

64j PREFACE
As he offered his body on the cross, his perfect sacrifice fulfilled all others. As he gave himself into your hands for our salvation, he showed himself to be the priest, the altar, and the lamb of sacrifice.

Roman Missal

64k AFTER COMMUNION
God our Father, whose Son was born into the world to free us from sin and death, and to bring us to everlasting life: purify us by his perfect sacrifice, that, when he comes in power and glory, we may greet him without shame or fear; through Jesus Christ our Lord. **Amen.**

Prayers for use at the Alternative Services, 324

641 BLESSING
May God the Father bless you, who has made a covenant with
us with sacrifice. **Amen.**
May God the Son bless you, who has opened up a new way for
us through the offering of his own body on the cross. **Amen.**
May God the Spirit bless you, who bears witness that our sins
are remembered no more. **Amen.**
May the holy and merciful Trinity accept our sacrifice of praise,
now and evermore. **Amen.**

Michael Counsell, from Hebrews 8.8; 9.7; 10.20, 15, 17; 13.15

---

65. SAINTS, ANGELS

See also LIFE, PETER

65a ALL SAINTSTIDE GREETING
Rejoice, people of God, praise the Lord. Let us keep the feast in
honour of all God's saints, in whose victory the angels rejoice
and glorify the Son of God. May the joy and peace of heaven be
with you.
The Lord bless you.
To our God belong victory, glory and power,
for right and just are his judgements.
Praise our God, all that serve him:
those who fear him, both small and great.
The Lord almighty has claimed his kingdom:
let us exult, rejoice, and give him glory.

The Promise of His Glory, p. 48

65b INVITATION TO CONFESS
We have come to Mount Zion, the city of the living God, the
heavenly Jerusalem, to myriads of angels, to God the judge of
all, and to Jesus the mediator of a new covenant. Let us confess
our sins in penitence and faith.

Hebrews 12.22–24, Michael Perham, *Enriching the Christian Year*, 9A1

65c CONFESSION
I confess to almighty God,
and to you, my brothers and sisters,
that I have sinned through my own fault
in my thoughts and in my words,
in what I have done,
and in what I have failed to do;

and I ask blessed Mary, ever virgin,
all the angels and saints,
and you, my brothers and sisters,
to pray for me to the Lord our God.

Roman Missal

65d ABSOLUTION

May God our Father forgive us our sins, and bring us to the fellowship of his table with his saints for ever. **Amen**

Stuart Thomas, in *Patterns for Worship*, 16D8

65e COLLECT

Almighty and everlasting God, you have kindled the flame of love in the hearts of the saints. Grant to us the same faith and power of love, that, as we rejoice in their triumphs, we may be sustained by their example and fellowship; through Christ our Lord. **Amen.**

Prayers for use at the Alternative Services

65f SUITABLE SCRIPTURE PASSAGES

Genesis 28.10–17; 2 Kings 6.8–17; Isaiah 25.6–9; Jeremiah 31.31–34; Daniel 7.1–3, 15–18; 10.4–21; Tobit 5.4–16; 12.6–22; Wisdom 3.1–9; Psalms 24.1–6; 34.1–10; 91.5–12; 103.17–22; 148; 149.
Matthew 4.1–11; 5.1–12; 18.1–6, 10; 26.47–53; Luke 2.8–15; 6.20–31; 22.39–43; John 1.43–51; 11.32–44; 1 Corinthians 1.1–9; Ephesians 1.11–23; Colossians 1.9–14; Hebrews 12.28 – 13.2; 1 John 3.1–13; Revelation 5.11–14; 7.9–17; 12.7–12; 21.1–6a.

65g AFFIRMATION OF FAITH

We believe that God the Creator is surrounded by the praises of heaven as they sing:
You are worthy, our Lord and our God,
to receive glory and honour and power,
for you created all things,
and the creation exists
only because you will it to.

We believe that God the Redeemer is followed by the multitudes he has saved as they sing:
You are worthy, for you were slain,
and by your death you have set us free,
from every race and language,
from every people and nation,
and made us a kingdom of priests.

We believe that God the Spirit fills the hearts of all with joy as
we sing:
From now on,
blest are those who die in the Lord.
Blest indeed, says the Spirit,
for they rest from their labours,
and enjoy the reward for their toil. Amen

Michael Counsell, from Revelation 4.11; 5.9–10; 14.13

65h INTERCESSION

With all the saints and angels, most holy Trinity, we bring you
praise and prayer.
We praise you for the lives of those who have served you in
ages past; for the example and the encouragement of the
church triumphant in heaven; and we pray to God the Spirit
that you will raise up lives of heroic holiness in the Church mil-
itant here on earth ... With all the saints and angels,
we bring you praise and prayer.

We praise you for giving to every nation its own culture and its
own dignity, and we pray to God the Son for the peacemakers
whom you called blest, that we may learn to live together in
harmony and peace ... With all the saints and angels,
we bring you praise and prayer.

We praise you for our families and neighbours, and for the
saintly lives we see around us, and we pray to God the Father
that, as each of your little ones has an angel in heaven who
beholds your face, you will give your angels charge over them
to keep them from harm ... With all the saints and angels,
we bring you praise and prayer.

We praise you for all those in the caring professions who minister to the needy, and we pray to God the Spirit that you will
inspire people today, as you have inspired the saints in every
age, to heal the sick, feed the hungry and visit those in prison
... With all the saints and angels,
we bring you praise and prayer.

We praise you for the lives of those who have served you on
earth and now praise you in heaven, and we pray to God the
holy and ever-living Trinity that you will receive into your eternal home those whom we remember today ... With all the
saints and angels,
we bring you praise and prayer.

Surrounded by a cloud of witnesses, of angels and the spirits of good people made perfect, we pray to the Father, in the Spirit, through Jesus Christ, who together live and reign in glory, for ever and ever. **Amen.**

Michael Counsell

AT THE PEACE

65i

May the God of peace make you perfect and holy, that you may be kept safe and blameless in spirit, soul and body, for the coming of our Lord Jesus Christ.

The Promise of His Glory, p. 54

65j

Hear again the song of the angels: Glory to God in the highest, and on earth peace.

Luke 2.14, Michael Perham, *Enriching the Christian Year*, 9G1

65k PREFACE

And now we give you thanks, most gracious God, surrounded by a great cloud of witnesses and glorified in the assembly of your saints. The glorious company of the apostles praise you. The noble fellowship of prophets praise you. The white-robed army of martyrs praise you. We, your holy Church, acclaim you. In communion with angels and archangels, and with all those who have served you in every age and worship you now in heaven, we raise our voice to proclaim your glory, for ever praising you and saying/singing ...

Te Deum, from *The Promise of His Glory*, p. 55*

65l AFTER COMMUNION

O God, our Father, we thank you for this sacrament. For all who down the centuries at this table have found the light that never fades, the joy that no one takes from them, the forgiveness of their sins, the love which is your love, the presence of their Lord; we thank you. **Amen.**

The Lord's Supper, p. 118*

65m BLESSING

God keep you in the fellowship of his saints. Christ protect you by the ministry of the angels. The Spirit make you holy in God's service; and the blessing ...

Michael Perham, *Enriching the Christian Year*, 9E1

66. SALVATION, ADOPTION, FREEDOM, REDEMPTION

See also FORGIVENESS, SACRIFICE

66a GREETING
In the name of Christ, who died and was raised by the glory of
the Father, we welcome you: grace, mercy and peace be with
you all.
And also with you.

Patterns for Worship, 6A1

66b INVITATION TO CONFESS
God so loved the world that he gave his only Son Jesus Christ
to save us from our sins, to be our advocate in heaven, and to
bring us to eternal life. Let us confess our sins, in penitence and
faith, firmly resolved to keep God's commandments and to live
in love and peace.

ASB, p. 120

66c CONFESSION
Let us return to the Lord our God and say to him:
Father,
we have sinned against heaven and against you.
We are not worthy to be called your children.
We turn to you again.
Have mercy on us,
bring us back to yourself
as those who once were dead
but now have life through Christ our Lord. Amen

Luke 15.21, 24, Stuart Thomas, in *Patterns for Worship*, 16C8

66d KYRIE
Let us call on God's loving mercy. Turn us again, O God our
Saviour, and let your anger cease from us. Lord have mercy;
Lord have mercy.
Show us your mercy, O Lord, and grant us your salvation.
Christ have mercy;
Christ have mercy.
Your salvation is near for those who fear you. Lord have mercy;
Lord have mercy.

Portsmouth Cathedral

66e ABSOLUTION

The Lord God set you free from the bondage of sin and fear; that in God's service you may find your freedom, and in God's will your peace; through Jesus Christ our Lord. **Amen.**

Adapted from *The Promise of His Glory*, p. 365

66f COLLECT

God of mercy and hope, in the struggle for freedom grant us strength; in decisions about freedom grant us guidance; in the dangers of freedom grant us protection; in the life of freedom grant us joy; and in the use of freedom grant us vision; for your name's sake. **Amen.**

Latin American Council of Churches, in *The Methodist Church (UK) Prayer Handbook 1993/94*

66g SUITABLE SCRIPTURE PASSAGES

Genesis 6.9–22; 7.24; 8.14–19; 8.1–19; Exodus 2.1–10; 14.10–31; 15.20–21; Job 42.1–6, 10–17; Isaiah 9.2–7; 42.1–9; 43.16–21; 51.1–6; 52.7–10; 58.1–9a; 61.10 – 62.5; 63.7–9; Jeremiah 31.7–14; Wisdom 10.15–21; Psalms 17.1–9; 22.19–28; 27.1, 4–9; 30; 34.1–8; 34.15–22; 37.1–11, 39–40; 40.1–11; 77.1–2, 11–20; 80.1–7, 17–19; 81.1–10; 85.1–2, 8–13; 90.12–17; 91.9–16; 96; 97; 98; 107.23–32; 111; 116.1–9, 12–19; 124; 126; 130; 136; 146.
Matthew 5.21–37; Luke 1.46–55 (Magnificat); 15.1–3, 11b–32; 19.1–10; Acts 4.5–12; Romans 1.1–7; 5.1–11; 6.12–23; 8.14–17; 8.18–25; 10.8b–13; 2 Corinthians 5.16–21; Galatians 4.4–7; 5.1, 13–25; Ephesians 1.3–14; 2.1–10; 2.11–22; Colossians 1.11–20; 1 Timothy 1.12–17; Titus 2.11–14; 3.4–7; Philemon 1–21; Hebrews 2.10–18; 5.1–10; 9.11–14; 9.24–28; 1 John 1.1 – 2.2; 3.1–7; 4.7–21.

66h INTERCESSION

We remember before God those who live in the pit of despair, asking that God will release them from their slavery. We think of those persecuted, imprisoned or tortured because of their beliefs; we think of those exploited, oppressed, discriminated against by their governments. We think of ... Saving God
Set your children free.

We think of those who are destitute, hungry or homeless, with no power to improve their lives; we think of those who are victims of warfare, natural disaster or epidemic. We think of ...
Saving God
Set your children free.

We think of those who are ill, who have chronic diseases or disabilities or who know they are to die; we think of those

whose lives are darkened by worry, depression or loss. We
think of ... Saving God
Set your children free.

And we pray for ourselves, bringing to God the despair we feel
when we are enslaved by the demands of others, by need, by
illness or by wrongdoing. Lord, hear our prayers and release us
into the glorious freedom of your children. In the name of our
crucified and risen Saviour. **Amen.**

Companion to the Lectionary 6, p. 133

66i AT THE PEACE
Christ is our peace. If anyone is in Christ, there is a new
creation. The old has passed away: behold, the new has come.

2 Corinthians 5.17, The Promise of His Glory, p. 237

66j PREFACE
Through Jesus Christ our Lord. By his birth we are reborn. In
his suffering we are freed from sin. By his rising from the dead
we rise to everlasting life. In his return to you in glory we enter
into your heavenly kingdom. And so, we join the angels and
the saints as they sing their unending hymn, for ever praising
you and saying/singing:...

Roman Missal*

66k THANKSGIVING
Almighty God, creator of the world and everything in it, Lord
of heaven and earth, you made the whole human race. You
have shown to us in Christ the mystery of your purpose: you
chose us all in Christ
to praise his glory.
We have heard the word of truth, the good news of salvation,
you have stamped us with the seal of your Spirit of promise:
you chose us all in Christ
to praise his glory.
He is the peace between us, and has broken down the barrier of
hostility. He has made us one new humanity and reconciled us
to you by the cross: you chose us all in Christ
to praise his glory.
Through him we come, by the Spirit, to you, our Father in heav-
en, to whom be all praise and glory now and for ever. **Amen.**

Adapted from Patterns for Worship, 16P20

661 BLESSING

Restore us again, O God of hosts, show us the light of your countenance and we shall be saved. Bless us and keep us, this *day/night* and always. **Amen.**

Celebrating Common Prayer, p. 85

---

67. SERVANT, SERVICE

67a GREETING

Praise our God, all you his servants:
those who fear him, both small and great.

Revelation 19.5, *Patterns for Worship*, 0A15, freely available

67b INVITATION TO CONFESS

We have come together as the family of God in our Father's presence to offer him praise and thanksgiving, to hear and receive his holy word, to bring before him the needs of the world, to ask his forgiveness of our sins, and to seek his grace, that through his Son Jesus Christ we may give ourselves to his service.

If we say we have no sin, we deceive ourselves, and the truth is not in us. If we confess our sins, God is faithful and just, and will forgive us our sins, and cleanse us from all unrighteousness.
Let us confess our sins to almighty God ...

ASB, p. 48

67c CONFESSION

In God there is forgiveness.
Loving and all-seeing God,
forgive us where we have failed to support one another
and to be what we claim to be.
Forgive us where we have failed to serve you;
and where our thoughts and actions
have been contrary to yours,
we ask your pardon. Amen.

A New Zealand Prayer Book, p. 479

67d ABSOLUTION

May the Father of all mercies cleanse us from our sins, and restore us in his service to the praise and glory of his name, through Jesus Christ our Lord. **Amen.**

After Michael Perry

67e COLLECT

Save us, Jesus, from hurrying away, because we do not wish to
help, because we know not how to help, because we dare not.
Inspire us to use our lives serving one another. **Amen.**

A New Zealand Prayer Book, p. 635

67f SUITABLE SCRIPTURE PASSAGES

Isaiah 42.1–9; 49.1–7; 50.4–9a; 51.1–6; 52.13 – 53.12; Psalm 123.
Matthew 25.14–30; Mark 9.30–37; 10.35–45; Luke 17.7–10; John
13.1–17, 31b–35; Philemon.

67g COMMITMENT TO SERVE GOD

Do you renounce Satan and all the spiritual forces of
wickedness that rebel against God?
I renounce them.
Do you renounce the evil powers of this world which corrupt
and destroy the creatures of God?
I renounce them.
Do you renounce all sinful desires that draw you from the love
of God?
I renounce them.

Do you turn to Jesus Christ and accept him as your Saviour?
I do.
Do you put your whole trust in his grace and love?
I do.
Do you promise to follow and obey him as your Lord?
I do.

Do you believe in God the Father?
I believe in God, the Father almighty,
creator of heaven and earth.

Do you believe in Jesus Christ, the Son of God?
I believe in Jesus Christ, his only Son, our Lord.
He was conceived by the power of the Holy Spirit
and born of the Virgin Mary.
He suffered under Pontius Pilate,
was crucified, died, and was buried.
He descended to the dead.
On the third day he rose again.
He ascended into heaven,
and is seated at the right hand of the Father.
He will come to judge the living and the dead.

Do you believe in God the Holy Spirit?
I believe in the Holy Spirit,
the holy catholic Church,
the communion of saints,
the forgiveness of sins,
the resurrection of the body,
and the life everlasting.

Will you continue in the apostles' teaching and fellowship, in the breaking of bread, and in the prayers?
I will, with God's help.
Will you persevere in resisting evil, and, whenever you fall into sin, repent and return to the Lord?
I will, with God's help.
Will you proclaim by word and example the Good News of God in Christ?
I will, with God's help.
Will you seek and serve Christ in all persons, loving your neighbour as yourself?
I will, with God's help.
Will you strive for justice and peace among all people, and respect the dignity of every human being?
I will, with God's help.

Deliver us, O Lord, from the way of sin and death.
Lord, hear our prayer.
Open our hearts to your grace and truth.
Lord, hear our prayer.
Fill us with your holy and life-giving Spirit.
Lord, hear our prayer.
Keep us in the faith and communion of your holy Church.
Lord, hear our prayer.
Teach us to love others in the power of the Spirit.
Lord, hear our prayer.
Send us into the world to witness to your love.
Lord, hear our prayer.
Bring us to the fullness of your peace and glory.
Lord, hear our prayer.

US BCP 1979, pp. 302–6

67h INTERCESSION
We pray for God to fill us with his Spirit, saying Lord, come to bless us
and fill us with your Spirit.

Generous God, we thank you for the *power* of your Holy Spirit. We ask that we may be strengthened to serve you better. Lord, ...

We thank you for the *wisdom* of your Holy Spirit. We ask you to help us understand better your will for us. Lord, ...

We thank you for the *peace* of your Holy Spirit. We ask you to keep us confident of your love wherever you call us. Lord, ...

We thank you for the *healing* of your Holy Spirit. We ask you to bring reconciliation and wholeness where there is division, sickness and sorrow. Lord, ...

We thank you for the *gifts* of your Holy Spirit. We ask you to equip us for the work you have given us. Lord, ...

We thank you for the *fruit* of your Holy Spirit. We ask you to reveal in our lives the love of Jesus. Lord, ...

We thank you for the *breath* of your Holy Spirit given on Easter Day. We ask you to keep the whole Church, living and departed, in the joy of eternal life. Lord, ...

Generous God, you sent your Holy Spirit upon your Messiah at the river Jordan, and upon the disciples in the upper room: in your mercy fill us with your Spirit,

hear our prayer,

and make us one in heart and mind

to serve you in Christ our Lord. Amen.

Kenneth Stevenson for Holy Trinity, Guildford, adapted in *Enriching the Christian Year*, 6C1

67i AT THE PEACE

Jesus said to his disciples, Peace be with you. As the Father has sent me, even so I send you.

John 20.21

67j PREFACE

And now we give you thanks because by your Holy Spirit you anointed your only Son to be servant of all and ordained that he should enter into his kingdom through suffering. In your wisdom and love you call your Church to serve the world, to share in Christ's suffering and to reveal his glory.

ASB, p. 155

67k AFTER COMMUNION

Gracious God, we thank you that in this sacrament you assure us of your goodness and love. Accept our sacrifice of praise and thanksgiving, and help us to grow in love and obedience, that we may serve you in the world, and finally be brought to that table where all your saints feast with you for ever. **Amen.**

A Prayer Book for Australia, p. 143

671 BLESSING
May the God of peace equip you with everything good for
doing his will, and do through you what pleases him. To Christ
be the glory for ever and ever! And may the blessing ...

Hebrews 13.20–21

---

68. THE SHEPHERD, SHEEP, THE LAMB

See also SACRIFICE

68a GREETING
Alleluia! The Lord our God, the almighty, is King!
**Happy are those who are invited
to the Lamb of God's wedding-feast. Alleluia!**

Revelation 19.6, 9

68b INVITATION TO CONFESS
The Son of Man came from heaven to seek and save his lost
sheep. There is more joy in heaven over one sinner who
repents, than over ninety-nine people who think they have no
need of forgiveness. Let us cry out to the Shepherd of our souls.

Michael Counsell, from Luke 19.10; 15.7; 1 Peter 2.25

68c GENERAL CONFESSION
**Almighty and most merciful Father,
we have wandered from your ways like lost sheep,
we have followed too much
the devices and desires of our own hearts,
we have offended against your holy laws.
We have left undone what we ought to have done;
and we have done what we ought not to have done.
Yet, good Lord, have mercy on us;
restore those who are penitent,
according to your promises
declared in Jesus Christ our Lord.
Grant, most merciful Father, for his sake,
that we may live godly, righteous and sober lives,
to the glory of your holy name. Amen**

BCP 1662, modernized in *A Prayer Book for Australia*, p. 4

68d ABSOLUTION
Praise the Lord, for he has heard your cry for mercy: in Christ
you are forgiven, he is your strength and shield – trust in him
and he will help you. Rejoice and give thanks to him in song,

for he is the strength of his people and will be your salvation.
He will save you and bless you; he will be your Shepherd and
care for you for ever. **Amen.**

Psalm 28.6–9, *Bible Praying*, 105

68e COLLECT
God and Father of our Lord Jesus Christ, though your people
walk in the valley of darkness, no evil should they fear; for they
follow in faith the call of the shepherd whom you have sent for
their hope and strength. Attune our minds to the sound of his
voice, lead our steps in the path he has shown, that we may
know the strength of his outstretched arm and enjoy the light of
your presence for ever. **Amen.**

Roman Missal

68f SUITABLE SCRIPTURE PASSAGES
2 Samuel 11.26 – 12.13a; Jeremiah 23.1–6; Ezekiel 34.11–16,
20–24; Psalms 23; 95.1–7a.
Matthew 25.31–46; Mark 6.30–34; Luke 2.1–21; 15.1–10; John
1.29–42; 10.1–10; 10.11–18; 10.22–30; 21.15–17; 1 Peter 2.19–25;
Revelation 5.1–19; 7.9–17; 19.6–10; 21.10, 22 – 22.5.

68g AFFIRMATION OF FAITH
(*May be sung to* Lux Eoi (*Sullivan*), Alleluia (*S. S. Wesley*), *or*
Abbot's Leigh (*C. Taylor*).)
We believe in God the Father,
God Almighty, by whose plan
earth and heaven sprang to being,
all created things began.
We believe in Christ the Saviour,
Son of God in human frame,
virgin-born, the child of Mary
upon whom the Spirit came.

Christ, who on the cross forsaken,
like a lamb to slaughter led,
suffered under Pontius Pilate,
he descended to the dead.
We believe in Jesus risen,
heaven's king to rule and reign,
to the Father's side ascended
till as judge he comes again.

We believe in God the Spirit;
in one church, below, above;

saints of God in one communion,
one in holiness and love.
So by faith, our sins forgiven,
Christ our Saviour, Lord and Friend,
we shall rise with him in glory
to the life that knows no end.

68h INTERCESSION

Lord God, in your love for all nations and races, give to each of them wise and faithful leaders. God of mercy:
Protect them with your love.
Lord God, in your love for Christ's body, the church, give faithfulness and love to all pastors and their congregations. God of mercy:
Protect them with your love.
Lord God, in your love for both the strong and the weak, give us a concern for all in need which brings healing to those who are ill and those who are well. God of mercy:
Protect them with your love.

Companion to the Lectionary 6, p. 209

68i AT THE PEACE

The Good Shepherd leads us into the ways of peace.

Michael Counsell

68j PREFACE

Through Jesus Christ our Lord, our paschal sacrifice. He is still our priest, our advocate who always pleads our cause. Christ is the victim who dies no more, the Lamb, once slain, who lives for ever.

Roman Missal*

68k PRAYER AFTER COMMUNION

Father, eternal shepherd, watch over the flock redeemed by the blood of Christ and lead us to the promised land. **Amen.**

Roman Missal

68l BLESSING

May Jesus, the Good Shepherd, lead you in pleasant pastures all your lives, that having passed through the valley of the shadow of death in his company, you may dwell with him for evermore; and the blessing ...

Michael Counsell, from Psalm 23.2, 4, 6

69. THE SPIRIT, THE ADVOCATE, THE COMFORTER, FRUIT, GIFTS, PENTECOST

See also GUIDANCE

69a OPENING RESPONSES
The Lord is here; **his Spirit is with us.**
We need not fear; **his Spirit is with us.**
We abide in peace; **his Spirit is with us.**
We are immersed in love; **his Spirit is with us.**
We continue in hope; **his Spirit is with us.**
We rejoice in faith; **his Spirit is with us.**
Lord, help us to know that you are here and with us now,
That your Spirit is with us and abides with us always.

The Open Gate, p. 15

69b INVOCATION OF THE HOLY SPIRIT
Come Holy Spirit, Source of Life.
Kindle in us the fire of your love.

Scottish Experimental Liturgy 1977

69c INVITATION TO CONFESS
Hear the teaching of Christ: you shall love the Lord your God with all your heart and with all your soul and with all your mind and with all your strength. This is the first commandment. And a second is this: you shall love your neighbour as yourself.
Spirit of God search our hearts.
Hear the teaching of Christ: a new commandment I give to you, that you love one another as I have loved you.
Spirit of God search our hearts.
(*Silence.*)
Let us confess our sins.

A New Zealand Prayer Book, p. 406

69d CONFESSION
Spirit of joy, through you, Christ lives in us and we in Christ. Forgive us when we forget you and when we fail to live in your joy.
Spirit of God, forgive us and lead us to life in you.
Spirit of love, you bond us in love both to yourself and to those around us in our families, our friends and our communities. Forgive us when we hurt those we love and when we turn away from the love of our friends.
Spirit of God, forgive us and lead us to life in you.

Spirit of peace, uniting us in the church with your life – giving grace and hope. Forgive us when we fail to proclaim your gospel and fail to carry your love into the world.
Spirit of God, forgive us and lead us to life in you.

Go Tell it on the Mountain

69e KYRIE

You raise the dead to life in the Spirit: Lord, have mercy;
Lord, have mercy.
You bring pardon and peace to the broken in heart: Christ, have mercy;
Christ, have mercy.
You make one by your Spirit the torn and divided: Lord, have mercy;
Lord, have mercy.

Portsmouth Cathedral

69f ABSOLUTION

May the Father forgive you by the death of his Son and strengthen you to live in the power of his Spirit all your days. **Amen.**

Patterns for Worship, 9D5

69g COLLECT

Spirit of truth whom the world can never grasp, touch our hearts with the shock of your coming; fill us with desire for your disturbing peace; and fill us with longing to speak your uncontainable word through Jesus Christ. **Amen.**

All Desires Known

69h SUITABLE SCRIPTURE PASSAGES

Genesis 1.1–5; Numbers 11.4–6, 10–16, 24–30; Deuteronomy 34.1–12; 1 Kings 19.1–18; 2 Kings 2.1–2, 6–14; Isaiah 42.1–9; 61.1–4, 8–11; Ezekiel 36.24–28; 37.1–14; Psalms 29; 104.24–34, 35b.
Matthew 3.13–17; 21.33–46; Luke 4.14–21; John 1.29–42; 3.1–17; 5.1–9; 7.37–39; 14.8–21; 15.1–17; 15.26–27; 16.4b–15; 16.12–13; 20.19–22; Acts 1.1–11; 2.1–21; 8.14–17; 10.34–43; 10.44–48; 11.1–18; 19.1–7; Romans 5.1–5; 8.1–11; 8.12–17; 12.1–8; 1 Corinthians 1.1–9; 2.1–12; 12.1–13; 2 Corinthians 1.18–22; 3.1–6; 3.12 – 4.2; 13.11–13; Galatians 5.1, 13–25; Ephesians 4.1–16; 1 John 4.7–21.

69i AFFIRMATION OF FAITH

**We believe in the one Holy Spirit,
giver of different spiritual gifts.
We believe in one Jesus Christ,**

Lord of various kinds of service.
We believe in one heavenly Father,
working in various ways.
We believe in one God,
Father Son and Holy Spirit. Amen

1 Corinthians 12.4, Bible Praying, 210

69j   INTERCESSION

We pray for the peace of the whole world, for the stability of the Holy Churches of God, and for the union of all. We will sing and praise your power.
Kyrie eleison.
We pray for this community, for the whole clergy and people, for all who minister and serve in the name of Christ. We will sing and praise your power.
Kyrie eleison.
We pray for this city and country, for all cities and nations, and for those who in faith dwell therein. We will sing and praise your power.
Kyrie eleison.
O Lord our God, accept this devout supplication of your people who pray unto you; and according to the multitude of your mercies, shed forth your bounties upon us and upon all your people which look unto you for rich mercy. We will sing and praise your power.
Kyrie eleison.
When the Most High came down and confused the tongues, he divided the nations; but when he distributed the tongues of fire, he called all to unity. Therefore, with one voice, we glorify the all-holy Spirit.
Amen. Our Father ...
Blessed are you, O Christ our God, who has revealed the fishermen as most wise by sending down upon them the Holy Spirit; through them you drew the world into your net. O Lover of All People, Glory to you!
Christ is in the midst of us:
He is and shall be.
Amen.

Ion Bria, in Let All the World ...

69k   AT THE PEACE

God has made us one in Christ. He has set his seal upon us, and as a pledge of what is to come has given the Spirit to dwell in our hearts.

2 Corinthians 1.22, The Promise of His Glory, p. 237

691 PREFACE
In you we live and move and have our being. Each day you show us a Father's love; your Holy Spirit, dwelling within us, gives us on earth the hope of unending joy. Your gift of the Holy Spirit, who raised Jesus from the dead, is the foretaste and promise of the paschal feast of heaven.

Roman Missal

69m AFTER COMMUNION
God of power, may the boldness of your Spirit transform us, may the gentleness of your Spirit lead us, may the gifts of your Spirit equip us to serve and worship you now and always. **Amen.**

A New Zealand Prayer Book, p. 541

69n BLESSING
May the God who dances in creation, who embraces us with human love, who shakes our lives like thunder, bless us and drive us out with power to fill the world with her justice. And may the blessing …

All Desires Known

---

70. SUFFERING

See also THE CROSS, HEALING, THE NEEDY

70a RESPONSIVE INTRODUCTION
We are hard pressed on every side, but not crushed; perplexed, but not in despair; persecuted, but not abandoned; struck down, but not destroyed. We always carry around in our body the death of Jesus:
so that the life of Jesus may be revealed.
We fix our eyes not on what is seen:
but on what is unseen and eternal.

2 Corinthians 4.8–10, Patterns for Worship, 5A9, freely available

70b INVITATION TO CONFESS
I set no store by life: I only want to finish the race and complete the task which the Lord Jesus assigned to me, of bearing witness to the gospel of God's grace.

The Promise of His Glory, p. 141

70c CONFESSION
Let us admit to God the sin which always confronts us.
Lord God,
we have sinned against you;

239

we have done evil in your sight.
We are sorry and repent.
Have mercy on us according to your love.
Wash away our wrongdoing and cleanse us from our sin.
Renew a right spirit within us
and restore us to the joy of your salvation,
through Jesus Christ our Lord. Amen.

Psalm 51.1–4,10–12, Stuart Thomas in *Patterns for Worship*, 4C2

70d ABSOLUTION
Receive God's forgiveness through our Lord Jesus Christ: he covers your weaknesses and carries your sorrows; he was pierced for your transgressions and crushed for your iniquities; he took your punishment upon himself to bring you peace: by his wounds you are healed. **Amen.**

Isaiah 53.4–5, *Bible Praying*, 148

70e COLLECT
Give to your suffering Church, O God, the sure knowledge of your ever watching eye. As your people, in their daily lives, bear the cost of following the path which your Son first trod to Calvary, so may they also know his fellowship on that path and at its end find peace and fulfilment in your glorious kingdom. **Amen.**

© The Church Mission Society

70f SUITABLE SCRIPTURE PASSAGES
Exodus 1.8 – 2.10; Job 1.1; 2.1–10; Isaiah 50.4–9a; 52.13 – 53.12; Jeremiah 20.7–13; Lamentations 1.1–6; 3.23–33; Psalms 31.9–16; 79.1–9; 137.
Matthew 2.13–23; 16.21–28; Mark 6.14–29; Luke 2.33–35; Romans 8.14–17; 2 Corinthians 4.13 – 5.1; 5.20b – 6.10; 6.1–13; 12.2–10; Philippians 1.21–30; 3.4b–14; 2 Timothy 2.8–15; Hebrews 1.1–4; 2.5–12; 2.10–18; 12.1–3; 1 Peter 4.12–14; 5.6–11; Revelation 7.9–17.

70g AFFIRMATION OF FAITH
If God is for us, who can be against us?
God did not even keep back his own Son,
but offered him for us all.
He gave us his Son,
will he not also freely give us everything else?
If we, whom God has chosen, were put on trial, no-one would be the prosecutor! God himself declares us not guilty!
Certainly Jesus is on our side:
he died and was raised to life,

and now stands before God pleading our case!
What, then, can separate us from the love of God? Can trouble
tear us from him, or hardship or persecution or hunger or
poverty or danger, or even death?
**No, in all these things we have complete victory
with the help of Jesus, who loved us!**
For I am certain that nothing can separate us from God's love:
nothing that happens to us while we are alive or when we die,
no evil powers,
nothing in the present or the future,
in the world above or the world below –
**nothing in all creation
can ever separate us from the love of God,
which is ours through Christ Jesus our Lord. Amen.**

Michael Counsell, from Romans 8.31–39

70h INTERCESSION
On the battlefields of war-torn …,
Be present, suffering Lord.
Where AIDS lays waste the bodies of the young,
Be present, suffering Lord.
At the table of hungry children in Asia,
Be present, suffering Lord.
Where work is hard and cruel in South America,
Be present, suffering Lord.
When old clothes refuse to keep out the Arctic cold,
Be present, suffering Lord.
In the face of racism and ethnic cleansing,
Be present, suffering Lord.
When faith is met by hate and love by rejection,
Be present, suffering Lord.
In our small sufferings,
Be present, Lord of glory. Amen.

© The Church Mission Society

70i AT THE PEACE
The God of hope fill you with all joy and peace in believing, so
that you may abound in hope through the power of the Holy
Spirit.

Romans 15.13

70j PREFACE
We give you thanks, O God, through your beloved Servant,
Jesus Christ. It is he whom you have sent in these last times to
save us and redeem us, and be the messenger of your will.

He is your Word, inseparable from you, through whom you made all things and in whom you take delight.

You sent him from heaven into the Virgin's womb, where he was conceived, and took flesh. Born of the Holy Spirit and the Virgin, he was revealed as your Son.

In fulfilment of your will he stretched out his hands in suffering, to release from suffering those who place their hope in you, and so he won for you a holy people. Of his own free choice he was handed over to his passion in order to make an end of death and to shatter the chains of the evil one; to trample underfoot the powers of hell and to lead the righteous into light; to establish the boundaries of death and to manifest the resurrection.

Hippolytus, ICEL

70k QUESTIONS TO CHRIST

Lord, what is the cost of one person's freedom?
Lord, what is the cost of safety for a child?
Lord, what does it cost to give a young man a future?
Lord, what does it cost to preserve a woman's dignity?
Lord, why did you pay so much for the words you spoke?
Lord, why were your actions for justice so expensive?
Lord, why did you pay so dearly for your dreams?
Lord, did you pay all that for me?
Lord, how much must I pay to follow you?
Amen.

© The Church Mission Society

70l BLESSING

To God be glory; to the angels honour; to Satan confusion; to the cross reverence; to the Church exaltation; to the departed quickening; to the penitent acceptance; to the sick and infirm recovery and healing; and to the four quarters of the world great peace and tranquillity; and on us who are weak and sinful may the compassion and mercies of our God come and overshadow us; and the blessing ...

Syriac prayer

71 THANKS, GRATITUDE

See also HARVEST

71a GREETING

Great is the Lord and worthy of all praise.
Amen! Praise and glory and wisdom,
thanksgiving and honour, power and might,
be to our God for ever and ever! Amen.

Revelation 5.13, A New Zealand Prayer Book, p. 35

71b INVITATION TO CONFESS

Happy are those whose wrong deeds are forgiven, whose sin is
pardoned.

Psalm 32.1

71c CONFESSION

Jesus said, Happy are those whose spirit is that of the poor.
We confess that we have behaved as though we were rich.
God help us to change.
Yours is the Kingdom of Heaven!
Jesus said, Happy are those who mourn.
We confess that we have cut ourselves off from the
sorrowful. God help us to change.
God will comfort you!
Jesus said, Happy are those who are humble.
We confess that we have been proud. God help us to change.
You will receive what God has promised!
Jesus said, Happy are those who hunger for justice.
We confess that we have condoned oppression. God help us
to change.
You will be satisfied!
Jesus said, Happy are those who are merciful.
We confess that we have been slow to forgive. God help us
to change.
God will be merciful to you!
Jesus said, Happy are those whose heart is pure.
We confess that our motives are mixed. God help us to
change.
You will see God!
Jesus said, Happy are those who work for peace.
We confess that we have left that to others. God help us to
change.
You are the children of God!
Jesus said, Happy are those who are persecuted.

We confess that we have kept silent to avoid mockery. God help us to change.
Rejoice and leap for joy! By your repentance you have chosen to receive the blessings which Jesus has promised.
Amen. Let us give thanks to God for he is good, and his mercy endures for ever.

Michael Counsell, Matthew 5.3–10; Psalm 107.1

71d ABSOLUTION
God desires that none should perish, but that all should turn to Christ, and live. In response to his call we acknowledge our sins. God pardons those who humbly repent, and truly believe the gospel. Therefore we have peace with God, through Jesus Christ. **Amen.**

A Prayer Book for Australia, p. 21

71e COLLECT
You have given so much to us, O Lord, give one thing more, a grateful heart, a heart whose pulse may be your praise; for Christ's sake. **Amen.**

George Herbert

71f SUITABLE SCRIPTURE PASSAGES
Isaiah 63.7–9; Psalms 16; 26.1–8; 50.7–15; 65; 89.1–4, 15–18; 105.1–6, 16–22, 45b; 107.1–3, 17–22; 116.1–4, 12–19; 137.1–5; 138; 144.2–11.
Mark 5.18–20; Luke 17.11–19; Romans 7.15–25a; 1 Corinthians 1.3–9; Ephesians 1.3–14; Colossians 3.12–17; 1 Thessalonians 1.1–10.

71g ENJOYMENT OF THE WORLD
Your enjoyment of the world is never right, till every morning you awake in heaven; see yourself in your Father's palace; and look upon the skies, the earth, and the air as celestial joys: having such a reverent esteem of all, as if you were among the angels. You never enjoy the world aright, till the sea itself flows in your veins, till you are clothed with the heavens, and crowned with the stars: and perceive yourself to be the sole heir of the whole world, and more than so, because people are in it who are every one sole heirs as well as you. Till you can sing and rejoice and delight in God, as misers do in gold, and kings in sceptres, you never enjoy the world. **Amen.**

Thomas Traherne

71h INTERCESSION FOR THE NATION
Almighty God, giver of all good things: We thank you for the natural majesty and beauty of this land. They restore us, though we often destroy them.
Heal us.
We thank you for the great resources of this nation. They make us rich, though we often exploit them.
Forgive us.
We thank you for the men and women who have made this country strong. They are models for us, though we often fall short of them.
Inspire us.
We thank you for the torch of liberty which has been lit in this land. It has drawn people from every nation, though we have often hidden from its light.
Enlighten us.
We thank you for the faith we have inherited in all its rich variety. It sustains our life, though we have been faithless again and again.
Renew us.
Help us, O Lord, to finish the good work here begun. Strengthen our efforts to blot out ignorance and prejudice, and to abolish poverty and crime. And hasten the day when all our people, with many voices in one united chorus, will glorify your holy Name. **Amen.**

US BCP 1979, p. 838

71i AT THE PEACE
All praise to God, who guides our feet into the ways of peace!

Luke 1.68, 79

71j LONGER PREFACE
God our maker, Abba, Father, we thank you for your glory, the majesty and splendour of the universe, this world, its many wonders and all its people. Even when we turn from you in sin, you reach out to us in healing love. In Jesus Christ you showed your full glory. He defeated sin and death on the cross, and by his resurrection he gave us life and joy. He united us in his Spirit, and brought us home to you. For such great love, we thank and praise you with all creation and all the powers of heaven, for ever praising you and saying/singing ...

Diocese of Southwark*

71k A LITANY OF THANKSGIVING
Let us give thanks to God our Father for all his gifts so freely bestowed upon us.

245

For the beauty and wonder of your creation, in earth and sky
and sea,
We thank you, Lord.
For all that is gracious in the lives of men and women,
revealing the image of Christ,
We thank you, Lord.
For our daily food and drink, our homes and families, and our
friends,
We thank you, Lord.
For minds to think, and hearts to love, and hands to serve,
We thank you, Lord.
For health and strength to work, and leisure to rest and play,
We thank you, Lord.
For the brave and courageous, who are patient in suffering and
faithful in adversity,
We thank you, Lord.
For all valiant seekers after truth, liberty and justice,
We thank you, Lord.
For the communion of saints, in all times and places,
We thank you, Lord.
Above all, we give you thanks for the great mercies and
promises given to us in Christ Jesus our Lord;
**To him be praise and glory, with you, O Father, and the Holy
Spirit, now and for ever. Amen.**

US BCP 1967, p. 837

711 BLESSING
Thanks be to God for his indescribable gifts; and the blessing ...

2 Corinthians 9.15

---

72. THE TRANSFIGURATION, GLORY

72a GREETING
Glory to the Father, and to the Son, and to the Holy Spirit:
**as it was in the beginning, is now, and will be for ever.
Amen.**

ICET

The Lord of glory be with you.
The Lord bless you.

Patterns for Worship, 0A8, source not identified

72b INVITATION TO CONFESS

When Christ appears we shall be like him, because we shall see him as he is. As he is pure, all who have grasped this hope make themselves pure. So let us confess our sins that mar his image in us.

1 John 3.2–3, Michael Perham, Enriching the Christian Year, 8A1

72c KYRIE

Your unfailing kindness, O Lord, is in the heavens, and your faithfulness reaches to the clouds: Lord have mercy.
Lord, have mercy.
Your righteousness is like the strong mountains, and your justice as the great deep: Christ, have mercy.
Christ, have mercy.
For with you is the well of life: and in your light shall we see light: Lord, have mercy.
Lord, have mercy

Psalm 36.5–6, 9, Michael Perham, Enriching the Christian Year, 8B1

72d ABSOLUTION

May the God of all healing and forgiveness draw *us* to himself, that *we* may behold the glory of his Son, the Word made flesh, and be cleansed from all *our* sins through Jesus Christ our Lord. **Amen.**

Kenneth Stevenson, Patterns for Worship, 2D1

72e COLLECT

Almighty God, on the holy mount you revealed to chosen witnesses your well–beloved Son, wonderfully transfigured: mercifully deliver us from the darkness of this world, and change us into his likeness from glory to glory; through Jesus Christ our Lord, who lives and reigns with you and the Holy Spirit, one God, now and for ever. **Amen.**

Canadian Book of Alternative Services, p. 418

72f SUITABLE SCRIPTURE PASSAGES

Exodus 24.12–18; 34.29–35; 2 Kings 2.1–12; Ezekiel 43.27 – 44.4; Daniel 7.9–10, 13–14; Psalms 2; 50.1–6; 96; 99.
Matthew 17.1–9; Mark 9.2–10; Luke 9.28–36; John 13.21–32; 2 Corinthians 3.12 – 4.2; 4.3–6; 1 Peter 4.12–14; 5.6–11; 2 Peter 1.16–19.

72g AFFIRMATION OF FAITH
We believe in God
who has spoken to us by his Son, Jesus Christ,
whom he appointed heir of all things,

through whom he made the worlds.
Christ is the radiance of God's glory,
the image of his being,
who upholds all things by his powerful word. Amen.

Hebrews 1.2–3, *Bible Praying*, 225

72h INTERCESSION

Lord of glory, it is good that you are here. In peace we make our prayer to you. In trust we confirm our faith in you. Help us to set our faces steadfastly where you would go with us. Lord, look with favour.
Lord, transfigure and heal.

Lord of glory, look with favour on your Church, proclaiming your beloved Son to the world and listening to the promptings of his Spirit … May it be renewed in holiness that it may reflect your glory. Lord, look with favour.
Lord, transfigure and heal.

Lord of glory, look with favour on the nations of the world, scarred by hatred, strife and war, and crying out to be changed by the touch of your hand … May they hear the good news like a lamp shining in a murky place. Lord, look with favour.
Lord, transfigure and heal.

Lord of glory, look with favour on those in need and distress, suffering as your Son has suffered and waiting for the salvation you promise … May the day break and Christ the Morning Star bring them the light of his presence. Lord, look with favour.
Lord, transfigure and heal.

Lord of glory, it is good if we suffer with you so that we shall be glorified with you. According to your promise bring all Christ's brothers and sisters … to see him with their own eyes in majesty and to be changed into his likeness from glory to glory. To him be praise, dominion and worship now and for all eternity. **Amen.**

Michael Perham, *Enriching the Christian Year*, 8C1

72i AT THE PEACE

Christ will transfigure our human body and give it a form like that of his own glorious body. We are the Body of Christ. We share his peace.

Philippians 3.21, Michael Perham, *Enriching the Christian Year*, 8G1

72j PREFACE

Before his passion you revealed the glory of Christ to his disciples, and your voice from heaven declared him your beloved Son.

The New Zealand Eucharistic Liturgy 1984

72k AFTER COMMUNION
Holy God, may we see your glory in the face of Jesus Christ.
May we who are partakers of his table reflect his life in word
and deed, that all the world may know his power to change
and save. We ask this in his name, Jesus Christ our Lord. **Amen.**

Canadian Book of Alternative Services, p. 419

72l BLESSING
Christ Jesus, the splendour of the Father and the image of his
being, draw you to himself that you may live in his light and
share his glory; and the blessing ...

Michael Perham, Enriching the Christian Year, 8E1

---

73. THE TRINITY, THE GREATNESS AND HOLINESS OF GOD AND OF JESUS

73a GREETING
The grace of our Lord Jesus Christ, and the love of God, and the
fellowship of the Holy Spirit, be with you all.
And also with you.

2 Corinthians 13.13

73b INVITATION TO CONFESS
Holy, holy, holy: when our eyes have seen the Lord of hosts we
echo the words of Isaiah, 'Woe is me! I am doomed.' We long
for the fire of God's cleansing to touch our unclean lips, for our
iniquity to be removed and our sin wiped out. So we meet
Father, Son and Holy Spirit with confession on our lips.

Isaiah 6.5, 7, Patterns for Worship, 9B11

73c KYRIE
Father, you come to meet us when we return to you. Lord, have
mercy:
Lord, have mercy.
Jesus, you died on the cross for our sins. Lord, have mercy:
Christ, have mercy.
Spirit, you give us life and peace. Lord, have mercy:
Lord have mercy.

Michael Perham, Enriching the Christian Year, 7B1

73d ABSOLUTION
God the Father says, your guilt is gone, and your sins are
forgiven. **Amen.**

God the Son says, I do not condemn you, go and sin no more.
Amen.
God the Spirit declares that we are God's children. **Amen.**

Michael Counsell, from Isaiah 6.7; John 8.11; Romans 8.16

73e COLLECT
O God our mystery, you bring us to life, call us to freedom, and
move between us with love. May we so participate in the dance
of your trinity, that our lives may resonate with you, now and
for ever. **Amen.**

All Desires Known

73f SUITABLE SCRIPTURE PASSAGES
Genesis 18.1–15; 1 Kings 18.20–21, 30–39; Job 23.1–9, 16–17;
38.1–11; Proverbs 8.1–4, 22–31; Isaiah 6.1–8; 40.12–17; 40.21–31;
44.6–8; Psalms 8; 19; 29; 48; 62.5–12; 77.1–2, 11–20; 96.1–9; 138.
Matthew 28.16–20; Mark 4.35–41; Luke 8.22–25; John 3.1–17;
10.22–30; 16.12–13; Romans 5.1–5; 8.12–17; 2 Corinthians
13.11–13; Revelation 1.4b–8.

73g FROM THE ATHANASIAN CREED
We proclaim the Church's faith in Jesus Christ:
We believe and declare that our Lord Jesus Christ,
the Son of God, is both divine and human.
God, of the being of the Father,
the only Son from before time began;
human from the being of his mother, born in the world.
Fully God and fully human;
human in both mind and body.
As God he is equal to the Father,
as human he is less than the Father.
Although he is both divine and human
he is not two beings but one Christ.
One, not by turning God into flesh,
but by taking humanity into God.
Truly one, not by mixing humanity with Godhead,
but by being one person.
For as mind and body form one human being
so the one Christ is both divine and human.
The Word became flesh and lived among us;
we have seen his glory,
the glory of the only Son from the Father,
full of grace and truth.

Patterns for Worship, 2F4

73h INTERCESSION

We come boldly to the throne of grace, praying to the almighty
God, Father, Son and holy Spirit for mercy and grace, saying
we plead before your throne in heaven.

Father of heaven, whose love profound
a ransom for our souls has found:
We pray for the world, created by your love, for its nations and
governments ... Extend to them your peace, pardoning love,
mercy and grace.
we plead before your throne in heaven.

Almighty Son, incarnate Word,
our Prophet, Priest, Redeemer, Lord:
We pray for the Church, created for your glory, for its ministry
to reflect those works of yours ... Extend to us your salvation,
growth, mercy and grace.
we plead before your throne in heaven.

Eternal Spirit, by whose breath
the soul is raised from sin and death:
We pray for families and individuals, created in your image, for
the lonely, the bereaved, the sick and the dying ... Breathe on
them the breath of life and bring them to your mercy and grace.
we plead before your throne in heaven.

Mysterious Godhead, three in one,
Jehovah – Father, Spirit, Son:
We pray for ourselves, for your Church, for all whom we
remember before you ... Bring us all to bow before your throne
in heaven, to receive life and pardon, mercy and grace for all
eternity as we worship you, saying
Holy, holy, holy Lord,
God of power and might,
heaven and earth are full of your glory.
Hosanna in the highest. Amen.

Trevor Lloyd, *Enriching the Christian Year*, 7C1, from Edward Cowper

73i AT THE PEACE

Peace to you from God our heavenly Father. Peace from his Son
Jesus Christ who is our peace. Peace from the Holy Spirit the
lifegiver.

Patterns for Worship, 9R10

73j PREFACE

Through him you have revealed to us your glory in the community of your love, three persons, one God, ever to be worshipped and adored.

A Prayer Book for Australia, p. 158

73k CANDLE-LIGHTING

1st Leader:

> I will light a light
> In the name of the Maker
> Who lit the world
> And breathed the breath of life for me.

(*A candle is lit and placed centrally*.)

2nd Leader:

> I will light a light
> In the name of the Son
> Who saved the world
> And stretched out his hand to me.

(*A candle is lit and placed centrally*.)

3rd Leader:

> I will light a light
> In the name of the Spirit
> Who encompasses the world
> And blesses my soul with yearning.

(*A candle is lit and placed centrally*.)

All:

> **We will light three lights**
> **For the Trinity of love:**
> **God above us,**
> **God beside us,**
> **God beneath us;**
> **The beginning,**
> **The end,**
> **The everlasting One**.

A Wee Worship Book, p. 37

73l BLESSING

May God whom Jesus called Abba embrace you in love for ever; may God the Servant bear your burdens with you; may God the Spirit grant you life in one another: so may the blessing of God, Abba, Servant, Spirit, be with you always. **Amen.**

A New Zealand Prayer Book, p. 545*

74. THE TRUTH, THE WAY,
THE TRUTH AND THE LIFE

See also FAITH, GUIDANCE, LIFE

74a OPENING RESPONSE
Whatever is true, whatever is noble, whatever is just and pure,
whatever is lovable and gracious, whatever is excellent and
admirable,
We will think on these things.

Philippians 4.8

74b INVITATION TO CONFESS
Friends in Christ, we come together to meet with God, and to
take our part in the building up of his Church. We will lift up
our hearts in thanks and praise, hear from God's holy word,
and pray for this world, and for ourselves. [Today ...] The Bible
tells us to approach God confidently, through our Lord Jesus
Christ. As we do so, we must confess our sins, seeking forgiveness through God's boundless goodness and mercy.
If we say that we have no sin, we deceive ourselves, and
the truth is not in us. But if we confess our sins, God is faithful
and just, and will forgive our sins and cleanse us from all
unrighteousness.
(*Silence.*)
So let us draw near to God with sincerity and confidence, and
pray together ...

1 John 1.8–9, A Prayer Book for Australia, p. 20

74c CONFESSION
Lord God,
In Jesus, you came in the body:
Flesh of our flesh, bone of our bone,
One with us in searing pain and delirious laughter.
We thank you that you did not remain an idea,
    even a religious idea,
But walked, wept and washed feet among us.
By your love,
Change our ideas, especially our religious ideas,
Into living signs of your work and will.
Through our lives and by our prayers,
your kingdom come.

A Wee Worship Book, p. 25

74d ABSOLUTION
This is a true saying, and worthy of belief by all people, that
Christ Jesus came into the world to save sinners. Let not his
coming here be in vain: believe that you have been saved from
your sin. **Amen.**

Michael Counsell, 1 Timothy 1.15

74e COLLECT
O Lord Jesus Christ, the Way, the Truth and the Life, grant that
we may never stray from you who are the Way, nor distrust you
who are the Truth, nor rest in any thing other than you, who are
the Life. Teach us by your Holy Spirit what to believe, what to
do, and wherein to take our rest. For your own name's sake we
ask it, O Jesus Christ our Lord. **Amen.**

Desiderius Erasmus

74f SUITABLE SCRIPTURE PASSAGES
Isaiah 59.9–15; Jeremiah 9.1–3; Psalm 25.1–10.
Matthew 5.21–37; John 1.1–14; 8.21–32; 14.1–17; 15.26–27,
16.4b–15; 2 Corinthians 3.12 – 4.2; Ephesians 4.13–16;
Philippians 4.8–9; 1 John 5.1–6.

74g AFFIRMATION OF FAITH
We believe in Jesus Christ,
the Son of God,
and we have this truth in our hearts:
God has given us eternal life,
and this life is in his Son.
Whoever has the Son has life;
whoever does not have the Son of God
does not have life.
We believe
that the Son of God has come,
and has given us wisdom
to know the true God. Amen.

1 John 5.10–12, 20, *Bible Praying*, 229

74h INTERCESSION
O Lord, voices surround us, always clamouring, directing,
imploring, accusing; and our own voices are too strident. May
we be quiet and listen, so that you may speak.
In miracle; in the wonders of human courage and hope and
endurance and sacrifice that we meet in ordinary people.
O Lord, speak to us:
help us to listen.

In Spirit; in the mysteries beyond our comprehension, in the
faith that defies all mortal order, in the resurrection truth.
O Lord, speak to us:
help us to listen.
In joy; in laughter, in human warmth, in triumph over pain, in
the experience of beauty. O Lord, speak to us:
help us to listen.
Speak, O Lord, that we may listen,
and tell what great things you have done for us,
in Jesus' name. Amen.

Editors, *Prayers for the People*, 25.41

74i AT THE PEACE
Grace, mercy and peace from God the Father and from Jesus
Christ, the Father's Son, be with you in truth and love. **Amen.**

2 John 3, *Bible Praying*, 26

74j LONGER PREFACE
It is the joy of our salvation, God of the universe, to give you
thanks through Jesus Christ. You said, 'Let there be light'; there
was light. Your light shines on in our darkness. For you the
earth has brought forth life in all its forms. You have created us
to hear your Word, to do your will and to be fulfilled in your
love. It is right to thank you. You sent your Son to be for us the
way we need to follow and the truth we need to know. You sent
your Son to give his life to release us from our sin. His cross has
taken our guilt away. You send your Holy Spirit to strengthen
and to guide, to warn and to revive your Church. Therefore
with all your witnesses who surround us on every side, countless as heaven's stars, we praise you for our creation and our
calling, with loving and joyful hearts, for ever praising you and
saying / singing ...

A New Zealand Prayer Book, p. 485*

74k AFTER COMMUNION
Bountiful God, at this table you graciously feed us with the
bread of life and the cup of eternal salvation. May we who have
reached out our hands to receive this sacrament be strengthened in your service; we who have sung your praises tell of
your glory and truth in our lives; we who have seen the greatness of your love see you face to face in your kingdom and
come to worship you with all your saints for ever. **Amen.**

A Prayer Book for Australia, p. 143, from the *Malabar Liturgy*

741 A MORNING BLESSING
Lord, set your blessing on us
As we begin this day together.
Confirm in us the truth by which we rightly live;
Confront us with the truth from which we wrongly turn.
We ask not for what we want
But for what you know we need,
As we offer this day and ourselves for you and to you
Through Jesus Christ our Saviour.
Amen.

A Wee Worship Book, p. 16

75. THE UNITY OF THE CHURCH

See also THE CHURCH

75a SENTENCE
Jesus said 'I am the good shepherd. There are other sheep of
mine that I must also bring home. Then all will listen to my
voice, and there shall be one flock under the one Shepherd.'

John 10.16

75b INVITATION TO CONFESS
We have come together as God's family to offer him our peni-
tence and praise, and to pray for the recovery of the unity of
Christ's Church and for the renewal of our common life. The
Lord is full of gentleness and compassion. Let us then ask his
forgiveness of our sins.

The Promise of His Glory, p. 246

75c CONFESSION
**We confess to God almighty, the Father, the Son and the Holy
Spirit, and to all our fellow members in the Body of Christ,
that we have sinned in thought, word and deed, and in what
we have left undone.**
(*Silence.*)
**Most loving Father, where sin has divided and scattered, may
your love make one again; where sin has brought weakness,
may your power heal and strengthen; where sin has brought
death, may your Spirit raise to new life.**

Scottish Experimental Liturgy 1977

75d KYRIE

God the Father of all, your Church is not catholic because we do not seek to comprehend within one family all the ways in which you are understood. Forgive us and make us truly catholic. Lord, have mercy:
Lord, have mercy.

God the Son who died for all, your Church is not evangelical because the gospel of your universal love is concealed by our narrowness and prejudice. Forgive us and make us truly evangelical. Christ, have mercy:
Christ, have mercy.

God the Spirit, you work through all and are in all. Your Church is not charismatic because we have pretended that our gifts are better than other people's, and have not made them subservient to the best gift of love. Forgive us and make us truly charismatic. Lord, have mercy:
Lord, have mercy.

Michael Counsell

75e ABSOLUTION

God through his forgiveness draws you closer to him, and in him closer to one another. **Amen.**

Michael Counsell

75f COLLECT

**Lord God, we thank you for calling us into the company
of those who trust in Christ
and seek to obey his will.
May your Spirit guide and strengthen us
in mission and service to your world;
for we are strangers no longer
but pilgrims together on the way to your Kingdom. Amen**

The Inter-Church Process

75g SUITABLE SCRIPTURE PASSAGES

Jeremiah 33.6–9a; Ezekiel 37.15–28; Psalm 133.
John 15.1–5; 17.11b–26; Romans 10.8b–13; 12.3–21; 1 Corinthians 1.10–18; 3.1–9; 10.14–17; 12.1–11; 12.12–31a; Galatians 3.23–29; Ephesians 1.15–23; 2.11–22; 4.1–16; 5.21–32; Philippians 4.1–9; Colossians 1.15–28; 2.16–19; 3.1–17.

75h THE CALL TO UNITY

It is our conviction that, as a matter of policy at all levels and in all places, our churches must now move from cooperation to clear commitment to each other, in search of the unity for which Christ prayed and in common evangelism and service of the world.

By God's grace will you do your best to hold the Christian faith
and to continue in the Apostles' teaching and fellowship?
We will.
Will you, together with other Christians in this place and
community proclaim the good news by word and deed,
serving Christ in all people?
We will.
Will you, together with other Christians in this place and
community, work for justice and peace, honouring God in all
that he has made?
We will.
Will you, together with other Christians in this place and
community, pray and work for the unity of all Christian
people?
We will.
As the seed grows secretly in the earth,
as the yeast rises in the dough,
may the power of God be at work in us.
May we be like a city set on a hill,
like a lamp shining in the darkness.
May we witness together with all Christians
to the glory of God and the fulfilment of his Kingdom.

Council of Churches for Britain and Ireland

75i INTERCESSION
In faith let us pray to God our Father, his Son Jesus Christ, and
the Holy Spirit.
Kyrie eleison.
For the Church of God throughout the world, let us invoke the
Spirit.
Kyrie eleison.
For the leaders of the nations, that they may establish and
defend justice and peace, let us pray for the wisdom of God.
Kyrie eleison.
For those who suffer oppression or violence, let us invoke the
power of the Deliverer.
Kyrie eleison.
That the churches may discover again their visible unity in the
one baptism which incorporates them in Christ, let us pray for
the love of Christ.
Kyrie eleison.
That the churches may attain communion in the eucharist
around one table, let us pray for the strength of Christ.
Kyrie eleison.

That the churches may recognize each other's ministries in the service of their one Lord, let us pray for the peace of Christ.
Kyrie eleison.
(*Free prayer of the congregation may follow.*)
Into your hands, O Lord, we commend all for whom we pray, trusting in your mercy; through your Son, Jesus Christ, our Lord. **Amen.**

Lima Liturgy

75j AT THE PEACE
Blessed be Christ the Prince of Peace
who breaks down the walls that divide.
The peace of God be always with you.
Praise to Christ who unites us in peace.

A New Zealand Prayer Book, p. 485

75k PREFACE
And now we give you thanks because of the unity that you have given us in your Son and that you are the God and Father of us all, above all and through all and in all.

ASB, p. 158

75l THANKSGIVING
We give you thanks, almighty God, we praise you for your work within this world through our Lord Jesus Christ. Because even in our divided humanity, separated from each other as we are, we experience now and then the reconciliation which comes from you. Your Spirit moves the hearts of enemies who find a way to speak to each other, of adversaries who finally shake hands, of people looking for a common ground for understanding. It is your work whenever peace ends a time of hatred, wherever vengeance is overcome by the Spirit of forgiveness. Our thanks to you and praise can never end. We ask: accept us in your Son; grant us, in this holy meal, the Spirit he has promised: the Spirit of unity that takes away whatever divides us, the Spirit that keeps us in communion with all your people on earth. Make your Church to become a sign of unity among all people, an instrument of your peace. **Amen.**

Roman Missal

75m BLESSING
May God, who gives patience and encouragement, give you a spirit of unity to live in harmony as you follow Jesus Christ, so that with one voice you may glorify the God and Father of our Lord Jesus Christ; and the blessing ...

Romans 15.5–6, Patterns for Worship, 12T33*

76. WISDOM

76a RESPONSE
To those who are called,
**Christ is the power of God
and the wisdom of God.**

1 Corinthians 1.24

76b A FOOL'S PRAYER
Lord, you call us to confess our sins,
but I don't often tell you what a fool I've been.
It would be a relief to tell someone.
So many things I could have done for you,
but I failed, by making senseless decisions.
I tried to speak your word,
but it was misunderstood, because I expressed it foolishly.
I have harmed other people,
when I was too stupid to foresee the effects of what I had done;
and broken fellowship with them,
through not knowing how silly my speech would sound.
Lord, how can you love such a fool?
And yet, foolish as it may seem,
I really believe you do love me.
Do you? You do! Thank God. **Amen.**

Michael Counsell

76c KYRIE
God of our ancestors, merciful Ruler, you made all things with
your word, and ordained the human race through your
wisdom, that we should have dominion over the creatures
which you have made; we confess that we have misused that
authority; Lord, have mercy.
Lord, have mercy.
Jesus Christ, the wisdom of God and the power of God, you
redeemed us that we might order the world according to
equity and righteousness, and execute justice with an upright
heart; yet we have withheld justice from those who cry out for
it; Christ, have mercy.
Christ, have mercy.
Holy Spirit, you have sent Wisdom out of your holy heavens,
and from the throne of your glory, that she may labour with us
and know what is pleasing to you, yet we have refused to
accept the spirit of wisdom; Lord, have mercy.
Lord, have mercy.

Michael Counsell, from *The Wisdom of Solomon*, Chapter 9

76d ABSOLUTION

God's wisdom is pure, peaceable, gentle, and full of mercy; God's wise plans for you begin by mercifully forgiving all your sins. **Amen.**

Michael Counsell, from James 3.17

76e COLLECT

Hidden God, whose wisdom compels our love and unsettles all our values; fill us with desire to search for her truth, that we may transform the world becoming fools for her sake, through Jesus Christ. **Amen.**

All Desires Known

76f SUITABLE SCRIPTURE PASSAGES

1 Kings 2.10–12; 3.3–14; 3.5–12; Proverbs 1.20–33; 8.1–21; 8.22–36; 9.1–6; Ecclesiastes 1.2, 12–14; 2.18–23; Wisdom 6.12–16; 6.17–20; 7.26 – 8.1; 10.15–21; Ecclesiasticus 24.1–12; Baruch 3.9–15, 32 – 4.4; Psalms 49.1–12; 111.

Matthew 25.1–13; Mark 9.2–9; Luke 12.13–21; 1 Corinthians 1.18–31; 2.1–12; Ephesians 5.15–20; James 3.13 – 4.3, 7–8a.

76g AFFIRMATION OF FAITH

Leader	We believe in God
All	**Who made the world, loves it and smiles on it;**
Women	Who created human beings each to be different and asked them to get on with each other;
Men	Who took the risk of leaving us alone, knowing that one day our differences might threaten the earth's safety;
All	**who trusts us in full knowledge of our frailness.**
Leader	We believe in Jesus Christ
Women	Who came among us insignificantly, Who grew among us uneventfully, Who walked among us incognito;
Men	Who, to change the world, became redundant and called others away from security;
Women	Who befriended those whose company would discredit him;
Men	Who pardoned those who deserved to be condemned;
Women	Who healed those who were hopeless cases;
Men	Who spoke the deepest truths in the language of the living room;
Leader	who contradicted common sense by accepting the cross and taking on the grave and being liberated to live on the third day;

All   **Who calls us, now as then,**
               to a life which is absurd
               by the standards of the world.

Leader We believe in the Holy Spirit

All   **through whom God surprises, disappoints,**
               cajoles and questions us;

Women Who is the bringer of strength
               and source of humour;

Men   Who leads us to discover
               the truth we avoid;

Leader who is a paradox –
               ever present yet unpredictable.

All   **And we believe**
               that the foolishness of God
               is wiser than the wisdom of the world:
               and we rejoice
               that God has made it so.

A Wee Worship Book, p. 41

76h PRAYER FOR WISDOM

Grant unto us, O God, to find the wisdom which is from above. Give us the wisdom which is pure, that we may never use our minds to think or plan an evil thing; the wisdom which is peaceable that we may live in friendship with all and in bitterness with none; the wisdom which is gentle, that we may ever be quicker to sympathise than to criticise, and to praise than to condemn; the wisdom which is open to reason, that we may not be stubborn and self-willed, but willing to listen to and to obey the truth; the wisdom which is full of mercy, that we may be as kind to others as we would wish them to be to us; the wisdom which is full of good fruits, that our lives may be lovely with the beauty of holiness. **Amen.**

Epilogues and Prayers, p. 188*

76i AT THE PEACE

Happy are those who find wisdom, and who gain understanding; her ways are ways of pleasantness, and all her paths are peace.

Proverbs 3.13, 17

76j PREFACE

When your children sinned and wandered far from your friendship, you reunited them with yourself through the blood of your Son and the power of the Holy Spirit. You gather them into your Church to be one as you, Father, are one with your

Son and the Holy Spirit. You call them to be your people, to praise your wisdom in all your works. You make them the body of Christ and the dwelling-place of the Holy Spirit.

*Roman Missal**

76k THANKSGIVING

Blessed are you, Sovereign God, source of light, giver of all things good! In your presence wisdom has prepared a feast; she calls the foolish to leave the way of darkness; she welcomes us with truth and goodness. In Jesus your light has shone out; his cross has brought peace to the sinful. Your Spirit has opened our hearts; with all the saints we share your light. Refuge of the weary, hope of the dying, blessed are you, Sovereign God, light in darkness. **Amen.**

The Promise of His Glory, p. 18

76l BLESSING

May holy Wisdom, kind to humanity, steadfast, sure and free, the breath of the power of God; may she who makes all things new, in every age, enter our souls, and make us friends of God. And may the blessing ...

*All Desires Known**

---

77. WOMEN

See also MARY THE VIRGIN, MOTHERING SUNDAY

77a RESPONSE

Lord, who shall live in your house,
who shall share your holy home?
**Those who lead an unselfish life,
and do the things that are right,
and speak the truth from their heart.**

Psalm 15.1–2

77b CONFESSION AND MUTUAL ABSOLUTION

O God, you have searched us out and known us, and all that we are is open to you. We confess that we have sinned: we have used our power to dominate and our weakness to manipulate; we have evaded responsibility and failed to confront evil; we have denied dignity to ourselves and to our sisters (each other), and fallen into despair.
**We turn to you, O God;
we renounce evil;**

we claim your love;
we choose to be made whole.

(In turn, around the circle, we say for each other: 'Woman/man, your sins are forgiven; be at peace.' This can be accompanied by a gesture such as taking hands, or making the sign of the cross on the forehead.)

All Desires Known

77c COLLECT

O God whose word is life, and whose delight is to answer our cry, give us faith like the Syro-Phoenician woman, who refused to remain an outsider; that we too may have the wit to argue and demand that our daughters be made whole, through Jesus Christ. **Amen.**

All Desires Known

77d SUITABLE SCRIPTURE PASSAGES

Genesis 2.18–24; 21.8–21; Exodus 2.1–10; 1 Samuel 1.20–28; Esther 7.1–6, 9–10; 9.20–22; Proverbs 31.10–31; Isaiah 49.8–16a; 66.10–14; Zephaniah 3.14–20; Psalms 71.1–6; 127.1–4; 139.1–6, 13–18.
Matthew 26.6–13; 28.1–10; Mark 5.21–43; 7.24–30; Luke 1.26–38; 1.39–56; 2.33–35; 7.36 – 8.3; 15.1–10; John 4.5–15, 19–26, 39–42; 8.1–11; 19.25–27; 20.1–18; Acts 9.36–43; 16.9–15; 4.4–7; Ephesians 5.21–33; 1 Peter 3.1–7; Revelation 12.1–5a.

77e STATEMENT OF FAITH

I believe
that women are equal in ability
to men;
I believe
that just because my mother accepted a subservient role,
it does not mean that I must too;
I believe
that if I do not fight for the rights of my sister,
then she will always be oppressed;
I believe
that limitless horizons lie before my daughter,
not just a few traditional choices;
I believe
that I have much to contribute to the world,
and I alone possess my particular talents and abilities;
I believe
that each woman is an individual,
not a stereotype.

Rene Parmar

h Reading - Luke 2 v 1-7
The birth of Jesus

hepherds watched their flocks by night.

Reading - Luke 2, v 8-14
e shepherds and the angels

4 - As with gladness men of old

Reading - Matthew 2 v 1-11
e men are led by the star to Jesus

No 15 - In the bleak midwinter

enth Reading - John 1 v 1-14
The Word made Flesh

the World - O come all ye faithfull

Prayer and Blessing

o 2 - Hark the herald angels sing

PRAYERS FOR OPPRESSED WOMEN
77f

Lord, who made time for the unimportant people and children, we pray for the removal of oppressive traditions that enslave and subordinate women whom you created in your image. **Amen.**

V. Premasagar

77g

O God, Creator of the heavens and earth, we pray for women throughout the world. Bless them. Help them and us to see one another through eyes enlightened by understanding and compassion. Release us from prejudices in order to receive with respect and attention the stories from our sisters. Open our ears to the cries of a suffering world and to the healing melodies of peace. Empower us to be instruments in bringing about your justice and equality everywhere. **Amen.**

World Conference of Women, 1995

77h AT THE PEACE
May the peace which Mary knew when she held her child in her arms, sustain you to Calvary and beyond.

Michael Counsell

77i EUCHARISTIC PRAYER
Eternal Wisdom, source of our being, and goal of all our longing, we praise you and give you thanks because you have created us, women and men, together in your image to cherish your world and to seek your face. Divided and disfigured by sin, while we were yet helpless, you emptied yourself of power, and took upon you our unprotected flesh. You laboured with us upon the cross, and have brought us forth to the hope of resurrection.

Therefore, with the woman who gave you birth, the women who befriended you and fed you, who argued with you and touched you, the woman who anointed you for death, the women who met you, risen from the dead, and with all your lovers throughout the ages, we praise you saying:
**Holy, holy, holy,
vulnerable God,
heaven and earth are full of your glory;
hosanna in the highest.
Blessed is the one
who comes in the name of God;
hosanna in the highest.**

Blessed is our brother Jesus, who, before his suffering, earnestly desired to eat with his companions the passover of liberation; who, on the night that he was betrayed, took bread, gave thanks, broke it, and said: 'This is my body which is for you. Do this to remember me.' In the same way also the cup, after supper, saying: 'This cup is the new covenant in my blood. Do this, whenever you drink it, to remember me.'
Christ has died. Christ is risen. Christ will come again.

Therefore, as we eat this bread and drink this cup, we are proclaiming Christ's death until he comes. In the body broken and the blood poured out, we restore to memory and hope the broken and unremembered victims of tyranny and sin; and we long for the bread of tomorrow and the wine of the age to come. Come then, life-giving Spirit of our God, brood over these bodily things, and make us one body with Christ; that we may labour with creation to be delivered from its bondage to decay into the glorious liberty of all the children of God. **Amen.**

All Desires Known

77j LITANY OF TRANSFORMATION

O flaming Spirit of love,
we cry to you in the midst of the struggles of our lives!
O sacred fire, empower us!
Together we release our anger and our rage.
Transform them into the power of your compassion.
O sacred fire, empower us!
Together we release our fears. Transform them into courage.
O sacred fire, empower us!
Together we release our despair. Transform it into hope.
O sacred fire, empower us!
Together we release our doubts. Transform them into wisdom.
O sacred fire, empower us!
We offer to you our broken sisterhood.
We offer to you our broken brotherhood.
Help us remember the wholeness that you intended.
O God of fire,
burn within us,
heal us, strengthen us,
remake us,
empower us with your passion for justice!
Amen.

Victoria Walton, for The Saskatchewan Christian Feminist Network

77k BLESSING
Holy and compassionate God:
so direct our strength
and inspire our weakness
that we may enter with power
into the movement of your whole creation
towards wholeness, justice and peace. Amen
And may the blessing of God,
Creator, Sufferer, and Love-giver ...

Christ Church Cathedral, Vancouver*

---

78. THE WORLD, THE UNITED NATIONS

See also THE NEEDY, PEACE

78a RESPONSE
God loves the world so much
that he sent us his only Son,
who prays for those who are in the world but not of the world
that God will keep us safe.
The body of Christ is in the world, not to condemn the world,
but that the world through Christ might be saved.

Michael Counsell, from John 3.16–17; 18.11–12

78b INVITATION TO CONFESS
We have rebelled against God most high and put him to the test. We did not obey his commandments, but were rebellious and disloyal like those who lived before us, unreliable as a crooked arrow. So let us make our confession to our loving heavenly Father.

Michael Counsell, from Psalm 78.56–57

78c CONFESSION
Lord God, our maker and our redeemer, this is your world and we are your people: come among us and save us. We have wilfully misused your gifts of creation; Lord be merciful:
forgive us our sin.
We have seen the ill-treatment of others and have not gone to their aid; Lord be merciful:
forgive us our sin.
We have condoned evil and dishonesty and failed to strive for justice; Lord be merciful:
forgive us our sin.

We have heard the good news of Christ, but have failed to share
it with others; Lord be merciful:
forgive us our sin.
We have not loved you with all our heart, nor our neighbours
as ourselves; Lord be merciful:
forgive us our sin.

Adapted from Michael Perry

78d KYRIE
Father Creator, we have raped and abused your world. Lord,
have mercy;
Lord, have mercy.
Jesus Saviour, we have ignored your great love. Christ, have
mercy;
Christ, have mercy.
Spirit, Sustainer of all, we have sought to live without you.
Lord, have mercy;
Lord, have mercy.

The Open Gate, p. 56

78e ABSOLUTION
May God who loved the world so much that he sent his Son to
be our Saviour forgive *us our* sins and make *us* holy to serve
him in the world, through Jesus Christ our Lord. **Amen.**

Patterns for Worship, 13D7

COLLECTS
78f

Gather us or scatter us, O Lord, according to your will. Build us
into one church: a church with open doors and large windows,
a church which takes the world seriously, ready to work and to
suffer, and even to bleed for it. **Amen.**

Hungarian, source unknown

78g

Gracious God, let your will for us all be known. Let all be part-
ners in shaping the future with a faith that quarrels with the
present for the sake of what yet might be. **Amen.**

From Taiwan, source unknown

78h SUITABLE SCRIPTURE PASSAGES
Exodus   18.1–12;   22.21–27;   23.6–9;   Leviticus   19.33–34;
Deuteronomy 1.9–16; 10.12–19; 23.7–8; 24.14–15; 1 Chronicles
29.14–15; Job 31.31–32; Malachi 3.1–5; Psalms 24; 146.5–10.
Matthew 2.13–23; 25.31–45; John 9.1–41; 12.44–50; 15.17 – 16.4;
17.6–19; Acts 17.26–28; Hebrews 10.5–10; 13.1–3.

78i AFFIRMATION OF FAITH
We affirm our faith in one God;
**Source of all life, greater than all names and forms,
our inmost self, closer than any.
Upon this one God we depend for all we are
and all we ever will be.**
And we affirm our faith in Christ.
**Who has shown us the way to true life.
By breaking the bond of human bondage,
through his self-giving life and death
and by his rising again,
he has given us hope for a new humanity,
hope for the healing of earth's life.**
And we affirm our faith in the living Spirit of God.
**Through whom we awaken to God's purpose for the world,
and share in the freedom, joy and peace
of the children of God.
For by his Spirit God's love has flooded our lives,
shaping us into a community of forgiven
and freely accepted brothers and sisters,
set apart for God's service.
Risen with Christ we share in his work
for God's world of everlasting life,
justice and peace. Amen.**

The Church of South India

78j INTERCESSIONS
O God the Father of our Lord Jesus Christ, in whom you chose
us, before the foundation of the world, and destined us in love
to be your own: help us to pray for all your children.
For the life of the world; that your peace may be known and
may prevail. For ...
Lord hear us. **Lord, graciously hear us.**
For all who suffer injury, death or loss; that they may know the
hope to which you call us:
Lord hear us. **Lord, graciously hear us.**
For all who exercise rule and authority; that they may
acknowledge your power:
Lord hear us. **Lord, graciously hear us.**
For the Church which is Christ's body; that it may live for the
praise of your glory:
Lord hear us. **Lord, graciously hear us.**
O God, you exerted your strength and power when you raised
Christ from the dead, putting everything in subjection under

his feet: accept the prayers which we offer in his name for the world you have created and redeemed; through him in whom you have set forth the mystery of your will, to unite all things in heaven and on earth, your Son, our Lord Jesus Christ. **Amen.**

Scottish Liturgy 1982

78k AT THE PEACE
God has called us to live in peace.

1 Corinthians 7.17, *Patterns for Worship*, 0R26, freely available

78l PREFACE
You made the world, and love your creation. Your Son's dying and rising have set us free from sin and death. By your Spirit you make us your friends.

Additional Eucharistic Prayers

78m AFTER COMMUNION
Father, your steadfast purpose is the completion of all things in your Son. May we who have received the pledges of the kingdom, live by faith, walk in hope and be renewed in love, until the world reflects your glory and you are all in all; through Jesus Christ our Lord. **Amen.**

Scottish Liturgy 1982

78n BLESSING
Go now into the world in peace. Hold fast to that which is good. Do not repay evil with evil. Encourage the faint-hearted, help the weak, be patient with everyone. Rejoice always, pray constantly, give thanks in all circumstances. And the blessing …

Michael Counsell, 1 Thessalonians 5.13–22

THE REVISED COMMON LECTIONARY AMENDED, SUNDAY LECTIONARY FOR THE PRINCIPAL SERVICE

(Reprinted by permission of the Central Board of Finance
of the Church of England)

*The Revised Common Lectionary is not based on themes, but on consecutive
reading of Scripture; nevertheless the numbers in brackets correspond to the
themes used in this book, and have been suggested to guide preachers and
those who plan liturgy, understanding that they should not feel bound to
these themes.*

YEAR A, the Year of Matthew

(Year A begins on Advent Sunday in 1999, 2002, 2005, etc.)

ADVENT
FIRST SUNDAY OF ADVENT (1)
Isaiah 2.1–5 Nations will seek the temple (19), Peace (51), Evangelism (23)
    Psalm 122 Let us go up to the temple (19), Peace (51)
Romans 13.11–14 Lay aside the Works (62) of darkness, Light (40)
Matthew 24.36–44 The coming of the Son of Man, Readiness (58)

SECOND SUNDAY OF ADVENT (1)
Isaiah 11.1–10 A shoot from the stump of Jesse, Justice (36)
    Psalm 72.1–7, 18–19 Give the King (37) your Righteousness (36)
Romans 15.4–13 Hope from the Bible (8)
Matthew 3.1–12 John the Baptist (58) preaches Repentance (60)

THIRD SUNDAY OF ADVENT (1)
Isaiah 35.1–10 Healing (32) in the desert
    Psalm 146.5–10, *or Canticle:* Magnificat, God's Justice (36)
James 5.7–10 Wait in Patience (52)
Matthew 11.2–11 Jesus' teaching about John the Baptist (58)

FOURTH SUNDAY OF ADVENT (1)
Isaiah 7.10–16 The sign of Immanuel, Incarnation (10)
    Psalm 80.1–7, 17–19 Restore your people, Salvation (66)
Romans 1.1–7 Sent to preach the gospel of Salvation (66)
Matthew 1.18–25 The birth of Jesus, Joseph's dream, Incarnation (10)

CHRISTMAS
CHRISTMAS DAY (10) (25 December) Years A, B & C
*Any of the following sets of readings may be used on the evening of Christmas
Eve and on Christmas Day. Set III should be used at some service during the
celebration.*

I
Isaiah 9.2–7 A child is born, Salvation (66)
   Psalm 96 Tell of his Salvation (66)
Titus 2.11–14 Salvation (66) has come
Luke 2.1–14 [15–20] Birth, Shepherds (68), Christmas (10)
II
Isaiah 62.6–12 Prepare a way, Readiness (58)
   Psalm 97 God comes to rescue his people, Salvation (66)
Titus 3.4–7 Salvation (66) by Grace (29)
Luke 2.[1–7] 8–20 Shepherds (68), Christmas (10)
III
Isaiah 52.7–10 Messenger of Peace (51), Salvation (66)
   Psalm 98 God's victory
Hebrews 1.1–4 [5–12] God speaks through a Son, Incarnation (10)
John 1.1–14 The Word (8) became flesh, Incarnation (10)

FIRST SUNDAY OF CHRISTMAS (10)
Isaiah 63.7–9 God's presence brings Salvation (66)
   Psalm 148 Let all Creation (16) praise the Lord
Hebrews 2.10–18 The Suffering (70) of Jesus brings Salvation (66)
Matthew 2.13–23 Flight into Egypt, Suffering (70), Needy (46)

SECOND SUNDAY OF CHRISTMAS (10)
Jeremiah 31.7–14 God will send Salvation (66)
   Psalm 147.12–20 God's Word (8) brings Peace (51)
or Ecclesiasticus 24.1–12 God's Wisdom (76) comes to earth
   Canticle: Wisdom 10.15–21 Salvation (66), Wisdom, Church (11)
Ephesians 1.3–14 God's plan to gather everything in Christ, Adoption (66)
John 1.[1–9] 10–18 God gave Grace (29) through Jesus, Incarnation (10)

EPIPHANY
THE EPIPHANY (21) (6 January) Years A, B & C
   The Wise men (76), Evangelism (23)
Isaiah 60.1–6 Bringing gold and incense
   Psalm 72.[1–9] 10–15 Kings will bow before him
Ephesians 3.1–12 Preaching to Gentiles
Matthew 2.1–12 Visit of the Magi

THE BAPTISM OF CHRIST (7)
Isaiah 42.1–9 God gives his Spirit (69) to his Servant (67)
   Psalm 29 The voice of the Lord is over the waters, Spirit (69)
Acts 10.34–43 Anointing by the Holy Spirit (69)
Matthew 3.13–17 The Baptism (7) and anointing of Jesus

SECOND SUNDAY OF EPIPHANY (21)
Isaiah 49.1–7 The Servant (67) a Light (40) to the nations, Evangelism (23)
   Psalm 40.1–11 I spoke of your Salvation (66), Evangelism (23)
1 Corinthians 1.1–9 Called to be Saints (65), Grace (29), Spiritual gifts (69)
John 1.29–42 Andrew brings Peter (53), Evangelism (23), Holy Spirit (69)

THIRD SUNDAY OF EPIPHANY (21)
Isaiah 9.1–4 The people who walked in darkness have seen Light (40)
　Psalm 27.1, 4–9 The Lord is my Light (40) and my Salvation (66)
1 Corinthians 1.10–18 Unity (75) through Baptism (7)
Matthew 4.12–23 Call (14) of Fishermen (27) disciples to Evangelism (23)

FOURTH SUNDAY OF EPIPHANY (21)
1 Kings 17.8–16 The widow's oil-jug, Providence (56)
　Psalm 36.5–10 God's steadfast Love (41)
1 Corinthians 1.18–31 Christ the Wisdom (76) of God
John 2.1 –11 Water into wine, Family (26), Eucharist (22)

THE PRESENTATION OF CHRIST (40) (2 February) Years A, B & C
Malachi 3.1–5 The Lord shall come to his Temple (19)
　Psalm 24.[1–6] 7–10 Open the Temple gates for the Lord
Hebrews 2.14–18 Jesus became like the descendants of Abraham
Luke 2.22–40 The Presentation of Christ in the Temple (19), Light (40)

ORDINARY TIME
PROPER 1 *Sunday between 3 and 9 February inclusive (if earlier than 2 before Lent)*
Isaiah 58.1–9a [9b–12] The fast (38) God wants: Freedom (66), Justice (36)
　Psalm 112.1–9 [10] Happy are those who do good Works (62)
1 Corinthians 2.1–12 [13–16] The Spirit (69) of Wisdom (76)
Matthew 5.13–20 Light (40), Commandments (13), Righteousness (62)

PROPER 2 *Sunday between 10 and 16 February inclusive (if earlier than 2 before Lent)*
Deuteronomy 30.15–20 *or* Ecclesiasticus 15.15–20 Choose Life (39)
　Psalm 119.1–8 Walk in the Law (13) of the Lord, Word (8)
1 Corinthians 3.1–9 Unity (75) between followers of Paul and Apollos
Matthew 5.21–37 Judgement (35) Forgiveness (28) Family (26) Truth (74)

PROPER 3 *Sunday between 17 and 23 February inclusive (if earlier than 2 before Lent)*
Leviticus 19.1–2, 9–18 Love (41) your Needy (46) neighbour
　Psalm 119.33–40 Trust (25) in God's Word (8)
1 Corinthians 3.10–11, 16–23 Building God's Church (11), Temple (19)
Matthew 5.38–48 Love (41) your enemies, Conflict (38), Forgiveness (28)

SECOND SUNDAY BEFORE LENT
Genesis 1.1–2.3 The Creation (16)
　Psalm 136 *or* Psalm 136.1–9, 23–26 Creation (16), Salvation (66)
Romans 8.18–25 The Creation (16) waits for Salvation (66)
Matthew 6.25–34 Lilies of the field, Providence (56), Assurance (5)

SUNDAY BEFORE LENT
Exodus 24.12–18 God appears to Moses on Mount Sinai
　Psalm 2 You are my son, *or* Psalm 99 A pillar of cloud
2 Peter 1.16–21 We ourselves heard this voice
Matthew 17.1–9 The Transfiguration (72)

Year A

LENT
ASH WEDNESDAY (38) Years A, B & C
Joel 2.1–2, 12–17 Rend your hearts, Repentance (60)
or Isaiah 58.1–12 Care for the Needy (46)
  Psalm 51.1–17 Cleanse me from my Sin (35), Forgiveness (28)
2 Corinthians 5.20b–6.10 Suffering (70) of an apostle (53), Ministry (43)
Matthew 6.1–6, 16–21 Secret fasting
or John 8.1–11 Adultery, Sin (35), Women (77), Forgiveness (28)

FIRST SUNDAY OF LENT (38)
Genesis 2.15–17; 3.1–7 The Fall (35)
  Psalm 32 Happy are those who know God's Forgiveness (28)
Romans 5.1–19 Christ's Obedience (47) cancels Adam's Judgement (35)
Matthew 4.1–11 The Temptation of Christ

SECOND SUNDAY OF LENT (38)
Genesis 12.1–4a Abram begins his journey of Faith (25)
  Psalm 121 I lift my eyes to the hills, Assurance (5), Faith (25)
Romans 4.1–5, 13–17 Abraham was Justified (62) by Faith (25)
John 3.1–17 Born again, Conversion (14)

THIRD SUNDAY OF LENT (38)
Exodus 17.1–7 Water from the rock, Baptism (7)
  Psalm 95 Worship, testing God
Romans 5.1–11 Reconciliation (28) to God
John 4.5–42 The Samaritan woman (77) at the well, Baptism (7)

FOURTH SUNDAY OF LENT (38)
1 Samuel 16.1–13 Samuel anoints David as King (37)
  Psalm 23 The Lord is my Shepherd (68), King (37)
Ephesians 5.8–14 Live as children of Light (40)
John 9.1–41 The Light (40) of the World (78)

Or: *MOTHERING SUNDAY (44)* Years A, B & C
  Family (26), Women (77), Children (9)
Exodus 2.1–10 His Mother (44) hides Moses, Adoption (66)
or 1 Samuel 1.20–28 His Mother (44) offers Samuel to the Lord
  Psalm 34.11–20 Advice to the young to be Righteous (62)
  or Psalm 127.1–4 Children (9) a gift from the Lord
2 Corinthians 1.3–7 Helping others because God helps us
or Colossians 3.12–17 Love (41) and care
Luke 2.33–35 Simeon predicts Mary's (42) Suffering (70)
or John 19.25–27 Mary (42) is your Mother (44)

FIFTH SUNDAY OF LENT (38) *(Passiontide)* *(17)*
Ezekiel 37.1–14 The valley of dry bones, Spirit (69), Death (18)
  Psalm 130 Out of the depths, Forgiveness (28), Assurance (5)
Romans 8.6–11 The Spirit (69) gives Life (39)
John 11.1–45 The Resurrection (61) of Lazarus

PALM SUNDAY (49)
Liturgy of the Palms:
Matthew 21.1–11 Triumphal Entry
    Psalm 118.1–2, 19–29 Procession to the Temple (19)
Liturgy of the Passion:
Isaiah 50.4–9a Servant (67), Cross (17), Suffering (70)
    Psalm 31.9–16 Assurance (5) in Suffering (70)
Philippians 2.5–11 Jesus' Obedience (47) unto Death (18), Humility (33)
Matthew 26.14 –27.66 The Last Supper to the Burial, Eucharist (22)
or Matthew 27.11–24 The Trial to the Death (18) on the Cross (17)

MONDAY OF HOLY WEEK
Isaiah 42.1–9 The Servant (67) brings Salvation (66)
    Psalm 36.5–11 Defend me against the wicked, Providence (56)
Hebrews 9.11–15 The Sacrifice (64) of the new Covenant (15)
John 12.1–11 Mary anoints Jesus' feet for his Death (18)

TUESDAY OF HOLY WEEK
Isaiah 49.1–7 The Servant (67) a Light (40) to the nations, Evangelism (23)
    Psalm 71.1–14 Rescue me from the wicked
1 Corinthians 1.18–31 The Cross (17) the power and Wisdom (76) of God
John 12.20–36 Death (18) of a seed, Resurrection (61) of a great harvest

WEDNESDAY OF HOLY WEEK
Isaiah 50.4–9a I gave my back to the smiters, Servant (67), Cross (17)
    Psalm 70 Those who say Aha! Aha!
Hebrews 12.1–3 Suffering (70) and Perseverance (52) on the Cross (17)
John 13.21–32 Judas betrays Jesus, Glory (72)

MAUNDY THURSDAY (22) Eucharist
Exodus 12.1–4 [5–10] 11–14 The Passover
    Psalm 116.1–2, 12–19 The cup of Salvation (66)
1 Corinthians 11.23–26 The last supper
John 13.1–17, 31b–35 Foot washing, Humility (33) of a Servant (67)

GOOD FRIDAY, Cross (17)
Isaiah 52.13 –53.12 The Suffering (70) Servant (67)
    Psalm 22 Why have you forsaken me?
Hebrews 10.16–25 *or* Hebrews 4.14–16; 5.7–9 Jesus the Priest (43)
John 18.1 –19.42 The blood of the Covenant (15)

EASTER EVE, Resurrection (61)
These readings are for use at services other than the Easter Vigil.
Job 14.1–14 Hide me in Sheol, Death (18)
or Lamentations 3.1–9, 19–24 New every morning, Assurance (5)
    Psalm 31.1–4, 15–16 Rescue me speedily
1 Peter 4.1–8 The gospel proclaimed to the Dead (18)
Matthew 27.57–66 *or* John 19.38–42 The Burial of Jesus, Death (18)

EASTER
EASTER DAY (61)
The following readings and psalms are provided for use at the Easter Vigil.
A minimum of three Old Testament readings should be chosen.
The reading from Exodus 14 should always be used.

Genesis 1.1–2.4a Creation (16)   Psalm 136.1–9, 23–26
Genesis 7.1–5, 11–18; 8.6–18; 9.8–13 Noah, Baptism (7)   Psalm 46
Genesis 22.1–18 Sacrifice (64) of Isaac   Psalm 16
Exodus 14.10–31; 15.20–21 The exodus   *Cant.:* Exodus 15.1b-13, 17–18
Isaiah 55.1–11 Come to the waters, Baptism (7)   *Canticle:* Isaiah 12.2–6
Baruch 3.9–15, 32 –4.4 God gives the Light (40) of Wisdom (76)
or Proverbs 8.1–8, 19–21; 9.4b–6 Wisdom (76)   Psalm 19
Ezekiel 36.24–28 I will sprinkle clean water on you   Psalms 42 & 43
Ezekiel 37.1–14 The valley of dry bones   Psalm 143
Zephaniah 3.14–20 I will bring you home   Psalm 98
Romans 6.3–11 Baptism (7), Death (18), Resurrection (61)   Psalm 114
Matthew 28.1–10 The empty tomb

The following readings and psalm are provided for use at the principal Easter Day service.
Acts 10.34–43 Peter (53) Witnesses (23) to the Resurrection (61)
or Jeremiah 31.1–6 An everlasting Love (41)
     Psalm 118.1–2, 14–24 I shall not die but live, Death (18), Life (39)
Colossians 3.1–4 Resurrection (61) with Christ
or Acts 10.34–43 Peter (53) Witnesses (23) to the Resurrection (61)
John 20.1–18 Magdalene at the tomb, Women (77)
or Matthew 28.1–10 The Women (77) see Jesus

For those who require an Old Testament reading on the Sundays in Eastertide, provision is made in the table below. If used, the reading from Acts must be used as the second reading.

SECOND SUNDAY OF EASTER (61)
Acts 2.14a, 22–32 Peter (53) Witnesses (23) to the Resurrection (61)
     Psalm 16 You show me the path of Life (39)
1 Peter 1.3–9 Hope from the Resurrection (61)
John 20.19–31 The upper room, Thomas's Resurrection (61) Faith (25)

THIRD SUNDAY OF EASTER (61)
Acts 2.14a, 36–41 The response to Peter's preaching (53), Baptism (7)
     Psalm 116.1–4, 12–19 Thanks (71) Salvation (66) Eucharist (22)
1 Peter 1.17–23 Born anew, Resurrection (61), Conversion (14)
Luke 24.13–35 The road to Emmaus, Word (8), Resurrection (61)

FOURTH SUNDAY OF EASTER (61)
Acts 2.42–47 Life in the early Church (11)
     Psalm 23 The Lord my Shepherd (68), Resurrection (61) Life (39)
1 Peter 2.19–25 Christ the Shepherd (68) of your souls
John 10.1–10 I am the good Shepherd (68)

FIFTH SUNDAY OF EASTER (61)
Acts 7.55–60 The Death (18) and Faith (25) of Stephen
    Psalm 31.1–5, 15–16 Deliver me
1 Peter 2.2–10 Living stones in the Church (11), God's Temple (19)
John 14.1–14 I will prepare a place for you, Death (18), Resurrection (61)

SIXTH SUNDAY OF EASTER (61)
Acts 17.22–31 Paul Witnesses (23) to the Resurrection (61) in Athens
    Psalm 66.8–20 God brought us out
1 Peter 3.13–22 Christ preached to the spirits, Death (18), Baptism (7)
John 14.15–21 The promise of the Holy Spirit (69) the Advocate

ASCENSION DAY (4) Years A, B & C King (37)
The reading from Acts must be used as either the first or second reading
Acts 1.1–11 The Ascension (4) *or* Daniel 7.9–14 The Son of Man
    Psalm 47 God has gone up, *or* Psalm 93 The Lord is King (37)
Ephesians 1.15–23 Christ is seated beside God; *or* Acts 1.1–11
Luke 24.44–53 The Ascension (4)

SEVENTH SUNDAY OF EASTER Ascension (4), King (37)
Acts 1.6–14 The Ascension (4)
    Psalm 68.1–10, 32–35 Let God arise
1 Peter 4.12–14; 5.6–11 Share Christ's Suffering (70) and his Glory (72)
John 17.1–11 Father, glorify your Son, The Church (11), Parenthood (50)

OLD TESTAMENT READINGS FOR
SUNDAYS IN EASTERTIDE, Years A, B & C
Easter 2 Exodus 14.10–31; 15.20–21 The exodus, Salvation (66)
Easter 3 Zephaniah 3.14–20 Assurance (5), the Lord is in your midst
Easter 4 Genesis 7 Noah goes into the ark, Baptism (7)
Easter 5 Genesis 8.1–19 Noah comes out of the ark, Salvation (66)
Easter 6 Genesis 8.20 –9.17 The Covenant (15) of the rainbow
Easter 7 Ezekiel 36.24–28 I will put my Spirit (69) in you

PENTECOST (69) (Whit Sunday) The Holy Spirit
The reading from Acts must be used as either the first or second reading.
Acts 2.1–21 The day of Pentecost (69)
or Numbers 11.24–30 The elders receive the Spirit (69), Authority (6)
    Psalm 104.24–34, 35b The Spirit (69) in Creation (16)
1 Corinthians 12.3b–13 Different gifts, one Spirit (69)
or Acts 2.1–21 The day of Pentecost (69)
John 20.19–23 Jesus breathes the Holy Spirit (69)
or John 7.37–39 Living water of the Spirit (69)

ORDINARY TIME
TRINITY SUNDAY (73)
Isaiah 40.12–17, 27–31 The greatness of God
    Psalm 8 Stewardship of Nature (45), Ecology (20), Possessions (54)
2 Corinthians 13.11–13 God, Jesus & the Holy Spirit (69), Parenthood (50)
Matthew 28.16–20 Baptism (7), name of the Trinity (73), Evangelism (23)

If the Sunday between 24 & 28 May inclusive follows Trinity Sunday, Proper 3 (above) is used.

PROPER 4 *Sunday between 29 May and 4 June inclusive (if after Trinity Sunday)*
Genesis 6.9–22; 7.24; 8.14–19 Noah, Salvation (66), Baptism (7)
　　Psalm 46 Our refuge and strength, Assurance (5), Baptism (7)
or Deuteronomy 11.18–21, 26–28 Choose blessing, Conversion (14)
　　Psalm 31.1–5, 19–24 Providence (56)
Romans 1.16–17; 3.22b–28 [29–31] Justified (62), Grace (29), Faith (25)
Matthew 7.21–29 The house on the rock, the Words (8) of Jesus

PROPER 5 *Sunday between 5 and 11 June inclusive (if after Trinity Sunday)*
Genesis 12.1–9 Abram sets out in Faith (25)
　　Psalm 33.1–12 The Word (8) in Creation (16)
or Hosea 5.15 –6.6 Return to the Lord, Repentance (60), Conversion (14)
　　Psalm 50.7–15 A Sacrifice (64) of Thanks (71)
Romans 4.13–25 Abraham's Faith (25), not Works (62) of the Law (13)
Matthew 9.9–13, 18–26 Healing (32), Forgiveness (28), Faith (25)

PROPER 6 *Sunday between 12 and 18 June inclusive (if after Trinity Sunday)*
Genesis 18.1–15 [21.1–7] Abraham, Trinity (73)
　　Psalm 116.1–2, 12–19 Thanks (71), Eucharist (22)
or Exodus 19.2–8a A Kingdom (37) of priests, Ministry (43)
　　Psalm 100 Worship in the Temple (19)
Romans 5.1–8 While we were Sinners (35), Cross (17), Salvation (66)
Matthew 9.35 –10.8 [9–23] Witness (23) to the Kingdom (37), Ministry (43)

PROPER 7 *Sunday between 19 and 25 June inclusive (if after Trinity Sunday)*
Genesis 21.8–21 Hagar, Women (77), Family (26), Race (57)
　　Psalm 86.1–10, 16–17 All nations, Evangelism (23)
or Jeremiah 20.7–13 Jeremiah's Prayer (55), Suffering (70), Assurance (5)
　　Psalm 69.7–10 [11–15] 16–18 Zeal for the Temple (19)
Romans 6.1b–11 Dead to sin (35) and alive to God, Righteousness (62)
Matthew 10.24–29 His eye on the sparrow, Assurance (5), Providence (56)

PROPER 8 *Sunday between 26 June and 2 July inclusive*
Genesis 22.1–14 The Sacrifice (64) of Isaac
　　Psalm 13 How long? Faith (25)
or Jeremiah 28.5–9 True prophecy, Word (8), Peace (51)
　　Psalm 89.1–4, 15–18 Covenant (15) with David, Thanks (71)
Romans 6.12–23 Freed from Sin (35), Life (39), Righteousness (62)
Matthew 10.40–42 A cup of cold water, Good Works (62), the Needy (46)

PROPER 9 *Sunday between 3 and 9 July inclusive*
Genesis 24.34–38, 42–49, 58–67 Rebecca betrothed
　　Psalm 45.10–17 Royal wedding, Family (26)
　　or Canticle: Song of Solomon 2.8–13,
　　Love (41) and springtime, Family (26), Nature (45)
or Zechariah 9.9–12 Rejoice, Joy (34)
　　Psalm 145.8–14 God's Kingdom (37) and Love (41)

Romans 7.15–25a Law of Judgement (35), Law (13) of God, Thanks (71)
Matthew 11.16–19 John the Baptist (58), Fast (38), Call (14)

PROPER 10 *Sunday between 10 and 16 July inclusive*
Genesis 25.19–34 Esau sells his birthright, Family (26)
   Psalm 119.105–112 Your Word (8) a lamp, Light (40)
or Isaiah 55.10–13 God's Word (8) brings Joy (34), Nature (45)
   Psalm 65.[1–8] 9–13 Joy (34) of Harvest (31), Nature (45)
Romans 8.1–11 Flesh, Law (13)and Spirit (69)
Matthew 13.1–9, 18–23 Parable of the sower, Word (8), Evangelism (23)

PROPER 11 *Sunday between 17 and 23 July inclusive*
Genesis 28.10–19a Jacob's ladder, Angels (65) Temple (19), Guidance (30)
   Psalm 139.1–12, 23–24 Ascension (4), Heaven (39)
or Wisdom of Solomon 12.13, 16–19 Righteousness (62), Love (41)
or Isaiah 44.6–8 Witnesses (23) to the one God, Trinity (73)
   Psalm 86.11–17 God's Grace (29)
Romans 8.12–25 Children of God, Creation (16), Hope (1)
Matthew 13.24–30, 36–43 Weeds: God's Judgement (35) and Patience (52)

PROPER 12 *Sunday between 24 and 30 July inclusive*
Genesis 29.15–28 Jacob Loves (41) Rachel, Family (26)
   Psalm 105.1–11, 45b Authority (6), Eucharist (22), Thanks (71)
   or Psalm 128 Family (26), Possessions (54)
   or 1 Kings 3.5–12 Solomon's Prayer (55) for Wisdom (76)
   Psalm 119.129–136 Word (8), Light (40)
Romans 8.26–39 All things work together for good, Providence (56)
Matthew 13.31–33, 44–52 Parables of the Kingdom (37)

PROPER 13 *Sunday between 31 July and 6 August inclusive*
Genesis 32.22–31 Wrestling Jacob, Prayer (55), Covenant (15)
   Psalm 17.1–7, 15 Guidance (30), Righteousness (62)
or Isaiah 55.1–5 Come to me, Call (14), Eucharist (22), Repentance (60)
   Psalm 145.8–9, 14–21 Providence (56), Prayer (55)
Romans 9.1–5 Christians and Jews (48)
Matthew 14.13–21 Feeding the five thousand, Eucharist (22)

PROPER 14 *Sunday between 7 and 13 August inclusive*
Genesis 37.1–4, 12–28 Joseph and his Family (26)
   Psalm 105.1–6, 16–22, 45b Thanks (71), Joseph in Authority (6)
or 1 Kings 19.9–18 A still small voice, Spirit (69), Prayer (55), Call (14)
   Psalm 85.8–13 Love (41), Works (62), Peace (51), Faith (25)
Romans 10.5–15 Justification (62), Law (13), Faith (25), Word (8)
Matthew 14.22–33 Walking on water, Faith (25)

PROPER 15 *Sunday between 14 and 20 August inclusive*
Genesis 45.1–15 Joseph and his Family (26)
   Psalm 133 Victory
or Isaiah 56.1, 6–8 Temple (19) a house of Prayer (55) for Evangelism (23)
   Psalm 67 Harvest (31), Thanks (71), Evangelism (23), Race (57)
Romans 11.1–2a, 29–32 God and Israel, Providence (56), Other Faiths (48)

Matthew 15.[10–20] 21–28 Crumbs from the table,
Faith (25), Evangelism (23), Healing (32), Eucharist (22)

PROPER 16 *Sunday between 21 and 27 August inclusive*
Exodus 1.8 –2.10 Moses in the bulrushes, Suffering (70), Providence (56)
Psalm 124 Salvation (66), Providence (56)
or Isaiah 51.1–6 The Servant (67) a Light (40) to the peoples,
Evangelism (23), Salvation (66)
Psalm 138 Temple (19), Prayer (55), Evangelism (23)
Romans 12.1–8 Sacrifice (64), Humility (33), Spirit (69)
Matthew 16.13–20 Peter (53) recognises the Messiah. Faith (25), King (37)

PROPER 17 *Sunday between 28 August and 3 September inclusive*
Exodus 3.1–15 The burning bush, Call (14), Covenant (15)
Psalm 105.1–6, 23–26, 45c Moses
or Jeremiah 15.15–21 Jeremiah's call (14), Word (8)
Psalm 26.1–8 Works (62), Temple (19), Thanks (71)
Romans 12.9–21 Love (41) in action, Righteousness (62)
Matthew 16.21–28 Take up your Cross (17), Suffering (70), Sin (35)

PROPER 18 *Sunday between 4 and 10 September inclusive*
Exodus 12.1–14 Passover, Eucharist (22), Sacrifice (64)
Psalm 149 Praise, Judgement (35)
or Ezekiel 33.7–11 Turn back from evil, Repentance (60)
Psalm 119.33–40 Law (13), Repentance (60)
Romans 13.8–14 Love (41) fulfils the Commandments (13)
Matthew 18.15–20 Where two or three agree, Prayer (55)

PROPER 19 *Sunday between 11 and 17 September inclusive*
Exodus 14.19–31 The exodus. Salvation (66), Baptism (7)
Psalm 114 The exodus
or Canticle: Exodus 15.1b–11, 20–21 The exodus
or Genesis 50.15–21 God turns evil to good, Providence (56), Family (26)
Psalm 103.[1–7] 8–13 God's Love (41) and Parenthood (50)
Romans 14.1–12 Tolerance and Judgement (35)
Matthew 18.21–35 Forgiveness (28) seventy times seven

PROPER 20 *Sunday between 18 and 24 September inclusive*
Exodus 16.2–15 Manna, Providence (56), Eucharist (22)
Psalm 105.1–6, 37–45 Manna
or Jonah 3.10 –4.11 Anger (35), Evangelism (23), Love (41), Prayer (55)
Psalm 145.1–8 God's Love (41)
Philippians 1.21–30 Death (18), Call (14), Works (62), Suffering (70)
Matthew 20.1–16 Vineyard Labourers, Justice (36) Grace (29) Needy (46)

PROPER 21 *Sunday between 25 September and 1 October inclusive*
Exodus 17.1–7 Water from the rock, Baptism (7)
Psalm 78.1–4, 12–16 Water from the rock, Baptism (7)
or Ezekiel 18.1–4, 25–32 Individual Responsibility, Repentance (60)
Psalm 25.1–9 Faith (25),
Guidance (30), Repentance (60), Humility (33), Sin (35)

Philippians 2.1–13 Incarnation (10), Humility (33), Ascension (4)
Matthew 21.23–32 Baptist's Authority (6), Obedience (47), Sinners (35)

PROPER 22 *Sunday between 2 and 8 October inclusive*
Exodus 20.1–4, 7–9, 12–20 The Ten Commandments (13)
   Psalm 19 The Heavens (39) declare, Creation (16), Law (13)
or Isaiah 5.1–7 Song of the vine, Creation (16), Righteousness (62)
   Psalm 80.7–15 The vine, Providence (56)
Philippians 3.4b–14 Persevere (52), Works (62), Faith (25), Suffering (70)
Matthew 21.33–46 The vine, Kingdom (37), Judgement (35), Spirit (69)

PROPER 23 *Sunday between 9 and 15 October inclusive*
Exodus 32.1–14 The golden calf, Judgement (35), Prayer (55)
   Psalm 106.1–6, 19–23 Judgement (35), Repentance (60)
or Isaiah 25.1–9 A refuge for the Needy (46), Death (18), Temple (19)
   Psalm 23 The Lord's my Shepherd (68), Providence (56)
Philippians 4.1–9 Rejoice in the Lord, Unity (75), Joy (34), Peace (51)
Matthew 22.1–14 The wedding banquet, Evangelism (23), Judgement (35)

PROPER 24 *Sunday between 16 and 22 October inclusive*
Exodus 33.12–23 Moses sees God's back
   Psalm 99 Moses' Prayer (55)
or Isaiah 45.1–7 God uses Cyrus, Authority (6)
   Psalm 96.1–9 [10–13] Creation (16)
1 Thessalonians 1.1–10 Thanks (71) for the Church (11), Conversion (14)
Matthew 22.15–22 Give to those in Authority (6) what belongs to them

PROPER 25 *Sunday between 23 and 29 October inclusive*
Deuteronomy 34.1–12 The Death (18) of Moses, Spirit (69)
   Psalm 90.1–6, 13–17 Prayer (55), Providence (56), Faith (25)
or Leviticus 19.1–2, 15–18 Love (41) of the Needy (46)
   Psalm 1 Law (13), Righteousness (62)
1 Thessalonians 2.1–8 Paul's Love (41) for the Church (11)
Matthew 22.34–46 Love (41) God and Love your Needy (46) neighbour

Or: **BIBLE SUNDAY (8)**
Nehemiah 8.1–4a [5–6] 8–12 Ezra reads the Commandments (13)
   Psalm 119.9–16 Meditation on the Commandments (13)
Colossians 3.12–17 Let the Word (8) dwell in you
Matthew 24.30–35 My Words (8) will not pass away

DEDICATION FESTIVAL (19) *First Sunday in October or Last Sunday after Trinity*
1 Kings 8.22–30 Solomon dedicates the Temple
or Revelation 21.9–14 The new Jerusalem
   Psalm 122 Let us go to the house of the Lord
Hebrews 12.18–24 You have come to Mount Zion, the Church (11)
Matthew 21.12–16 Cleansing the Temple, Judgement (35)

ALL SAINTS' SUNDAY (65)
Sunday between 30 October and 5 November inclusive
Revelation 7.9–17 The crowd before God's throne
   Psalm 34.1–10 Happy are those who find God, Providence (56)

1 John 3.1–13 A child of God does not continue to Sin (35)
Matthew 5.1–12 The beatitudes

Or: **FOURTH SUNDAY BEFORE ADVENT**
*Sunday between 31 October and 5 November inclusive. For use if the feast of All
Saints was celebrated on 1 November and alternative propers are needed.*
Micah 3.5–12 Judgement (35) on society, The City (12)
    Psalm 43 I will go to God's altar, Eucharist (22)
1 Thessalonians 2.9–13 A Call (14) to Righteousness (62)
Matthew 24.1–14 Predictions of the Coming of Christ (1)

THIRD SUNDAY BEFORE ADVENT *Sunday between 6 and 12 November inclusive*
Wisdom of Solomon 6.12–16 Wisdom (76) described
    Canticle: Wisdom of Solomon 6.17–20 Divine Wisdom (76)
or Amos 5.18–24 Let Justice (36) roll down
    Psalm 70 A Prayer (55) for help
1 Thessalonians 4.13–18 The Resurrection (61) from Death (18)
Matthew 25.1–13 Wise (76) and foolish bridesmaids, Readiness (58)

SECOND SUNDAY BEFORE ADVENT *Sunday between 13 and 19 November
inclusive*
Zephaniah 1.7, 12–18 The Day of Judgement (35)
    Psalm 90.1–8 [9–11] 12 The shortness of Life (39)
1 Thessalonians 5.1–11 The day of the Lord, Advent (1), Readiness (58)
Matthew 25.14–30 The parable of the talents, Readiness (58)

CHRIST THE KING (37) *Sunday between 20 and 26 November inclusive*
Ezekiel 34.11–16, 20–24 God the Shepherd (68)
    Psalm 95.1–7a We are his sheep, he is our Shepherd (68)
Ephesians 1.15–23 Christ the head of all, Church (11), Evangelism (23)
Matthew 25.31–46 Sheep (68) Judge (35) Needy (46) Other Faiths (25)

YEAR B, The Year of Mark

(Year B begins on Advent Sunday in 1997, 2000, 2003 etc.)

ADVENT
FIRST SUNDAY OF ADVENT (1)
Isaiah 64.1–9 Rend the heavens, Repentance (60), Judgement (35)
    Psalm 80.1–7 Repentance (60), Salvation (66)
1 Corinthians 1.3–9 Blameless on the Day of the Lord, Advent (1)
Mark 13.24–37 Readiness (58) for the coming of the Son of Man

SECOND SUNDAY OF ADVENT (1)
Isaiah 40.1–11 Comfort my people, Readiness (58)
    Psalm 85.1–2, 8–13 Salvation (66) is at hand
2 Peter 3.8–15a The Day of the Lord like a thief, Advent (1), Readiness (58)
Mark 1.1–8 John the Baptist (58), the voice in the wilderness

THIRD SUNDAY OF ADVENT (1)
Isaiah 61.1–4, 8–11 The year of the Lord's favour, Spirit (69), Justice (36)
    Psalm 126 or *Canticle:* Magnificat, Justice (36)
1 Thessalonians 5.16–24 At the coming of Jesus, Advent (1), Readiness (58)
John 1.6–8, 19–28 Words of John the Baptist (58), Light (40), Baptism (7)

FOURTH SUNDAY OF ADVENT (1)
2 Samuel 7.1–11, 16 God promises King (37) David Peace (51)
    Canticle: Magnificat, *or* Psalm 89.1–4, 19–26 Covenant (15)
Romans 16.25–27 The mystery promised long ago
Luke 1.26–38 The Annunciation to Mary (42), Incarnation (10)

CHRISTMAS
CHRISTMAS DAY (10) (25 December) *As in year A*

FIRST SUNDAY OF CHRISTMAS (10)
Isaiah 61.10 –62.3 Garments of Salvation (66)
    Psalm 148 Old and young (9) praise God, Nature (45)
Galatians 4.4–7 God sent his Son, born of a Woman (77), Adoption (66)
Luke 2.15–21 The Shepherds (68) visit Bethlehem

SECOND SUNDAY OF CHRISTMAS (10)
Jeremiah 31.7–14 God will send Salvation (66).
    Psalm 147.12–20 God's Word (8) brings Peace (51)
or Ecclesiasticus 24.1–12 God's Wisdom (76) comes to earth.
    Canticle: Wisdom 10.15–21, Salvation (66), Wisdom, Church (11)
Ephesians 1.3–14 Gather everything in Christ, Adoption (66), Church (11)
John 1.[1–9] 10–18 God gave Grace (29) through Jesus, Incarnation (10)

EPIPHANY
THE EPIPHANY (21) (6 January) *As in Year A*

THE BAPTISM OF CHRIST (7)
Genesis 1.1–5 The Spirit (69) over the waters
    Psalm 29 The voice of the Lord over the waters
Acts 19.1–7 Baptism (7) and the Spirit (69)
Mark 1.4–11 The Baptism (7) of Jesus

SECOND SUNDAY OF EPIPHANY (21)
1 Samuel 3.1–10 [11–20] The child Samuel in the Temple (19)
    Psalm 139.1–6, 13–18 God knows us, Providence (56)
Revelation 5.1–10 Worthy is the Lamb (68), Music (3)
John 1.43–51 'You are the Son of God,' Revelation (21)

THIRD SUNDAY OF EPIPHANY (21)
Genesis 14.17–20 Melchizedek brought bread and wine, Eucharist (22)
    Psalm 128 God will bless your Family (26)
Revelation 19.6–10 The Family (26) feast of the Lamb (68)
John 2.1–11 A wedding at Cana, Family (26), Baptism (7), Eucharist (22)

FOURTH SUNDAY OF EPIPHANY (21)
Deuteronomy 18.15–20 God will raise up a prophet, Word (8)
　Psalm 111 Salvation (66)
Revelation 12.1–5a A Woman (77) in heaven, Mary (42)
Mark 1.21–28 Demons recognise Christ, Revelation (21)

THE PRESENTATION OF CHRIST (2 February) *As in year A*

ORDINARY TIME
PROPER 1 *Sunday between 3 and 9 February inclusive (if earlier than 2 before Lent)*
Isaiah 40.21–31 God's greatness, Creation (16), Grace (29)
　Psalm 147.1–11, 20c Creation (16), Providence (56), Healing (32)
1 Corinthians 9.16–23 Evangelism (23), Other Faiths (48), Law (13)
Mark 1.29–39 Jesus' Healing (32) and preaching

PROPER 2 *Sunday between 10 and 16 February inclusive (if earlier than 2 before Lent)*
2 Kings 5.1–14 Naaman Healed (32), Race (57), Other Faiths (48)
　Psalm 30 Salvation (66) from Death (18), Grace (29), Joy (34)
1 Corinthians 9.24–27 The Perseverance (52) of athletes
Mark 1.40–45 Healing (32) a leper, Evangelism (23)

PROPER 3 *Sunday between 17 and 23 February inclusive (if earlier than 2 before Lent)*
Isaiah 43.18–25 God's Forgiveness (28)
　Psalm 41 Care for the Needy (46), Healing (32), Providence (56)
2 Corinthians 1.18–22 Jesus is the Yes to God's promises, Spirit (69)
Mark 2.1–12 Healing (32) and Forgiveness (28) of a paralysed man

SECOND SUNDAY BEFORE LENT
Proverbs 8.1, 22–31 Wisdom (76) in Creation (16)
　Psalm 104.24-end Creation (16)
Colossians 1.15–20 The head,
Church (11), Creation (16), Forgiveness (28), Peace (51), Cross (17)
John 1.1–14 The Word (8) in Creation (16)

SUNDAY BEFORE LENT
2 Kings 2.1–12 Elisha sees Elijah's Ascensin in Glory
　Psalm 50.1–6 God speaks from heaven, Word (8)
2 Corinthians 4.3–6 The Glory of God in the face of Jesus
Mark 9.2–9 The Transfiguration (72)

LENT
ASH WEDNESDAY (38) *As in Year A*

FIRST SUNDAY OF LENT (38)
Genesis 9.8–17 Noah's Covenant (15) Nature (45) Grace (29)
　Psalm 25.1–10 God's Grace (29) and Forgiveness (28)
1 Petr 3.18–22 Jesus speaks to Noah's generation, Baptism (7) Death (18)
Mark 1.9–15 The Baptism (7) and temptation of Jesus, Repentance (60)

SECOND SUNDAY OF LENT (38)
Genesis 17.1–7, 15–16 The Covenant (15) with Abraham
　Psalm 22.23–31 Witnessing (23) Grace (29) to all, Death (18)

Romans 4.13–25 The Covenant (15) with Abraham was through Faith (25)
Mark 8.31–38 Take up your Cross (17)

THIRD SUNDAY OF LENT (38)
Exodus 20.1–7 The first four Commandments (13)
    Psalm 19 The heavens declare greatness, Nature (45), Law (13)
1 Corinthians 1.18–25 The Cross (17) is greater than human Wisdom (76)
John 2.13–22 Cleansing the Temple (19), Judgement (35)

FOURTH SUNDAY OF LENT (38)
Numbers 21.4–9 The bronze serpent, Healing (32)
    Psalm 107.1–3, 17–22 Thanks (71) for Healing (32)
Ephesians 2.1–10 Salvation (66) by Grace (29), Faith (25), Works (62)
John 3.14–21 Moses lifted the serpent, Life (39) Light (40) Judgement (35)

Or: MOTHERING SUNDAY (44) As in Year A

FIFTH SUNDAY OF LENT (38) *(Passiontide) (17)*
Jeremiah 31.31–34 New Covenant (15), Forgiveness (28), Law (13)
    Psalm 51.1–2 Forgiveness (28), *or* Psalm 119.1–16 Law (13)
Hebrews 5.5–10 Jesus the Mediator of a new Covenant (15)
John 12.20–33 The Death (18) of the seed, Judgement (35), Cross (17)

PALM SUNDAY (49)
Liturgy of the Palms:
Mark 11.1–11 or John 12.12–16 Triumphal Entry
    Psalm 118.1–2, 19–29 Procession to the Temple (19)
Liturgy of the Passion:
Isaiah 50.4–9a I gave my back to the smiters, Servant (67), Cross (17)
    Psalm 31.9–16 Assurance (5) in Suffering (70)
Philippians 2.5–11 Jesus' Obedience (47) unto Death (18).Humility (33)
Mark 14.1 –15.47 The Last Supper to the Burial, Eucharist (22)
or Mark 15.1–39 [40–47] The Trial to the Death (18) on the Cross (17)

HOLY WEEK TO EASTER DAY *As in Year A*

SECOND SUNDAY OF EASTER (61)
Acts 4.32–35 Witnessing (23) to the Resurrection (61), The Needy (46)
    Psalm 133 Unity (75), Life (39)
1 John 1.1 –2.2 Word (8) of Life (39) Light (40) Forgiveness (28)
John 20.19–31 Upper room, Faith (25), Peace (51), Life (39)

THIRD SUNDAY OF EASTER (61)
Acts 3.12–19 Witnessing (23) to the Resurrection (61), Repentance (60)
    Psalm 4 Joy (34), Light (40), Providence (56)
1 John 3.1–7 Adoption (66)
Luke 24.36b–48 The Upper Room,
Fish (27), Bible (8), Repentance (60), Forgiveness (28), Evangelism (23)

FOURTH SUNDAY OF EASTER (61)
Acts 4.5–12 Peter's (53) Witness (23) to Resurrection (61), Salvation (66)
    Psalm 23 The Lord is my Shepherd (68)

1 John 3.16–24 Law (13), Faith (25), Love (41), the Needy (46)
John 10.11–18 The good Shepherd (68)

FIFTH SUNDAY OF EASTER (61)

Acts 8.26–40 Baptism (7) of an Ethiopian, Bible (8) Witness (23) Race (57)
    Psalm 22.25–31 The Needy (46), Evangelism (23), Death (18)
1 John 4.7–21 Love (41) one another, Spirit (69), God's Love (41)
John 15.1–8 The true vine, Church (11), Eucharist (22)

SIXTH SUNDAY OF EASTER (61)

Acts 10.44–48 Baptism (7) of gentiles, Spirit (69) Race (57) Witness (23)
    Psalm 98 Salvation (66), Evangelism (23), Justice (36)
1 John 5.1–6 Love (41), Commandments (13)
John 15.9–17 The Commandment (13)to Love (41).Death (18)

ASCENSION DAY (4) *As in Year A*

SEVENTH SUNDAY OF EASTER (61)

Acts 1.15–17, 21–26 Choosing Matthias, Authority (6), Ministry (43)
    Psalm 1 Righteousness (62)
1 John 5.9–13 Faith (25), Life (39)
John 17.6–19 The World (78), Providence (56), Joy (34), Word (8)

OLD TESTAMENT READINGS FOR SUNDAYS IN EASTERTIDE as in Year A

PENTECOST (69) (Whit Sunday) The Holy Spirit
The Reading from Acts must be used as either the first or second Reading.
Acts 2.1–21 The day of Pentecost (69), *or* Ezekiel 37.1–14 Valley of bones
    Psalm 104.24–34, 35b The Spirit (69) in Creation (16)
Romans 8.22–27 The Spirit's (69) Prayer (55), *or* Acts 2.1–21 Pentecost (69)
John 15.26–27; 16.4b–15 The Advocate, Truth (74), Evangelism (23)

ORDINARY TIME
TRINITY SUNDAY (73)
Isaiah 6.1–8 Holy, holy, holy, God's greatness and call (14)
    Psalm 29 God's greatness
Romans 8.12–17 The Spirit (69) makes us heirs of God, with Christ
John 3.1–17 Born of the Spirit (69)

*If the Sunday between 24 & 28 May inclusive follows Trinity Sunday, Proper 3
(above) is used.*

PROPER 4 *Sunday between 29 May and 4 June inclusive (if after Trinity Sunday)*
1 Samuel 3.1–10 [11–20] Samuel hears God's call (14), Children (9)
    Psalm 139.1–6, 13–18 Known in the womb, Providence (56)
or Deuteronomy 5.12–15 Commandments 5–10 (13)
    Psalm 81.1–10 Salvation (66), Law (13), Sabbath (63)
2 Corinthians 4.5–12 Clay pots, Ministry (43), Life (39), Light (40)
Mark 2.23 –3.6 Healing (32) on the Sabbath (63), Commandments (13)

PROPER 5 *Sunday between 5 and 11 June inclusive (if after Trinity Sunday)*
1 Samuel 8.4–11 [12–15] 16–20 [11.14–15] King (37) Saul anointed
   Psalm 138 God's greatness
or Genesis 3.8–15 God in the Garden of Eden
   Psalm 130 Hope for Salvation (66)
2 Corinthians 4.13 –5.1 Grace (29), Suffering (70), Resurrection (61)
Mark 3.20–35 Family (26), Obedience (47)

PROPER 6 *Sunday between 12 and 18 June inclusive (if after Trinity Sunday)*
1 Samuel 15.34 –16.13 David's call (14), anointed King (37)
   Psalm 20 Give victory to the King (37)
or Ezekiel 17.22–24 God's call (14)
   Psalm 92.1–4, 12–15 Righteousness (62)
2 Corinthians 5.6–10 [11–13] 14–17 Faith (25), Life (39), Death (18)
Mark 4.26–34 Parables of the Kingdom (37)

PROPER 7 *Sunday between 19 and 25 June inclusive (if after Trinity Sunday)*
1 Samuel 17.[1a, 4–11, 19–23] 32–49 David and Goliath, Providence (56)
   Psalm 9.9–20 God lifts me from Death (18), Providence (56)
or 1 Samuel 17.57–18.5, 10–16 David and Jonathan
   Psalm 133 Unity (75)
or Job 38.1–11 God's greatness in Creation (16)
   Psalm 107.23–32 Protection (56) from the storm, Salvation (66)
2 Corinthians 6.1–13 The Suffering (70) of the Apostles (53),
   Ministry (43) Providence (56)
Mark 4.35–41 Stilling the storm, Providence (56)

PROPER 8 *Sunday between 26 June and 2 July inclusive*
2 Samuel 1.1, 17–27 David's lament over Saul and Jonathan, Death (18)
   Psalm 130 Out of the depths, Faith (25), Death (18)
or Wisdom of Solomon 1.13–15; 2.23–24 Made for Life (39) not Death (18)
   Canticle: Lamentations 3.23–33 New every morning,
   Suffering (70), God's Love (41)
   or Psalm 30 Healing (32), Death (18), Life (39)
2 Corinthians 8.7–15 Giving to the Needy (46), Possessions (54)
Mark 5.21–43 Healing (32) Jairus' child (9), a sick Woman's (77) Faith (25)
Lamentations 3.23–33 *may be used as the First Reading in place of* Wisdom
1.13–15; 2.23–24

PROPER 9 *Sunday between 3 and 9 July inclusive*
2 Samuel 5.1–5, 9–10 David's victory over the City (12)
   Psalm 48 God's Protection (56) of the City (12)
or Ezekiel 2.1–5 Speak the Word (8), ignore Disobedience (47)
   Psalm 123 Hope for God's Grace (29) with Obedience (47)
2 Corinthians 12.2–10 God's Grace (29) is sufficient in Suffering (70)
Mark 6.1–13 Jesus rejected, Obedience (47) Evangelism (23) Ministry (43)

PROPER 10 *Sunday between 10 and 16 July inclusive*
2 Samuel 6.1–5, 12b–19 The ark comes to the City (12) Arts (3) Festival (63)
   Psalm 24 Lift up your heads, City (12)

Year B

or Amos 7.7–15 The plumbline: Judgement (35) on the City (12)
  Psalm 85.8–13 Peace (51) Faith (25) Works (62) Harvest (31)
Ephesians 1.3–14 Called (14) to Adoption (66)
Mark 6.14–29 Herod beheads the Baptist (58) Suffering (70) Authority (6)

PROPER 11 *Sunday between 17 and 23 July inclusive*
2 Samuel 7.1–14a King (37) David not to build the Temple (19)
  Psalm 89.20–37 Covenant (15) with King (37) David
or Jeremiah 23.1–6 Promise of a Righteous (62) King (37) & Shepherd (68)
  Psalm 23 The Lord is my Shepherd (68)
Ephesians 2.11–22 Unity (75) and Forgiveness (28), Jew & Gentile,
  Evangelism (23), Race (57), Other Faiths (48)
Mark 6.30–34, 53–56 Feeding the 5000, Eucharist (22), Providence (56)

PROPER 12 *Sunday between 24 and 30 July inclusive*
2 Samuel 11.1–15 David and Bathsheba, Family (26)
  Psalm 14, Repentance (60), the Needy (46)
or 2 Kings 4.42–44 Elisha feeds a crowd, Eucharist (22), Providence (56)
  Psalm 145.10–18 Prayer (55), Providence (56), Eucharist (22)
Ephesians 3.14–21 Prayer (55) and Providence (56)
John 6.1–21 Feeding the five thousand, Eucharist (22), Providence (56)

PROPER 13 *Sunday between 31 July and 6 August inclusive*
2 Samuel 11.26–12.13a The parable of the one ewe Lamb (68),
  Repentance (60), Forgiveness (28), Justice (36)
  Psalm 51.1–12 Forgiveness (28)
or Exodus 16.2–4, 9–15 The manna, Eucharist (22), Providence (56)
  Psalm 78.23–29 The manna
Ephesians 4.1–16 Gifts of the Spirit (69), Unity (75) of the Church (11)
John 6.24–35 I am the bread of Life (39), Eucharist (22)

PROPER 14 *Sunday between 7 and 13 August inclusive*
2 Samuel 18.5–9, 15, 31–33 David's grief over Absalom's Death (18)
  Psalm 130 Grief, Forgiveness (28)
or 1 Kings 19.4–8 God gives Elijah food, Providence (56)
  Psalm 34.1–8 Prayer (55) and Providence (56)
Ephesians 4.25 –5.2 Love (41), Forgiveness (28), and Righteousness (62)
John 6.35, 41–51 I am the bread of Life (39), Eucharist (22)

PROPER 15 *Sunday between 14 and 20 August inclusive*
1 Kings 2.10–12; 3.3–14 Solomon's dream, Wisdom (76), Authority (6)
  Psalm 111 The beginning of Wisdom (76)
or Proverbs 9.1–6 Wisdom's (76) Call (14)
  Psalm 34.9–14 Providence (56), Works (62), Peace (51)
Ephesians 5.15–20 Wisdom (76), Works (62), the Arts (3)
John 6.51–58 Eat and live, Eucharist (22), Life (39)

PROPER 16 *Sunday between 21 and 27 August inclusive*
1 Kings 8.[1, 6, 10–11] 22–30, 41–43 Solomon Prays (55), Evangelism (23)
  Psalm 84 How lovely is your Temple! (19)
or Joshua 24.1–2a, 14–18 Choose the Lord, Conversion (14)

Psalm 34.15–22 The Lord's Salvation (66)
Ephesians 6.10–20 The Armour of God (56), Perseverance (52)
John 6.56–69 Faith (25) and Life (39)

PROPER 17 *Sunday between 28 August and 3 September inclusive*
Song of Solomon 2.8–13 Love (41) in springtime, Family (26), Nature (45)
    Psalm 45.1–2, 6–9 The King's (37) wedding, Family (26)
or Deuteronomy 4.1–2, 6–9 Teach Family (26) Obedience (47) to Law (13)
    Psalm 15 Temple (19), Works (62)
James 1.17–24 Doers of the Word (8), Righteousness (62)
Mark 7.1–8, 14–15, 21–23 Inner cleanness, Righteousness (62)

PROPER 18 *Sunday between 4 and 10 September inclusive*
Proverbs 22.1–2, 8–9, 22–23 The Needy (46)
    Psalm 125 God rewards the Righteous (62)
or Isaiah 35.4–7a Water in the desert, Healing (32), Baptism (7)
    Psalm 146 Healing (32) and Salvation (66)
James 2.1–10 [11–13] 14–17 Grace (29) to the Needy (46), Works (62)
Mark 7.24–37 Crumbs from the table, Healing (32) the deaf, Witness (23)

PROPER 19 *Sunday between 11 and 17 September inclusive*
Proverbs 1.20–33 Wisdom's (76) call (14)
    Psalm 19 Law (13), Works (62), Nature (45)
    or Canticle: Wisdom of Solomon 7.26 –8.1 Wisdom (76)
or Isaiah 50.4–9a Suffering (70)
    Psalm 116.1–9 Salvation (66) from Death (18)
James 3.1–12 Controlling the tongue, Righteousness (62)
Mark 8.27–38 Take up your Cross (17)

PROPER 20 *Sunday between 18 and 24 September inclusive*
Proverbs 31.10–31 A good wife, Family (26), Women (77), Works (62)
    Psalm 1 A good person, Righteousness (62)
or Wisdom (76) of Solomon 1.16 –2.1, 12–22 Conflict (38)
or Jeremiah 11.18–20 Conflict (38)
    Psalm 54 Conflict (38)
James 3.13 –4.3, 7–8a Wisdom (76) and Works (62)
Mark 9.30–37 Be like Children (9), Humility (33) Service (67) Family (26)

PROPER 21 *Sunday between 25 September and 1 October inclusive*
Esther 7.1–6, 9–10; 9.20–22 Esther's victory, Women (77)
    Psalm 124 Salvation (66)
or Numbers 11.4–6, 10–16, 24–29 The Spirit (69) on leaders, Authority (6)
    Psalm 19.7–14 Law (13), Guidance (30), Forgiveness (28)
James 5.13–20 Prayer (55) Healing (32) Repentance (60) Conversion (14)
Mark 9.38–50 Causes of offence, Temptation (38)

PROPER 22 *Sunday between 2 and 8 October inclusive*
Job 1.1; 2.1–10 Job tested by Suffering (70)
    Psalm 26 Righteousness (62)
or Genesis 2.18–24 Creation (16) of Eve, Family (26), Women (77)
    Psalm 8 Creation (16) and Ecology (20)

Hebrews 1.1–4; 2.5–12 Creation (16) of humankind, Suffering (70)
Mark 10.2–16 Family (26) and Children (9)

PROPER 23 *Sunday between 9 and 15 October inclusive*
Job 23.1–9, 16–17 God's greatness and Justice (36)
    Psalm 22.1–15 Faith (25) and Assurance (5)
or Amos 5.6–7, 10–15 Justice (36) for the Needy (46)
    Psalm 90.12–17 Salvation (66)
Hebrews 4.12–16 Word (8) Incarnation (10) Temptation (38) Temple (19)
Mark 10.17–31 Possessions (54)

PROPER 24 *Sunday between 16 and 22 October inclusive*
Job 38.1–7, [34–41] Creation (16)
    Psalm 104.1–9, 24, 35c Creation (16)
or Isaiah 53.4–12 The Suffering (70) Servant (67)
    Psalm 91.9–16 Providence (56), Salvation (66)
Hebrews 5.1–10 Christ a priest (43), Salvation (66), Incarnation (10)
Mark 10.35–45 Humility (33) and Service (67)

PROPER 25 *Sunday between 23 and 29 October inclusive*
Job 42.1–6, 10–17 Repentance (60) and Forgiveness (28)
    Psalm 34.1–8 [19–22] Salvation (66)
or Jeremiah 31.7–9 Salvation (66)
    Psalm 126 Forgiveness (28) Salvation (66) Harvest (31) Joy (34)
Hebrews 7.23–28 Christ our high priest, Prayer (55), Ministry (43)
Mark 10.46–52 Healing (32) of a blind man

Or: **BIBLE SUNDAY (8)**
Isaiah 55.1–11 My Word (8) shall not return empty, Call (14)
    Psalm 19.7–14 The Law (13) of the Lord is perfect
2 Timothy 3.14 –4.5 All Scripture (8) is inspired
John 5.36b–47 Search the Scriptures (8)

DEDICATION FESTIVAL (19) *First Sunday in October or Last Sunday after Trinity*
Genesis 28.11–18 This is the house of God
or Revelation 21.9–14 The new City (12) of Jerusalem
    Psalm 122 Let us go up to the house of the Lord
1 Peter 2.1–10 Living stones in God's Temple, the Church (11)
John 10.22–29 The Dedication Festival (19) in the Temple

ALL SAINTS' SUNDAY (65) *Sunday between 30 October and 5 November inclusive*
Wisdom 3.1–9 The righteous in God's hand
or Isaiah 25.1–9 A refuge for the Needy (46), Death (18), Temple (19)
    Psalm 24.1–6 Open the Temple gates for the Lord
Revelation 21.1–6a The new Jerusalem
John 11.32–44 The Resurrection (61) of Lazarus

Or: **FOURTH SUNDAY BEFORE ADVENT**
*Sunday between 31 October and 5 November inclusive. For use if the feast of All
Saints was celebrated on 1 November and alternative propers are needed.*
Deuteronomy 6.1–9 Love (41) God, teach the Law (13) to Children (9)

Psalm 119.1–8 Joy (34) in the Commandments (13)
Hebrews 9.11–14 Salvation (66) through the Sacrifice (64) of Christ
Mark 12.28–34 Law (13) to Love (41) God, Love the Needy (46)

THIRD SUNDAY BEFORE ADVENT *Sunday between 6 and 12 November inclusive*
Jonah 3.1–5, 10 God's Forgiveness (28) of Nineveh, Evangelism (23)
    Psalm 62.5–12 God's greatness and Love (41)
Hebrews 9.24–28 Salvation (66) through Christ
Mark 1.14–20 Fish (27) for people, Evangelism (23)

SECOND SUNDAY BEFORE ADVENT *Sunday between 13 and 19 November inclusive*
Daniel 12.1–3 Conflict (38) and Resurrection (61)
    Psalm 16 Death (18), Resurrection (61) and Life (39)
Hebrews 10.11–14 [15–18] 19–25 Assurance (5) and Faith (25)
Mark 13.1–8 Conflict (38)

CHRIST THE KING (37) *Sunday between 20 and 26 November inclusive*
Daniel 7.9–10, 13–14 The Kingship (37) of Christ
    Psalm 93 The Lord is King (37)
Revelation 1.4b–8 The greatness of Christ
John 18.33–37 Are you the King (37)?

YEAR C, the Year of Luke

(Year C begins on Advent Sunday in 1998, 2001, 2004, etc.)

ADVENT
FIRST SUNDAY OF ADVENT (1)
Jeremiah 33.14–16 A King (37) is promised
    Psalm 25.1–10 Waiting for God, Readiness (58)
1 Thessalonians 3.9–13 Prayer (55) to be blameless at the coming of Christ
Luke 21.25–36 The coming of Christ

SECOND SUNDAY OF ADVENT (1)
Baruch 5.1–9 God will lead his people with Joy (34), Church (11)
or Malachi 3.1–4 A messenger to prepare the way
    Canticle: Benedictus, The birth of John the Baptist (58)
Philippians 1.3–11 Completion by the day of Christ
Luke 3.1–6 John the Baptist (58)

THIRD SUNDAY OF ADVENT (1)
Zephaniah 3.14–20 Sing, daughter Zion, God is in your midst,
    Joy (34), the Arts (3), Women (77)
    Canticle: Isaiah 12.2–6 Great in your midst
Philippians 4.4–7 Rejoice in the Lord, Joy (34)
Luke 3.7–18 The witness of John the Baptist (58), Evangelism (23)

FOURTH SUNDAY OF ADVENT (1)

Micah 5.2–5a A leader from Bethlehem, Authority (6), Incarnation (10)
  Canticle: Magnificat, Incarnation (10), Mary (42)
  or Psalm 80.1–7, Come with Salvation (66)
Hebrews 10.5–10 When Christ came into the World (78), Incarnation (10)
Luke 1.39–45 Mary (42) visits Elizabeth, Women (77)

CHRISTMAS
CHRISTMAS DAY (10) (25 December) *As in Year A*

FIRST SUNDAY OF CHRISTMAS (10)

1 Samuel 2.18–20 Giving Children (9) to God
  Psalm 148 Young and old together
Colossians 3.12–17 The Word (8) of God, The Arts (3)
Luke 2.41–52 The Child Jesus in the Temple (19)

SECOND SUNDAY OF CHRISTMAS (10)

Jeremiah 31.7–14 God will send Salvation (66)
  Psalm 147.12–20 God's Word (8) brings Peace (51)
or Ecclesiasticus 24.1–12 God's Wisdom (76) comes to earth
  Canticle: Wisdom 10.15–21 Salvation (66), Wisdom, Church (11)
Ephesians 1.3–14 God's plan to gather everything in Christ, Salvation (66)
John 1.[1–9] 10–18 God gave Grace (29) through Jesus, Incarnation (10)

EPIPHANY
THE EPIPHANY (21) (6 January) *As in Year A*

THE BAPTISM OF CHRIST (7)

Isaiah 43.1–7 When you pass through the waters
  Psalm 29 The voice of the Lord is over the waters
Acts 8.14–17 Baptism (7) and the Holy Spirit (69)
Luke 3.15–17, 21–22 The Baptism (7) of Jesus

SECOND SUNDAY OF EPIPHANY (21)

Isaiah 62.1–5 Nations shall see your Salvation (66), Evangelism (23)
  Psalm 36.5–10 All peoples, Evangelism (23)
1 Corinthians 12.1–11 Many gifts, one Spirit (69), Unity (75)
John 2.1–11 The wedding at Cana, Family (26), Eucharist (22)

THIRD SUNDAY OF EPIPHANY (21)

Nehemiah 8.1–3, 5–6, 8–10 Joy (34) in the Commandments (13)
  Psalm 19 The heavens declare, Nature (45), Law (13)
1 Corinthians 12.12–31a The Unity (75) of Christ's body the Church (11)
Luke 4.14–21 Jesus reads the Bible (8) at Nazareth, Spirit (69)

FOURTH SUNDAY OF EPIPHANY (21)

Ezekiel 43.27 –44.4 The Glory (72) of the Lord filled the Temple (19)
  Psalm 48 The greatness of God, The Temple (19)
1 Corinthians 13.1–13 Love (41)
Luke 2.22–40 The presentation of Christ in the Temple (19), Light (40)

THE PRESENTATION OF CHRIST (2 February) *As in Year A*

ORDINARY TIME
PROPER 1 *Sunday between 3 and 9 February inclusive (if earlier than 2 before Lent)*
Isaiah 6.1–8 [9–13] Holy, holy, holy, The greatness of God, Vocation (14)
  Psalm 138 Faith (25)
1 Corinthians 15.1–11 The Resurrection (61) of Christ
Luke 5.1–11 Fish (27) for people, Evangelism (23), Ministry (43)

PROPER 2 *Sunday between 10 and 16 February inclusive (if earlier than 2 before Lent)*
Jeremiah 17.5–10 A tree planted by the water, Faith (25), Works (62)
  Psalm 1 Works (62)
1 Corinthians 15.12–20 Faith (25) in the Resurrection (61)
Luke 6.17–26 Blessed are the poor, The Needy (46)

PROPER 3 *Sunday between 17 and 23 February inclusive (if earlier than 2 before Lent)*
Genesis 45.3–11, 15 Joseph and his Family (26)
  Psalm 37.1–11, 39–40 Salvation (66)
1 Corinthians 15.35–38, 42–50 Adam (47), seeds and Resurrection (61)
Luke 6.27–38 Love (41) your enemies, Conflict (38)

SECOND SUNDAY BEFORE LENT
Genesis 2.4b–9, 15–25 Creation (16)
  Psalm 65 Creation (16), Harvest (31)
Revelation 4 The living creatures cry 'Holy!' Nature (45)
Luke 8.22–25 Stilling the storm, Nature (45)

SUNDAY BEFORE LENT
Exodus 34.29–35 Moses' face is shining
  Psalm 99 God spoke his Word (8) in the cloud
2 Corinthians 3.12 –4.2 The Spirit (69) unveils God's Truth (74)
Luke 9.28–36 [37–43] The Transfiguration (72)

LENT
ASH WEDNESDAY (38) *As in Year A*

FIRST SUNDAY OF LENT (38)
Deuteronomy 26.1–11 First-fruits, Harvest (31)
  Psalm 91.1–2, 9–16 God's Providence (56)
Romans 10.8b–13 Faith (25), Salvation (66) and Unity (75)
Luke 4.1–13 The temptation of Jesus

SECOND SUNDAY OF LENT (38)
Genesis 15.1–12, 17–18 God's promise to Abraham
  Psalm 27 Faith (25), Providence (56), Temple (19)
Philippians 3.17–4.1 Citizens of heaven (39), City (12), Perseverance (52)
Luke 13.31–35 Jesus' lament over the City (12)

THIRD SUNDAY OF LENT (38)
Isaiah 55.1–9 A call to conversion (14)
  Psalm 63.1–8 Faith (25), Providence (56)
1 Corinthians 10.1–13 Temptation (38)
Luke 13.1–9 The parable of the fig tree, Works (62)

FOURTH SUNDAY OF LENT (38)
Joshua 5.9–12 Eating the Passover in Canaan, Sabbath (63)
Psalm 32 Repentance (60)
2 Corinthians 5.16–21 Forgiveness (28)
Luke 15.1–3, 11b–32 The prodigal son, Forgiveness (28), Parenthood (50)

Or: MOTHERING SUNDAY (44) As in year A

FIFTH SUNDAY OF LENT (38) *(Passiontide)* (17)
Isaiah 43.16–21 Salvation (66)
Psalm 126 Salvation (66), Joy (34)
Philippians 3.4b–14 Perseverance (52)
John 12.1–8 Mary and Martha, Works (62) and Prayer (55)

PALM SUNDAY (49)
Liturgy of the Palms:
Luke 19.28–40 The Triumphal Entry
Psalm 118.1–2, 19–29 Procession to the Temple (19)
Liturgy of the Passion:
Isaiah 50.4–9a I gave my back to the smiters, Servant (67), Cross (17)
Psalm 31.9–16 Assurance (5) in Suffering (70)
Philippians 2.5–11 Jesus' Obedience (47) unto Death (18), Humility (33)
Luke 22.14 –23.56 The Last Supper to the Burial, Eucharist (22)
or Luke 23.1–49 The Trial before Pilate to the Death (18) on the Cross (17)

HOLY WEEK TO EASTER DAY *As in Year A*

SECOND SUNDAY OF EASTER (61)
Acts 5.27–32 Peter (53) Witnesses (23) to the Resurrection (61)
Psalm 118.14–29 I shall not die but live, Life (39)
or Psalm 150 Praise in Heaven (39), The Arts (3)
Revelation 1.4–8 The firstborn from the dead
John 20.19–31 The upper room, Thomas's Faith (25)

THIRD SUNDAY OF EASTER (61)
Acts 9.1–6 [7–20] Paul's conversion (14)
Psalm 30 God brought me up from Death (18)
Revelation 5.11–14 Worshipping the Lamb (68), The Arts (3)
John 21.1–19 Fishing (27), Evangelism (23) and Eucharist (22)

FOURTH SUNDAY OF EASTER (61)
Acts 9.36–43 Peter (53) raises Tabitha, Women (77)
Psalm 23 The Lord is my Shepherd (68)
Revelation 7.9–17 The Lamb their Shepherd (68), Suffering (70)
John 10.22–30 My Sheep (68) hear my voice, Parenthood (50) Trinity (73)

FIFTH SUNDAY OF EASTER (61)
Acts 11.1–18 Baptism (7) of the Gentiles, Spirit (69), Evangelism (23)
Psalm 148 Nature (45) praising God
Revelation 21.1–6 Death (18) will be no more
John 13.31–35 The Commandment (13) to Love (41)

SIXTH SUNDAY OF EASTER (61)
Acts 16.9–15 Baptism (7) of Lydia, Women (77), Evangelism (23)
    Psalm 67 Evangelism (23), Harvest (31)
Revelation 21.10, 22 –22.5 Lamb (68) Light (40) Healing (32) Baptism (7)
John 14.23–29 Going to the Father, Parenthood (50)
or John 5.1–9 Spirit (69), Baptism (7)

ASCENSION DAY (4) *as in Year A*

SEVENTH SUNDAY OF EASTER (61)
Acts 16.16–34 Baptism (7) of a jailer, Conversion (14), Evangelism (23)
    Psalm 97 The Lord is King (37)
Revelation 22.12–14, 16–17, 20–21 Come! The coming of Christ (1)
John 17.20–26 Church (11) Unity (75) and Love (41)

OLD TESTAMENT READINGS FOR SUNDAYS IN EASTERTIDE as in Year A

PENTECOST (69) (Whit Sunday) The Holy Spirit
The reading from Acts must be used as either the first or second reading.
Acts 2.1–21 The day of Pentecost (69)
or Genesis 11.1–9 The tower of Babylon, Language and Race (57)
    Psalm 104.24–34, 35b The Spirit (69) in Creation (16)
Romans 8.14–17 Spirit (69) Adoption (66) Guidance (30) Suffering (70)
or Acts 2.1–21 The day of Pentecost (69)
John 14.8–17 [25–27] The Spirit (69) of Truth (74)

ORDINARY TIME
TRINITY SUNDAY (73)
Proverbs 8.1–4, 22–31 Wisdom's (76) call (14), Wisdom in Creation (16)
    Psalm 8 The greatness of God, God in Nature (45)
Romans 5.1–5 God's Love (41) and Spirit (69)
John 16.12–13 Spirit (69), Father and Jesus, Parenthood (50)

If the Sunday between 24 & 28 May inclusive follows Trinity Sunday, Proper 3 (above) is used.

PROPER 4 *Sunday between 29 May and 4 June inclusive (if after Trinity Sunday)*
1 Kings 18.20–21 [22–29] 30–39 Elijah & Baal, Assurance (5), Prayer (55)
    Psalm 96 Praise God all nations, Evangelism (23)
or 1 Kings 8.22–23, 41–43 Solomon's Prayer (55) for Evangelism (23)
    Psalm 96.1–9 God's greatness
Galatians 1.1–12 No other gospel
Luke 7.1–10 Healing (32) a centurion's boy, Evangelism (23), Authority (6)

PROPER 5 *Sunday between 5 and 11 June inclusive (if after Trinity Sunday)*
1 Kings 17.8–16 [17–24] The widow's jar, Providence (56), The Needy (46)
    Psalm 146 God upholds the widows
or 1 Kings 17.17–24 Elijah heals the widow's Child (9), Resurrection (61)
    Psalm 30 Resurrection (61) from Death (18)
Galatians 1.11–24 Paul's Conversion (14) and Authority (6)
Luke 7.11–17 The Resurrection (61) of a Child (9) at Nain, The Needy (46)

PROPER 6 *Sunday between 12 and 18 June inclusive (if after Trinity Sunday)*
1 Kings 21.1–10 [11–14] 15–21a Naboth's vineyard, Justice (36)
    Psalm 5.1–8 God's Justice (36)
or 2 Samuel 11.26 –12.10, 13–15 David's Repentance (60)
    Psalm 32 Forgiveness (28)
Galatians 2.15–21 Law (13), Faith (25) and Grace (29)
Luke 7.36 –8.3 A Woman's (77) Repentance (60), Forgiveness (28)

PROPER 7 *Sunday between 19 and 25 June inclusive (if after Trinity Sunday)*
1 Kings 19.1–4 [5–7] 8–15a The still small voice, Spirit (69)
    Psalms 42 & 43 Faith (25), hope, Eucharist (22)
or Isaiah 65.1–9 God's Judgement (35)
    Psalm 22.19–28 Salvation (66)
Galatians 3.23–29 The Law (13) our tutor till Faith (25) comes,
    Unity (75), Baptism (7), Evangelism (23)
Luke 8.26–39 Demons sent into pigs, Healing (32)

PROPER 8 *Sunday between 26 June and 2 July inclusive*
2 Kings 2.1–2, 6–14 Elijah's Spirit (69) given to Elisha
    Psalm 77.1–2, 11–20 God's greatness in Salvation (66)
or 1 Kings 19.15–16, 19–21 Elijah's Authority (6) to call followers
    Psalm 16 Thanks (71)
Galatians 5.1, 13–25 The fruit of the Spirit (69), Salvation (66), Peace (51)
Luke 9.51–62 The call (14) to follow Christ.

PROPER 9 *Sunday between 3 and 9 July inclusive*
2 Kings 5.1–14 Naaman's Healing (32) from leprosy
    Psalm 30 Healing (32), Forgiveness (28), Resurrection (61)
or Isaiah 66.10–14 The Motherhood (50) of God, Women (77)
    Psalm 66.1–9 God's Grace (29)
Galatians 6.[1–6] 7–16 Righteousness (62)
Luke 10.1–11, 16–20 Evangelism (23) by the 70 Apostles (53), Ministry (43)

PROPER 10 *Sunday between 10 and 16 July inclusive*
Amos 7.7–17 The Plumbline, Judgement (35) on the City (12)
    Psalm 82 Justice (36)
or Deuteronomy 30.9–14 The Word (8) is near you
    Psalm 25.1–10 Truth (74), Guidance (30)
Colossians 1.1–14 Prayer (55), Faith (25), Works (62), Forgiveness (28)
Luke 10.25–37 The good Samaritan, neighbour to the Needy (46),
    Love (41)

PROPER 11 *Sunday between 17 and 23 July inclusive*
Amos 8.1–12 Justice (36) for the Needy (46)
    Psalm 52 Justice (36) for the Needy (46)
or Genesis 18.1–10a The oaks of Mamre, Trinity (73)
    Psalm 15 Justice (36)
Colossians 1.15–28 Christ the head of the Church (11)
Luke 10.38–42 Martha and Mary, Works (62) and Prayer (55)

PROPER 12 *Sunday between 24 and 30 July inclusive*
Hosea 1.2–10 Hosea's Family (26), Forgiveness (28)
  Psalm 85 Forgiveness (28)
or Genesis 18.20–32 Abraham's Prayer (55) for Forgiveness (28) for Sodom
  Psalm 138 Prayer (55) for Grace (29), Thanks (71)
Colossians 2.6–15 [16–19] Resurrection (61) with Christ
Luke 11.1–13 Prayer (55)

PROPER 13 *Sunday between 31 July and 6 August inclusive*
Hosea 11.1–11 Parenthood (50) of God, Guidance (30)
  Psalm 107.1–9, 43 Guidance (30)
or Ecclesiastes 1.2, 12–14; 2.18–23 Vanity and Wisdom (76)
  Psalm 49.1–12 Wisdom (76) and Death (18)
Colossians 3.1–11 Righteousness (62), Unity (75)
Luke 12.13–21 The rich fool, Possessions (54), Wisdom (76)

PROPER 14 *Sunday between 7 and 13 August inclusive*
Isaiah 1.1, 10–20 Works (62), Obedience (47), Forgiveness (28)
  Psalm 50.1–8, 22–23 Covenant (15)
or Genesis 15.1–6 Promise to Abram, his Faith (25)
  Psalm 33.12–22 Faith (25)
Hebrews 11.1–3, 8–16 Abraham's Faith (25)
Luke 12.32–40 Treasure in Heaven (39), Readiness (58), Possessions (54)

PROPER 15 *Sunday between 14 and 20 August inclusive*
Isaiah 5.1–7 The song of the vineyard, Church (11)
  Psalm 80.1–2, 8–19 The vine
or Jeremiah 23.23–29 The Word (8) of God
  Psalm 82 Justice (36)
Hebrews 11.29 –12.2 Faith (25) and Perseverance (52)
Luke 12.49–56 Justice (36)

PROPER 16 *Sunday between 21 and 27 August inclusive*
Jeremiah 1.4–10 God's Word (8), Jeremiah's call (14)
  Psalm 71.1–6 Providence (56), Women (77)
or Isaiah 58.9b–14 The Needy (46)
  Psalm 103.1–8 Forgiveness (28) and Healing (32)
Hebrews 12.18–29 The mediator of a new Covenant (15), Sin (35)
Luke 13.10–17 Healing (32) on the Sabbath (63)

PROPER 17 *Sunday between 28 August and 3 September inclusive*
Jeremiah 2.4–13 Living water, God's Justice (36), Baptism (7)
  Psalm 81.1, 10–16 God's Justice (36)
or Ecclesiasticus 10.12–18 Sin and Judgement (35)
or Proverbs 25.6–7 Pride (35) and Humility (33)
  Psalm 112 Righteousness (62), the Needy (46)
Hebrews 13.1–8, 15–16 Righteousness (62)
Luke 14.1, 7–14 Pride (35) and Humility (33)

PROPER 18 *Sunday between 4 and 10 September inclusive*
Jeremiah 18.1–11 The potter, Judgement (35) and Forgiveness (28)
  Psalm 139.1–6, 13–18 God knows us
or Deuteronomy 30.15–20 Choose Life (39), Conversion (14)
  Psalm 1 Righteousness (62)
Philemon 1–21 The runaway slave, Salvation (66) and Forgiveness (28)
Luke 14.25–33 The Call (14) to take up the Cross (17)

PROPER 19 *Sunday between 11 and 17 September inclusive*
Jeremiah 4.11–12, 22–28 Judgement (35)
  Psalm 14 Judgement (35)
or Exodus 32.7–14 Judgement (35) and a Prayer (55) for Forgiveness (28)
  Psalm 51.1–10 Prayer (55) for Forgiveness (28)
1 Timothy 1.12–17 Christ brings Salvation (66), Sin (35), Forgiveness (28)
Luke 15.1–10 A lost sheep (68), a Woman's (77) lost coin, Forgiveness (28)

PROPER 20 *Sunday between 18 and 24 September inclusive*
Jeremiah 8.18 –9.1 Balm in Gilead, Healing (32) the Nation (59)
  Psalm 79.1–9 Suffering (70), Prayer (55) for Forgiveness (28)
or Amos 8.4–7 The Needy (46)
  Psalm 113 The Needy (46)
1 Timothy 2.1–7 Those in Authority (6)
Luke 16.1–13 The shrewd manager, Possessions (54), The Needy (46)

PROPER 21 *Sunday between 25 September and 1 October inclusive*
Jeremiah 32.1–3a, 6–15 Buying a field, Faith (25)
  Psalm 91.1–6, 14–16 Providence (56)
or Amos 6.1a, 4–7 Possessions (54)
  Psalm 146 The Needy (46)
1 Timothy 6.6–19 Possessions (54), the Needy (46)
Luke 16.19–31 A rich man and Lazarus, Possessions (54), the Needy (46)

PROPER 22 *Sunday between 2 and 8 October inclusive*
Lamentations 1.1–6 The Nation (59), Suffering (70)
  Canticle: Lamentations 3.19–16 New every morning,
  or Psalm 137 Suffering (70) in Babylon
or Habakkuk 1.1–4; 2.1–4 A watchman, Perseverance (52), Justice (36)
  Psalm 37.1–9 Faith (25) and Justice (36)
2 Timothy 1.1–14 Faith (25) and Justice (36)
Luke 17.5–10 Faith (25) and Obedience (47)

PROPER 23 *Sunday between 9 and 15 October inclusive*
Jeremiah 29.1, 4–7 The City (12)
  Psalm 66.1–12 Providence (56)
or 2 Kings 5.1–3, 7–15c Naaman's Healing (32) from leprosy
  Psalm 111 Providence (56)
2 Timothy 2.8–15 Suffering (70), Perseverance (52), the Word (8)
Luke 17.11–19 The Healing (32) of a leper and his Thanks (71)

PROPER 24 *Sunday between 16 and 22 October inclusive*
Jeremiah 31.27–34 The new Covenant (15)
   Psalm 119.97–104 The Commandments (13)
or Genesis 32.22–31 Wrestling Jacob, Perseverance (52)
   Psalm 121 Providence (56)
2 Timothy 3.14 –4.5 The Word (8)
Luke 18.1–8 Perseverance (52) in Prayer (55)

PROPER 25 *SUNDAY BETWEEN 23 AND 29 OCTOBER INCLUSIVE*
Joel 2.23–32 Harvest (31)
   Psalm 65 Harvest (31)
or Ecclesiasticus 35.12–17 The Needy (46), Justice (36)
or Jeremiah 14.7–10, 19–22 Repentance (60)
   Psalm 84.1–7 The Temple (19)
2 Timothy 4.6–8, 16–18 Perseverance (52) and Providence (56)
Luke 18.9–14 Pharisee's Pride (35), taxman's Humility (33), Prayer (55)

Or: BIBLE SUNDAY (8)
Isaiah 45.22–25 The Word (8) of God
   Psalm 119.129–136 The Word (8) of God
Romans 15.1–6 Hope from the Bible (8)
Luke 4.16–24 The Bible's (8) promise fulfilled

DEDICATION FESTIVAL (19) *First Sunday in October or Last Sunday after Trinity*
1 Chronicles 29.6–19 We have given you what is yours, Possessions (54)
   Psalm 122 Let us go up to the house of the Lord
Ephesians 2.19–22 Living stones in God's Temple (19), the Church (11)
John 2.13–22 Cleansing the Temple (19)

ALL SAINTS' SUNDAY (65)
Sunday between 30 October and 5 November inclusive
Daniel 7.1–3, 15–18 The people of God will receive power
   Psalm 149 The victory of God's people
Ephesians 1.11–23 Christ rules with the saints
Luke 6.20–31 The sermon on the plain

Or: **FOURTH SUNDAY BEFORE ADVENT**
Sunday between 31 October and 5 November inclusive. For use if the feast of All Saints was celebrated on 1 November and alternative propers are needed.
Isaiah 1.10–18 Forgiveness (28)
   Psalm 32.1–7 Forgiveness (28)
2 Thessalonians 1.1–12 Justice (36)
Luke 19.1–10 Salvation (66) for Zacchaeus

THIRD SUNDAY BEFORE ADVENT *Sunday between 6 and 12 November inclusive*
Job 19.23–27a My redeemer lives, Resurrection (61)
   Psalm 17.1–9 Prayer (55) for Salvation (66)
2 Thessalonians 2.1–5, 13–17 Perseverance (52)
Luke 20.27–38 Resurrection (61)

Year A

SECOND SUNDAY BEFORE ADVENT *Sunday between 13 and 19 November inclusive*
Malachi 4.1–2a Judgement (35)
    Psalm 98 A new song, Nature (45), the Arts (3)
2 Thessalonians 3.6–13 Perseverance (52), Works (62)
Luke 21.5–19 Perseverance (52)

CHRIST THE KING (37) *Sunday between 20 and 26 November inclusive*
Jeremiah 23.1–6 A Shepherd (68)
    Psalm 46 Providence (56)
Colossians 1.11–20 Forgiveness (28)
Luke 23.33–43 The thief on the Cross (17), Heaven (39)

INDEX OF
SUITABLE SCRIPTURES

Text in bold denotes biblical references; plain text the
corresponding chapter of this book.

INDEX OF SOURCES AND ACKNOWLEDGEMENTS

* in the text indicates that a prayer has been altered with the permission of the copyright holder.

this volume and others.
Acknowledgement is made for *Today's English Version,* © American Bible Society 1966, 1971, 1976. British usage edition (*Good News Bible*) published 1976 by the Bible Societies and Collins and used by permission of HarperCollins Publishers, 12a=35a

Bible Praying (Fount Paperbacks, HarperCollins*Religious*; prayers from *Bible Praying* are © 1992 Michael Perry / Jubilate Hymns, Southampton), 3 29g; 10 64i; 11 11a; 14 50i; 21 25a; 26 74i; 28 56i; 70 8c; 105 68d; 107 38e; 114 34d; 120 50c; 122 19d; 146 23d; 148 70d; 156 7d; 157 21d; 158 14d; 161 9d; 201 63h; 202 28h; 204 40g; 206 1h; 207 62e; 209 22h; 210 69i; 211 27h; 214 17g; 215 37g; 216 26g; 218 33e; 219 6g; 221 52f; 222 4g; 223 21g; 224 29e; 225 72g; 226 38h; 229 74g; 230 64g; 317 19c; 455 11k; 475 31

Biswas, Subir, in *Liturgy of Life* No. 103 (reprinted by permission of the Bishop of Calcutta) 30e

Blake, William (1757–1827) English poet, engraver and mystic ('The Divine Image' from *Songs of Innocence & of Experience*) 3g

Bonhoeffer, Dietrich (1906–45), German pastor and martyr, in *Letters and Papers from Prison* (the Enlarged Edition, SCM Press, 1971), p.11 55g

Book of Alternative Services, see Canadian *Book of Alternative Services*

Book of Common Prayer (English 1549, 1552 & 1662). Extracts from *The Book of Common Prayer* of 1662, the rights in which are vested in the Crown in perpetuity within the United Kingdom, are reproduced by permission of the Crown's Patentee, Cambridge University Press. *The Book of Common Prayer* is in the Public Domain outside of the UK. *BCP 1549* 2c, 55e, 55h; *BCP 1662* 13l, 47e, 68c. See also *Australian Prayer Book; Church of India, Pakistan, Burma and Ceylon; The Prayer Book as Proposed in 1928; Scottish BCP* and *US BCP 1979.*

Book of Dimma, (quoted in *The Edge of Glory,* p. 93) 39f

Brazil Experimental Liturgy 1972

(translated from the Portuguese in *Further Anglican Liturgies,* © 1975 Colin O. Buchanan, Grove Books, Nottingham), 22a

Bria, Ion, Director of the Sub-Unit for the Renewal of Congregational Life at the World Council of Churches, in *Let all the World ...* 69j

CAFOD, taken from the liturgy notes prepared for the 'Witness the Kingdom' Event 57k

The Calendar and Lessons (a Report by the Liturgical Commission of the Church of England General Synod 1969, copyright as for *ASB 1980*), 19e

Canadian *Book of Alternative Services* based on (or excerpted from) *The Book of Alternative Services of the Anglican Church of Canada,* © 1985 by the General Synod of the Anglican Church of Canada; used with permission), p.107 17k; p.118 24j; p.121 41h; p.123 14h; p.191 47b, 47d; p.193 15g; p.216 28a; p.219 1k; p.226 43j; p.276 50k; p.396 31e; p.399 38l; p.412 53l; p.418 36l, 72e; p.419 72k; p.671 19h; p.673 19j

Carmina Gadelica (edited Alexander Carmichael, Scottish Academic Press reprint 1983, Vol. 3), p.337 24n

Celebrating Common Prayer (© the European Province of the Society of Saint Francis, 1992, published by Mowbray, a Cassell imprint), p.38 62j; p.85 66l; p.108 24o; p.132 7l, 55l; p.145 41k; p.158 33j, 54j; p.183 48p

Celtic Blessing 51m

Christ Church Cathedral, Vancouver, Canada (in *A Service of Remembrance and Lament for Violence Committed against Women and for the Montreal Massacre,* 6 December 1994; used by permission), 77k

Christian Aid, see Kate Compton 51l; *Feast for Life* 31g,l; and *God of Life* 39a,b,c,; 46g

Church Family Worship (© Michael Perry/Jubilate Hymns)

The Church in Wales, source unknown 23l

The Church Mission Society (Anglican mission agency, © the Church Mission

More Prayers for Sundays

Liturgy and Death by Trevor Lloyd
(Grove Worship Booklet 28, 1974, ©
Trevor Lloyd), 56k

Liturgy of Life, an anthology compiled by
Donald Hilton based on patterns of
Christian worship (collection ©
Donald Hilton, 1991, published by
National Christian Education Council,
Birmingham), No.103 © Subir Biswas,
30e; No.147 © David J. Harding, 49d

The Liturgy of St John Chrysostom, in
general use in Orthodox Churches,
adapted in *Prayers for Sundays* 49h

Living Prayers for Today compiled by
Maureen Edwards (© 1996, repro-
duced with the permission of the
International Bible Reading
Association, Birmingham), No.93 2e;
No.162 18g

The Living Word (Redemptorist
Publications, Alton), *ASB* Year 2,
Advent 4 64b

Lloyd, Trevor, in *Enriching the Christian
Year* 14Q1 16m; 20B1 43c; 7C1 73h; in
Liturgy and Death 56k

The Lord's Supper by William Barclay (©
SCM Press, London), 65l

Luke, The Gospel according to 1.68,79 30g,
71i; 1.78–79 40i=58i; 2.10–11 10a; 2.14
10i, 65j; 2.29 2j, 24j, 40m; 2.46–55 42a;
13.29 57i; 15.21,24 66c; 19.10, 15.7 68b;
19.38 49a; 19.41 12b; 19.42 51k;
24.29–31 24l

Magnificat (Luke 2.46–55) 42a
Malabar, Liturgy of (Indian orthodox) 74k
A Manual of Eastern Orthodox Prayers
(SPCK, 1945), p.23 13e

Mark, The Gospel according to 2.17 35b;
3.35 26i; 4.34–35 44a; 9.35 33h; 12.17
54h

Mason, John (1645–94, English hymn-
writer) 3b

Matthew, The Gospel according to 4.17 37b;
4.19–20 14a; 5.3–10 71c; 5.9 51j; 5.24
26b, 28j; 6.25,33 54b; 11.4–6 39a;
18.20–21 49f; 23.37 45b,c, 51k; 25.45
46b; 28.19 23a

Medieval requiem mass introit 18a

Melanesian Prayer Book Draft (© 1984 the
Co-ordinator of the Committee on
Liturgy and Worship in the Church of
the Province of Melanesia) 7j

Memorials upon Several Occasions edited
by Eric Milner-White (1884–1964)
(published anonymously in 1933 by
A. R. Mowbray & Co., Oxford and
London, and subsequently repub-
lished as *After the Third Collect*), 39j

Methodist Church in Singapore (reprinted from *Now* with the permission of
the Methodist Publishing House), 43g

*The Methodist Church (UK) Prayer
Handbook 1993/94* 66f; see also *The
Companion to the Lectionary* and *The
Methodist Service Book.*

The Methodist Service Book. The Covenant
Service (© 1975 Methodist Conference
Office) is reproduced with the consent
of the Methodist Publishing House.
On 25 December 1747 and on many
other occasions John Wesley urged the
Methodists to renew their covenant
with God, and he used the words of
Joseph and Richard Alleine, which
have been revised to form this service:
15a,b,c,e

Mexican, source unknown 50e

Ministry at the Time of Death (© the
Central Board of Finance of the
Church of England, 1991), p.5 2g

Ministry to the Sick (© the Central Board
of Finance of the Church of England,
1983, reproduced with permission),
p.29 32c; p.44 32g

More Prayers for Today's Church by Dick
Willams (Kingsway Books, used by
permission of Canon Williams of
Liverpool), No.35 8n

Mozarabic (ancient Spanish liturgy) 51f

Munns, Sally (of West Wickham) 45l

My God, My Glory by Eric Milner-White
(SPCK, London, 1967) 13c

New Zealand: copyright material taken
from *The New Zealand Eucharistic
Liturgy 1984*, 32d, 72j; and *A New
Zealand Prayer Book – He Karakia
Mihinare o Aotearoa 1989* (used by per-
mission of the General Secretary, the
General Synod Office, Hastings, New
Zealand, of the Church in Aotearoa,
New Zealand and Polynesia, and of
HarperCollins San Francisco, who
hold the copyright for the USA,
Europe and Great Britain), p.35 71a;

Prayers for Sundays (© in the compilation 1994 Michael Counsell, HarperCollins*Religious*, London) 10e, 44i,l; 49h; 54i,l

Prayers for the Christian Year by William Barclay (© SCM Press, 1964) 53i

Prayers for the People (published 1992 by Marshall Pickering, an imprint of HarperCollins*Religious*, London; prayers from *Prayers for the People* are © the Editors / Jubilate Hymns, Southampton, 1992), 2.14 21c; 2.25 62f; 3.7 75a; 4.13 30b; 6.59 26k; 11.30 3k; 14.15 9c; 14.17 27c; 14.19 27f; 14.34 63l; 15.19 27d; 16.54 25k; 17.70 23k; 25.41 74h; 28.28 13h; 28.57 22b; 29.27 59h

Prayers for use at the Alternative Services (Mowbray, London and Oxford, © David Silk 1980) 35k, 46l, 64k, 65e

Premasagar, Rt Rev. Victor, reprinted from *Word for Today* (reproduced with the permission of the International Bible Reading Association, Birmingham) 77k

The Promise of His Glory, Services and Prayers for the Season from All Saints to Candlemas (Church House Publishing and Mowbray, a Cassell imprint, © the Central Board of Finance of the Church of England 1990, 1991), p.17 42k; p.18 76k; p.25 58e; p.48 65a; p.54 65i; p.55 65k; p.62 18b; p.72 18l; p.101 1m=42l; p.107 35d; p.118 13d; p.119 58l; p.125 58b; p.126 24d; p.132 35j; p.133 58j; p.135 37l; p.141 70b; p.144 24e,f; p.155 40a; p.165 10b; p.178 10h; p.179 42i; pp.182–3 10k; p.183 10l; p.185 10d; p.187 36i; p.202 52g; p.203 15i; p.226 21k; p.227 21l; p.229 7c; p.235 11g; p.237 66i, 69k; p.238 62h; p.241 23b, 54b; p.242 23c, 36d; p.244 21i, 23i, 28j; p.246 75b; p.249 6c, 45e; p.254 11f; p.275 21h; p.278 40j; p.283 60a; p.346 29c; p.364 51f; p.365 52c, 66e; and see Perham

Proverbs 3.13,17 76i

The Province of the Indian Ocean, quoted in *The SPCK Book of Christian Prayer* (© SPCK 1995, used by kind permission of the Bishop of the Seychelles) 23h

The Province of the West Indies, *The Book of Common Prayer for the Church in the Province of the West Indies* (© 1996,

used by kind permission of the Archbishop of the CPWI), p.129 31j

Psalms 4.8 24i; 15.1–2 2a, 77a; 15.3 2b; 15.7,1 2d; 23.2,4,6 68l; 28.6–9 68d; 31.5,7 24i; 31.9–16 38e; 32.1 71b; 36.5,6,9 72c; 46.10–11 5d; 51.1–4, 10–12 70c; 51.9–12 34d; 51.15 55a; 51.17 38b; 67.6–7 31a; 70.1 55a; 78.56–57 78b; 85.8 8k; 96.9, 85.10 3i; 103.3 28a; 103.4–5 20d; 103.8–13 50c; 103.9,13 44c; 103.11–13 19d; 107 46h, 71c; 118.24 63a; 119 64h; 119.62 13j; 119.105 13a; 119.165 13i=47i; 130.1–6 27c; 130.7–8 27d; 131.3 44c; 136 28a; 139.8 27b; 139.11 24i; 141.2 24a; 145.10, 149.5, 68.32, 115.1 3a; 145.13–16 63h; 147.14 31i; 148.12–13 9a

Queen's Park United Reformed Church, source unknown 9g

Revelation 1.5–8 64g; 4.11, 5.9–10, 14.13 65g; 5.9 36m; 5.13 71a; 7.9 57a; 19.5 67a; 19.6,9 68a; 22.20 1a

Revised Common Lectionary Amended © 1997 The Central Board of Finance of the Church of England, used by permission, pp.271–300.

Roman Missal, excerpts from the English translation of *The Roman Missal* (© 1973, International Committee on English in the Liturgy Inc. (ICEL); all rights reserved; altered and adapted with permission): *Mass* 18d, 18i, 29b, 50a, 65c; *Kyries* 1c, 18c, 28d, 32c, 35c, 42c; *Prefaces* 11i, 18j, 20j, 25i, 29h, 36k, 37j, 39i, 46j, 47j, 64j, 66j, 68j, 69l, 76j; *Prayers over the People and Solemn Blessings* 60k; *Propers* 22e, 37k, 68e,k; *Rite of Reconciliation* 28l,m, 75l

Romans, Letter of Paul to the 1.2–4 1h; 1.7 29g; 3.23 48b; 5.1–8 29i; 5.8 28b; 5.19 47a; 8.2,14–25 14j; 8.16 73d; 8.22 31b; 8.23–39 5k; 8.31–39 70g; 8.33–34 4d; 10.8–10 62e; 12.1 54a; 12.9,17,18 62g; 13.11–12 58a; 14.17 22j; 15.5,6 75m; 15.13 25k, 70i; 15.33 63j

St Barnabas' Church, Dulwich, London (prayer used in a Service of Unity in 1990; source unknown) 57b

St George's Church, Oakdale 31h, 38m, 42h, 44h

USPG (the United Society for the Propagation of the Gospel, an Anglican mission agency): see *A Still Place of Light* 57e; *Go Tell it on the Mountain* 34h, 69d; and *Let all the World …* 17h, 38c, 69j

Vaughan, Charles John (1816–97, Dean of Llandaff, Wales) 27e
Vowles, Rev. Patricia (Vicar of St Michael's, Camberwell), in *Let all the World …* 38c

Walker, Michael, in *Baptist Praise and Worship*, 420 7g (used by permission of Mrs A. M. Walker), 520 18k
Walton, Victoria, for *The Saskatchewan Christian Feminist Network* (used by permission) 77j
Webb, Pauline, see *Living Prayers for Today*, 162 (reproduced with the permission of the International Bible Reading Association, Birmingham) 18g
A Wee Worship Book (© the Wild Goose Resource Group, Iona Community, 840 Govan Road, Glasgow G51 3UU, Scotland), p.4 25b; p.6 6h; p.8 20k; p.9 37h; p.16 74l; p.17 28c, 45a; p.18 25f; pp.20–21 11b; p.23 50b; p.25 74c; p.32 1l; p.37 73k; p.41 76g; p.46 32a; p.47 32h
Wesley, John (1703–91, Anglican priest, founder of the Methodist movement), 15a,b,c,e
West Africa, *The Experimental Liturgy of the Church of the Province of West Africa 1980* (permission sought), 30i, 40c,d

Westcott, Brooke Fosse (1825–1901, Bishop of Durham) 5h
Westcott House, Cambridge, England (Theological College) 8m, 271
With All God's People – The New Ecumenical Prayer Cycle (1989 WCC Publications, Geneva, Switzerland) 57m
The Wisdom of Solomon, Apocrypha, chapter 9 76c
Wind and Fire by Margaret and Ian Fraser (Lagan, Inverness) 11d
Women's World Day of Prayer 1993 in *God's People: Instruments of Healing*, by the women of Guatemala, 571
Woodward, C. S., adapted in *Prayers for the People*, 14.15 9c
World Conference of Women, 1995 (a noonday prayer at Beijing, by permission of Ann Smith, Office of Women in Mission and Ministry, 815 Second Avenue, New York), 77g
World Council of Churches, (WCC Publications, Geneva, Switzerland) from *Jesus Christ, the Life of the World: A Worship Book* 48l; from Canberra Assembly 1991 44g, 52b; from *With All God's People – The New Ecumenical Prayer Cycle* 1989 57m
Written to Teach Us (© Bible Society 1995, used with permission) 8e,j

If any copyright has been infringed the editor and publishers apologize and will rectify it in future editions.

INDEX OF SUBJECTS